THE POLITICS OF POVERTY REDUCTION IN INDIA

THE POLITICS OF POVERTY REDUCTION IN INDIA

The UPA Government, 2004 to 2014

James Chiriyankandath
Diego Maiorano
James Manor
Louise Tillin

Orient BlackSwan

THE POLITICS OF POVERTY REDUCTION IN INDIA:
THE UPA GOVERNMENT, 2004 TO 2014

ORIENT BLACKSWAN PRIVATE LIMITED

Registered Office
3-6-752 Himayatnagar, Hyderabad 500 029, Telangana, India
e-mail: centraloffice@orientblackswan.com

Other Offices
Bengaluru, Bhopal, Chennai, Guwahati, Hyderabad, Jaipur, Kolkata
Lucknow, Mumbai, New Delhi, Noida, Patna, Visakhapatnam

First published by Orient Blackswan Private Limited 2020

ISBN 978-93-5287-848-2

030959

Typeset in
Constantia 10.5/13
by Le Studio Graphique, Gurgaon 122 007

Printed in India at
Akash Press, Delhi

Published by
Orient Blackswan Private Limited
3-6-752, Himayatnagar, Hyderabad 500 029, Telangana, India
e-mail: info@orientblackswan.com

To N. C. Saxena,

A wise advisor to our project

Contents

Abbreviations

AAY	Antyodaya Anna Yojana
AIFAWH	All India Federation of Anganwadi Workers and Helpers
AMRUT	Atal Mission for Rejuvenation and Urban Transformation
APL	above poverty line
ASER	*Annual State of Education Report*
ASHA	accredited social health activist
AMN	auxiliary midwife nurse
AWC	anganwadi centre
AWW	anganwadi worker
BATF	Bangalore Agenda Task Force
BDO	Block Development Officer
BJP	Bharatiya Janata Party
BPL	below poverty line
BSUP	Basic Services for the Urban Poor
CACP	Commission on Agricultural Costs and Prices
CAG	Comptroller and Auditor General
CBOs	community based organisations
CDPs	City Development Plans
CDPO	child development project officer
CEPT	Centre for Environmental Planning and Technology
CMP	Common Minimum Programme

CSD	Centre for Social Development
CSE	Centre for Sustainable Employment
CSMC	Central Sanctioning and Monitoring Committee
CSO	Central Statistical Organisation
CSS	Centrally Sponsored Schemes
DHAN	Development of Humane Action
DPRs	Detailed Project Reports
FAO	Food and Agriculture Organisation
FRA	Forest Rights Act
GDP	Gross Domestic Product
HDFC	Housing Development Finance Corporation
HLRN	Housing and Land Rights Network
HPEC	High Powered Expert Committee
IAS	Indian Administrative Service
ICDS	Integrated Child Development Services
IDPS	Institute of Development and Policy Studies
IT	information technology
IFPRI	International Food Policy Research Institute
IHSDP	Integrated Housing and Slum Development Programme
IMF	International Monetary Fund
IMR	infant mortality rate
GoI	Government of India
JNNURM	Jawaharlal Nehru National Urban Renewal Mission
MKSS	Mazdoor Kisan Shakti Sangathan
MGNREGA	Mahatma Gandhi National Rural Employment Guarantee Act
MHFW	Ministry of Health and Family Welfare
MHRD	Ministry of Human Resource Development
MIS	management information system
MoEFCC	Ministry of Environment, Forestry and Climate Change
MoHUPA	Ministry of Housing and Urban Poverty Alleviation
MoUD	Ministry of Urban Development
MP	member of Parliament

MSDE	Ministry of Skill Development and Entrepreneurship
MSP	Minimum Support Price
MWCD	Ministry of Women and Child Development
NAC	National Advisory Council
NDA	National Democratic Alliance
NDC	National Development Council
NDTV	New Delhi Television Limited
NFHS	National Family Health Survey
NFSA	National Food Security Act
NFSB	National Food Security Bill
NFFWP	National Food for Work Programme
NHRC	National Human Rights Commission
NIPFP	National Institute of Public Finance and Policy
NITI Aayog	National Institution for Transforming India
NIUA	National Institute of Urban Affairs
NNC	National Nutrition Conclave
NREP	National Rural Employment Programme
NRHM	National Rural Health Mission
NSDP	National Slum Development Programme
NSG	National Steering Group
NSSO	National Sample Survey Office
NSWC	National Social Watch Coalition
NULM	National Urban Livelihood Mission
OECD	Organisation for Economic Co-operation and Development
OPHI	Oxford Poverty and Human Development Initiative
PRIA	Participatory Research in Asia
PDS	Public Distribution System
PHC	Primary Health Centre
PIL	Public Interest Litigation
PM	Prime Minister
PMIUPEP	Prime Minister's Integrated Urban Poverty Eradication Programme
PMO	Prime Minister's Office

POCUS	Progress On Children Under Six Report
PPP	public–private partnership purchasing power parity
PUCL	People's Union of Civil Liberties
RAY	Rajiv Awas Yojana
RSBY	Rashtriya Swasthya Bima Yojana
RTE	Right of Children to Free and Compulsory Education (Act)
RTF	Right to Food (Campaign)
RTI	Right to Information (Act)
SC	Scheduled Caste
SHG	self-help group
SJSRY	Swarna Jayanti Shahari Rozgar Yojana
SN	supplementary nutrition
SPARC	Society for the Promotion of Area Resource Centres
SSA	Sarva Shiksha Abhiyan
ST	Scheduled Tribe
TAG	Technical Advisory Group
TPDS	Targeted Public Distribution System
UIDAI	Unique Identification Authority of India
UIDSSMT	Urban Infrastructure Development Scheme for Small and Medium Towns
UIG	urban infrastructure and governance
ULBs	urban local bodies
UNDP	United Nations Development Programme
UNICEF	United Nations Children's Fund (originally, United Nations International Children's Emergency Fund)
UPA	United Progressive Alliance
WDI	World Development Indicators
WHO	World Health Organization

Tables and Figure

Tables

Figure

Acknowledgements

We are grateful to Economic and Social Research Council (ESRC), United Kingdom (grant number ES/J012629/1), for a major grant under their 'Rising Powers' initiative which made our studies possible. Our work formed part of a larger project in which twenty researchers compared efforts by governments in Brazil, India, China and South Africa after 2002 to tackle poverty and inequality, and their impact. We benefited greatly from comparative insights provided by colleagues who analysed those other three countries, especially Steven Friedman, Marcus Andre Melo and Jane Duckett. We are also grateful to the School of Advanced Study, University of London, for serving as the host institution for the four-country project.

Important insights were gained from colleagues at the Savitribai Phule Pune University, which enabled one of us to present a series of lectures on the findings in this book, under the Government of India's Global Initiative of Academic Networks (GIAN) programme.

A great many people across India lent valuable assistance during our research. They are too numerous to list here, but we are especially grateful to Reetika Khera, Yogesh Kumar, the late K. C. Sivaramakrishnan and most notably, N. C. Saxena, to whom this book is dedicated.

Introduction

In 2004 the United Progressive Alliance (UPA) coalition led by the Congress Party unexpectedly came to power in India, promising to govern in the interests of the '*aam aadmi*' (common man). Over the next decade it introduced a raft of rights-based legislation and welfare programmes targeting mass poverty in a country with more people living below the poverty line than in the whole of sub-Saharan Africa. In this book, four specialists in Indian politics and public policy critically review five of the most important of these: on food security, rural employment, child nutrition and development, urban poverty, and forest inhabitants' rights. Between them, new policy initiatives in these fields contributed to a major expansion of India's social security provision beyond the small formal sector of its economy. While there were many continuities with older policies, some important elements of the new policies represented departures: in many instances, they focused on creating legal entitlements rather than discretionary disbursements. They also adopted new means of identifying beneficiaries which moved away from earlier attempts to target benefits to the 'below poverty line' population: an approach that had proved to be both inefficient and excluded some of the most vulnerable.[1]

This book is the first systematic review of the politics and policy-making that lay behind the array of anti-poverty programmes undertaken by the UPA coalition. It examines how far the UPA delivered on its promise to meet the needs of the poor. As one of the first systematic studies of the decade of UPA government, it also analyses official Indian thinking and policy-making on poverty in the early twenty-first century. Our analysis reveals the politics behind the design and implementation of these programmes, and the important roles played by senior political leaders, bureaucrats and civil society activists in influencing the UPA's adoption of a rights-based agenda.[2]

Collectively, the chapters in this book ask how—through what political and policy-making processes—social policies took the form they did and with what implications. The battles over the insertion, modification or deletion of specific provisions reveal a constellation of interests that shaped both the final form of these policies and their implementation on the ground. We ask how actors at the national level thought about the roles of central, state and local governments as the crucial arenas for policy implementation, as well as the roles of other bodies such as the courts, civil society organisations and the private sector in the achievement of policy goals. The views of government actors on the roles of these bodies in the implementation process helped to shape the way that policies were framed. Chapters in the book address the question of how policy designers tried to form or break (or failed to form or break) coalitions of interests among these actors and what strategies they used to advance or block legislation or specific provisions. They ask how perceptions of the availability of financial and human resources, and of local and state administrative capacity or incentives, shaped what was thought possible at the implementation stage. They also examine the implications of those things.

In other words, this book contributes to our understanding of why India's partly rights-based welfare regime assumed its present form. By unearthing the constellation of interests that shaped legislation and the reasons why specific policy provisions were inserted, modified or removed, we contribute to an explanation of the persistent gap between intent and outcomes of social policy in India—a puzzle that remains to be explored (Chopra 2014: 98). The existing literature has focused largely on the barriers to implementation over the 'last mile' such as issues around corruption and clientelism (see for e.g., Bardhan and Mookherjee 2006; Besley, Pande and Rao 2005; Markusson 2011; Shankar and Gaiha 2013; Jenkins and Manor 2017); poor workforce monitoring, giving rise to problems such as teacher absenteeism (Chaudhury et al. 2006; Rogers and Vegas 2009; Duflo et al. 2012); financial management (Banerjee et al. 2015); unequal power relations and the burden of bureaucracy on local government (Mathur 2016). Far less attention has been given to the interplay of political and policy processes at the policy formulation stage, which has a crucial impact on policy implementation. Some studies analyse the making of single initiatives (e.g. Chopra 2011a; Balarajan and Reich 2016; Rao 2017), while Das (2013) provides an overview of some important rights-based legislations enacted by UPA-I (its government between 2004 and 2009), but politics hardly finds a role in the analysis. Through in-depth assessments of the policy-making processes of five key policy initiatives, we stress the importance of political dynamics in explaining both the final shape of legislation and their implications on the ground.

THEMES OF THE BOOK

What explains the substantial expansion of India's welfare regime under the UPA? At first sight, the Indian case seems to support a long-standing theory: when left of Centre parties are in power, we see more redistribution and an expansion of welfare provisions.[3] Indeed, the Left Front's support to the UPA government was based on the implementation of the Common Minimum Programme (CMP), which included several policy initiatives that now form the backbone of India's social assistance architecture. The fact that, during the UPA's second term, when the Left Front was no longer supporting the government, the push to expand the welfare state decreased dramatically seems to confirm this view.

As the reader will note, however, the Left Front parties and politicians are not at the centre of our analysis. In fact, we show that, contrary to the expectations of theorists, the parties of the

Left played a limited role in the political and policy processes that led the Government of India to increase its efforts to tackle poverty and inequality. At times, as in the case of the Mahatma Gandhi National Rural Employment Guarantee Act (MGNREGA) and the Forest Rights Act (FRA), they played a small but important role in Parliament. But in the case of the other initiatives that we studied, their role was limited to not opposing the introduction or reform of policies—a role which they share with other parties. While there are complex reasons why the parties of the Left failed to play a substantial role in policy-making—including the struggle for power between the party's national leadership and the West Bengal unit of the Communist Party of India (Marxist), the largest component of the Left Front—what is important to note here is that the support of the Left Front to the UPA-I was helpful, but ultimately not crucial in the expansion of welfare programmes.

Perhaps more important than any direct role in the policy-making process was the indirect role that the Left Front parties played. In fact, the UPA government, and in particular Prime Minister Manmohan Singh, presented progressive legislation as a way to 'buy' the support of the Left for the nuclear deal with the United States—arguably Singh's top foreign policy priority during his term in office.[4] The strategy, eventually, did not work, and the Left Front withdrew its support to the government when the deal was signed in 2008. But his government nevertheless survived as did its progressive impetus—albeit at a reduced pace during Singh's second term. In fact, two of the initiatives that we analysed, the National Food Security Act (NFSA) and the reform of the Integrated Child Development Services (ICDS)—both with important financial implications—were adopted during the UPA's second term.

This does not mean that there were not stark differences in the politics of policy-making between the UPA-I and UPA-II governments, which largely explain the more limited effectiveness of the ruling coalition to push through progressive legislation during its second spell in power. First, as mentioned, the Left Front was no longer in the picture. Second, the primary engine of the introduction of new social policies during UPA-I, the National Advisory Council (NAC)—an advisory body constituted to act as a bridge between coalition partners—changed dramatically in its mandate and composition. The first NAC had the objective of monitoring the implementation of the CMP, which included a number of very specific policy promises to be adopted by the ruling coalition. But its second incarnation had the much more limited role of giving 'attention to the priorities stated in the address of the President of India to Parliament on 4 June 2009' (Gupta 2011) which was an exercise high in rhetoric and low in substance. Furthermore, the composition of the NAC changed quite dramatically and some of its most progressive members—including Aruna Roy, Jean Drèze and Harsh Mander—resigned over the course of the UPA's second term.

Second, the UPA was, in a way, a victim of its own success. The introduction of important policies like the MGNREGA, the Right to Information (RTI) Act, the Forest Rights Act and the universalisation of the Midday Meal scheme raised the stakes both for those who wanted the State to be more ambitious, and those who wanted it to step back. In other words, the nature and vigour of ideological debate about State investment in anti-poverty programmes itself changed, and this in turn altered the climate in which the later initiatives of UPA-II were negotiated. The advent of the global financial crisis further polarised the ideological debate as growth slowed down in India after 2011 and the government enacted a series of countercyclical measures that increased State expenditure (especially on infrastructure) and cut indirect taxation.

Third, UPA-II was tainted by a long list of scandals. In 2010, a Comptroller and Auditor General (CAG) report accused the government of causing the loss of Rs 1.76 lakh crore (US$ 25 billion) to the exchequer by under-charging telecom companies—in exchange for kickbacks—for the purchase of telecommunication spectrum. In 2012, the CAG estimated that the losses due to the fraudulent coal blocks auctioning system amounted to Rs 1.86 lakh crore (US$ 27 billion). Media reports estimated that a Commonwealth Games scam cost the exchequer around Rs 70,000 crore (US$ 10 billion). The losses due to these three scams alone—which do not include a rather long list of minor scams and a number of major scams involving state-level politicians belonging to the UPA like the chief ministers of Maharashtra, Ashok Chavan, and Andhra Pradesh, Y. S. Rajasekhara Reddy—could have financed the MGNREGA for more than a decade. Clearly, the legitimacy of the government was severely damaged, especially in the eyes of the middle classes, who tend to see spending on the poor as 'populism' or 'handouts'.

If the support of the Left Front was helpful but not critical in explaining the expansion of India's welfare state during the UPA's regime, what does? Our analysis of the political and policy processes of five key initiatives shows that three factors were particularly important. All three are expressions of India's democracy.

The first factor is party competition between the Congress and the Bharatiya Janata Party (BJP). The latter had experience of forming governments at the national level since 1998, thus proving that it had become a credible national alternative to the Grand Old Party. That realisation changed the Congress in a number of ways. First, it accepted that, if it wanted to rule India in the changed political scenario, it had to make alliances and renounce its 'natural right' to govern India on its own. It also made it clear that secularism was not an issue on which elections could be won, as the post-Ayodhya political landscape clearly demonstrated: the Congress needed to differentiate itself more from its rival. The BJP and the media offered the Congress the opportunity to do just that on a silver plate: the former by choosing as a campaign slogan 'India shining'; the latter by attributing the Congress victory in 2004 to a revolt of the rural poor against the BJP's arrogant electoral slogan which was intended to highlight how the BJP-led government had ensured high rates of economic growth, but failed to realise how little of this growth had 'trickled down' to the rural poor. The Congress knew that the 'revolt of the poor' argument was largely a myth (Manor 2011a); but it took the opportunity to give substance to decades of rhetorical commitment to the welfare of the poor and to prepare for the 2009 elections on the basis of a progressive track record.

The Congress Party thus decided to keep its feet in both shoes: on the one hand, it continued to promote a set of economic policies that promoted investments, economic growth and the interests of the better off; on the other, however, it decided to invest part of the fruits of economic growth in the welfare of the poor, to give economic reforms 'a human face' as the government's rhetoric put it. 'Invest' is a key word here, as much of the government's effort to promote the welfare of the poor also stemmed from the idea that investing in people's capabilities was a way to invest in the country's future economic growth—an idea that key actors in the NAC brought to the very heart of the policy-making machine.

Second, to understand not only why the welfare state expanded under the UPA, but also why it assumed the forms that it did, we must consider the breadth and openness of the policy community—that is, the full range of individuals and organisations involved in influencing policy. The creation of the NAC constituted a marked break with the past in this respect. Policy-making had always been conducted behind closed doors, with no or very limited involvement of civil society. Among the initiatives that we analyse, only the Jawaharlal Nehru National Urban Renewal Mission (JNNURM) was designed in this way—although even in this case, prominent social entrepreneurs were involved and played a crucial role in shaping the scheme.

For the other initiatives, however, the NAC functioned as a sounding board for ideas coming from civil society organisations and other allies of the poor (see Chopra 2011a). The UPA chairperson, Sonia Gandhi, included some very prominent and widely respected social activists like Aruna Roy and Jean Drèze who had strong connections with the network of civil society organisations that had lobbied the government for increased attention to the welfare of the poor for decades. The NAC also included other progressive members who were either part of government agencies (like Mihir Shah) or former bureaucrats (like N. C. Saxena). This ensured first that policies designed by the NAC were 'realistic' and implementable, but also that ideas coming from below reached the heart of the policy-making machine.

Importantly, the policy community was not only broader than in the past, but it was also fuzzy and fluid as its members played different and overlapping roles. Jean Drèze, for example, was a member of the NAC, but also part of the Right to Food (RTF) Campaign that played a key role in drafting, supporting and defending the MGNREGA, the NFSA and the ICDS. N. C. Saxena was member of the NAC, but also special commissioner of the Supreme Court in the Right to Food case, which played a determinant role in shaping the ICDS and the NFSA. Harsh Mander, another commissioner, was also a member of the NAC. Dipa Sinha served as an advisor to the commissioners of the Supreme Court, but was also a key member of the RTF Campaign. The UPA also recruited a few scholarly and progressive civil society activists to serve on the Planning Commission which operated as a potent 'think-tank', providing policy advice to the government. In short, the policy community was broad and open to ideas coming from allies of the poor and from a network of civil society organisations that had worked at the grassroots for decades and had vast experience of the failures of development programmes. This openness and the configuration of the policy community enabled these ideas to penetrate deep into policy-making circles that absorbed and reworked these ideas into concrete policy provisions.

At first glance, it seems surprising that the UPA was so open to ideas coming from below as it broke with a well-established 'tradition' of secrecy, opaqueness and self-referentiality in policy-making. However, it did so both for hard-nosed political reasons and out of altruism: in order to broaden its electoral base among poorer voters, and (just possibly) to make an unprecedented, historic impact on poverty and inequality.

Both reasons seem to have motivated the actions of the key actor in the political and policy processes that we analysed: the UPA's chairperson, Sonia Gandhi. This is in fact the third important factor that explains the emergence of a stronger and more inclusive welfare state in India: the role of senior political leaders in what is a consolidated, but weakly institutionalised and therefore leader-dependent democracy. Sonia Gandhi's role was important in a number of ways.

As the leader of the largest party in the ruling coalition, she played a key role in creating an opportunity to give substance to her own party's socio-democratic credentials. After Indira Gandhi won the 1971 elections with the slogan '*garibi hatao*' (abolish poverty), the Congress Party had supposedly made the fight against poverty its raison d'être. However, as we will discuss in Chapter 2, this had remained largely at the rhetorical level and previous Congress governments could claim very little in terms of reducing poverty and ameliorating the living conditions of the poor. Sonia Gandhi seized the opportunity provided by the narrative surrounding the Congress victory in 2004—that the results were largely an outcome of a revolt of the rural poor against globalisation and the 'India shining' model proposed by the BJP—and took a series of crucial steps to put her party on a different path. In particular, before the Congress could realise that the 'revolt of the rural poor' was largely a myth, she had set up the NAC and filled it with carefully selected progressive individuals with vast experience in development programmes that put the policy-making machine in motion.

Sonia Gandhi also used her influence to facilitate and promote social policies in several other ways. She ensured that the policy provisions that gave the legislation teeth stayed in the acts. Such interventions were crucial for both the MGNREGA and the FRA. But the ICDS and the NFSA were also defended in key interventions by Sonia Gandhi. She also let her party know that what came out of the NAC was what she herself supported. In the Congress culture, whatever 'Madam' decided became the official party line. While this was not sufficient, as we will see in the chapters dedicated to the MGNREGA, FRA, ICDS, and the NFSA, to avoid attempts by senior ministers (including from within the Congress Party) and bureaucrats—especially in the Finance Ministry—to dilute or undermine progressive legislation, her endorsement of particular policy provisions was important in ensuring that the Congress voted the way it did in Parliament. Furthermore, the fact that she set up the NAC and that she attended the meetings and followed its work quite closely—at least during the first term of the UPA, before she needed to be treated for a serious illness—gave the NAC authority that branches of the State apparatus found difficult to resist. The NAC was a fluid, agile and competent body with no clear constitutional authority, no fixed rules and terms of reference, but with enormous political influence nonetheless. This influence was largely explained by the weight that Sonia Gandhi threw behind it.

However, she was not the only actor who played a crucial role in the policy-making processes that we analysed. Other senior political leaders played a constructive role. Jairam Ramesh, for instance, was repeatedly mentioned in our interviews as a respected, progressive and knowledgeable Congress Party leader who enjoyed the confidence of Sonia Gandhi. One member of the NAC described him as 'the ringmaster', while an important member of the RTF Campaign told us that it became clear after awhile that convincing Ramesh of something was the most efficient way of convincing Sonia herself. Similarly, other politicians played important roles at crucial moments by spending some political capital to support specific pieces of the legislation, or by facilitating access to decision-makers, or by not opposing legislation.

In short, Sonia Gandhi and other senior leaders were able to use her influence within her party to break free from constraints that had hobbled India's efforts to tackle poverty in the previous decades. The key innovation that enabled this was the creation of the NAC.

In other cases, contributions to the emergence of a strengthened welfare regime were more ambiguous. The actions of then prime minister Manmohan Singh illustrate the point. He, for instance, decided not to oppose the passage of the MGNREGA on fiscal grounds after a member of the NAC, N. C. Saxena, showed him that the budgetary implications would not be too drastic. In the case of the ICDS, however, his role was more ambiguous. Singh was convinced that the sitting Minister for Women and Child Development, Renuka Chowdhury, was keen on providing pre-packaged food to the children instead of hot cooked meals as mandated by the Supreme Court and as advocated by virtually the entire policy community. Since Chowdhury's stubbornness was seen as a major impediment to the development of the policy, Singh decided to delay the reform of the scheme until after the 2009 election, when she was removed from the ministry. His decision helped reform the ICDS. But it also caused a significant delay that frustrated many in the policy community and jeopardised it because there was no guarantee that a post-2009 government would pursue the reform. In the case of the NFSA, the prime minister's position was much closer to fiscal conservatives in his government than to progressives in his party or in the NAC. During the second term of the UPA, when Singh had acquired a more solid position, and Sonia Gandhi was ill and did not follow policy developments closely, he was less inclined to back expensive social policies like the NFSA. The opposition of the Prime Minister's Office (PMO) was a serious obstacle that proved impossible for proponents of a universal food security act to overcome. The point here is that senior political leaders exert an important influence on policy-making and their backing of—or opposition to—social policies can crucially determine their fate and final shape.

While senior leaders are certainly important in policy-making, as the chapters in this book demonstrate, they are not free from constraints imposed by institutions and policy inheritances. On the contrary, all the policies that we analyse were built upon a policy infrastructure that was already present. In the case of the ICDS and the NFSA, the existence of a capillary implementation system already in place—the *anganwadi* centres and the Public Distribution System (PDS), respectively—crucially determined policy choices. When confronted with the option of scrapping the existing system and building a new one from scratch—a choice that policy-makers confronted in both cases—'path dependencies' tilted the balance in favour of reforming, expanding or improving the existing system.

This occurred not only out of administrative convenience but also because constellations of interests that are difficult to dismantle gravitate around policy architectures. The procurement system for food for the PDS is a case in point. The most innovative policy was the MGNREGA. The introduction of a management information system (MIS) to track all operations and ensure transparency, and the ban on contractors, were two innovations that constituted a marked break with the past. However, the MGNREGA itself was designed using Maharashtra's employment scheme and practices that had developed in Rajasthan as models, and by borrowing part of the policy infrastructure of the National Food for Work Programme (NFFWP).

It should be noted that in virtually all cases, pre-existing policies were not very promising: the PDS was notoriously inefficient and leaky (although some states had started to demonstrate that reforms were possible); the ICDS had been marked by severe shortcomings; the Food for Work Programme was known as 'the Loot-for-Work' scheme; the various policies for urban development had invariably been poorly implemented; and the acts and norms regulating forest areas had been used by the Forest Service to build an empire of their own rather than to guarantee rights to Adivasis and other forest dwellers. Nevertheless, it proved feasible to gradually improve or expand existing policies instead of dismantling existing systems and replacing them with completely new initiatives.

Two additional features of the political and policy processes that accompanied the emergence of the five policies that we analyse are worth mentioning. The first was the frequent absence of any significant parliamentary opposition to social policies. The MGNREGA was passed unanimously, while the ICDS, the JNNURM and the FRA met with virtually no political opposition in Parliament. Few political parties believed that they would acquire electoral capital by appearing to oppose anti-poverty programmes. Instead, the roadblocks came from within the UPA or from within the State apparatus. The ICDS, MGNREGA, and NFSA were all opposed by the Finance Ministry, the PMO and/or the Planning Commission on fiscal grounds. Ministries proposed dilutions of the latter two programmes which—if they had been included in the final versions that were enacted—would have thwarted the right to work and the right to food. The FRA, on the other hand, was met with firm opposition from the Forest Service which saw its power threatened by a strong rights-based act. Faulty drafting of that Act later enabled the Forest Service to undermine most of its provisions.

The second feature that is worth mentioning is the absence of any significant attempt to 'sell' the introduction of the new social policies to the strongest opponents of increased spending on the welfare of the poor: the upper and middle classes. This meant that, as Chapter 2 discusses, despite its mass scale, poverty did not become a salient political issue. One can perhaps argue that the continuation of policies that favoured the better off—low taxation, several incentives on savings, retirement schemes, tax exemptions and so forth—could be seen as an attempt to build a coalition around social policies. But the attempts at coalition-building ended there. No government campaign targeted the elites with the objective of easing their opposition. The vigorous debates in the media about the MGNREGA and the NFSA reflected the absence of any serious attempt to persuade the middle classes of the necessity of increased spending to tackle poverty and inequality. In contrast to Brazil, where the middle and upper classes largely favour increased spending on the welfare of the poor, this kind of 'social consciousness' is virtually absent in India, and no serious attempt to foster one was made by the ruling coalition.

Arguably, the need to build a broad coalition to support a stronger welfare state was not urgent. According to data collected by the International Monetary Fund (IMF), government revenues grew by more than 300 per cent between 2002 and 2012, or from 17.7 to 19.7 per cent of the Gross Domestic Product (GDP), (Maiorano and Manor 2017). This meant that the Indian government could afford to expand the welfare state without curbing benefits for the better off. It also made the increased financial commitment to the welfare of the poor both financially and politically feasible.

ISSUES BEYOND THE PURVIEW OF OUR ANALYSES

This book explores how the UPA governments tried to address five problems that contribute significantly to the persistence of extreme and widespread poverty and inequalities in India: lack of income security in rural areas; persisting food insecurity; management of natural resources in forest areas; astonishingly high levels of child malnutrition; and the long-standing neglect of urban poverty which co-exists with rapid growth in India's cities. After an introductory chapter which puts the poverty reduction effort of the government in historical perspective, each of the following chapters is dedicated to a specific policy introduced by the UPA governments: the MGNREGA; the NFSA; the FRA; the ICDS; and the JNNURM.

There are two important things that are—inevitably, because of a lack of space—not fully covered in this book. The first is the role of the state governments in both policy formulation and implementation. Second, the five policy initiatives covered in this book do not represent the entire poverty alleviation effort of the UPA governments.

While the focus of this book is on policy-making at the national level, it is difficult to overestimate the importance of the states in the shaping of India's welfare regime. In fact, it is much more appropriate to speak of different welfare regimes, in the plural, as each state has different social policy mixes and implementation arrangements, which produce a great deal of variety in policy and welfare outcomes (Tillin, Deshpande and Kailash 2015).

The importance of the states is threefold. First, some states directly contributed ideas and experience that shaped the policy formulation of Central government initiatives. For instance, the adoption of the RTI Act in 2005—which the UPA government saw as the bedrock of all its policy initiatives (more on this below)—was the final outcome of a two-decade long battle initiated by social activists in Rajasthan (Jenkins and Goetz 1999). Years of interactions (and frustration) with the state governments there to access government records constituted a fruitful learning experience which was used by those activists to design the comprehensive RTI law that was adopted just a year after the installation of the UPA government.

In other cases, programmes piloted in some states were scaled up at the national level, like Tamil Nadu's Midday Meal scheme or Andhra Pradesh's Aarogyasri (a health care insurance programme). In still other cases, state policies were used as the basis to formulate national-level legislation, like Maharashtra's employment guarantee scheme which was adapted and augmented to frame the MGNREGA. In these cases, the experience of civil servants and social activists with state-level schemes proved to be crucial to address known design and implementation problems, and to assess their feasibility and their political desirability.

Second, most of the initiatives covered in this book are Centrally Sponsored Schemes (CSS), designed and mostly funded by the Central government, but implemented by the states. Even though these programmes tend to be rather centralised—a tendency that was reinforced by the Modi government after 2014—the states have a certain degree of freedom to adapt central programmes to local conditions. Variety in implementation arrangements can be quite marked. For example, Andhra Pradesh has decided to implement the MGNREGA by excluding locally elected councils (*gram panchayats*), which, according to the national Act, were supposed to spend at least 50 per cent of the funds (Maiorano 2014). On a more positive note, Andhra Pradesh set up an independent society for the conduct of social audits of the MGNREGA, which was then adopted at the national level. Similarly, Maharashtra implemented the ICDS in 'mission mode', which bypassed normal implementation structures. The 'mission mode' was later adopted at the national level (see Chapter 6).

Third, local political dynamics result in strikingly different policy outcomes. This is partly due to the fact that the states have very different implementation capacities. But this does not explain why some states like Chhattisgarh—certainly not a prime example of a high capacity state—obtained significant results in the implementation of the MGNREGA, or reformed very successfully the PDS—a change that then inspired other state governments to reform their own PDS and indeed served as a model for the National Food Security Act (2013) (Tillin, Saxena and Singh Sisodia 2015). On the other hand, differences in implementation capacity do not explain why some high capacity states like Gujarat are unable to achieve significant results in social policy implementation. In fact, 'regional political settlements and leadership play a pivotal role' in shaping different welfare regimes and in determining policy outcomes (Tillin, Deshpande and Kailash 2015: 9). Each of the policies covered in this book—and those not covered—sometimes look radically different in different states.

Let us now turn to some of the social policies adopted by the UPA governments that are not analysed in this book. These covered different areas such as human capital formation (the Right to Education Act, 2009), health (the National Rural Health Mission), social security for informal workers (the Unorganised Workers' Social Security Act, 2008), food security (the scaling up of the Midday Meal scheme) and debt relief (the farmers' loan waiver, 2009). Moreover, at the beginning of its first term, the UPA adopted the already mentioned RTI. It is worth devoting a few words to some of these initiatives which, even if not perfectly designed or implemented, did have a substantial impact.

The RTI was intended to be the foundation upon which the UPA's idea of a rights-based welfare state was to be built. Aruna Roy (a former civil servant and one of the social activists from Rajasthan who had initiated the campaign for accessing public records as a right) came to the very first meeting of the NAC with a fully drafted RTI, which was quickly adopted by Parliament the following year.

The Act was a radical initiative in the Indian context where the bureaucracy—largely as a legacy of British colonial rule—had made of secrecy and opaqueness 'a veritable art form' (Das 2013: 2). This resulted in a strong allergy on the part of the State to transparency and downward accountability (Jenkins and

Manor 2017). The decision by the Indian State to open itself up to scrutiny was even more remarkable if one considers that many countries in the world were going in exactly the opposite direction in the wake of the 9/11 attacks in the US.

The RTI Act was intended to be an instrument that could potentially tilt the balance of power between common citizens and the State in favour of the former. In some cases, it did. There are often vocal confrontations between poor rural dwellers and local bureaucrats at public hearings where official records (obtained through the RTI, usually by civil society organisations) are read out in public, and corruption and other forms of misappropriation are exposed. One of the authors of this book saw officials returning—in public—at least part of the money that they had siphoned off.[5] In other cases, large-scale corruption networks have been exposed and eventually dismantled following investigations by RTI activists. In any case, there is evidence to suggest that the mere existence of the RTI may serve as a deterrent for corrupt bureaucrats and politicians.

However, like all policy initiatives in India, the RTI is not implemented fully or evenly across the states. Despite the 'poor-friendly' provisions of the law, studies found that awareness of the Act—let alone its usage—is low in rural areas and among disadvantaged communities (PRIA 2009). Also, bureaucratic resistance, insufficient staffing and poor grievance redressal mechanisms limit the impact of the Act as a tool to promote transparency and accountability (Roberts 2010). Those things are further weakened by the widespread tendency of the state governments to ignore or to implement only partially the provisions of the Act which require public authorities to display information proactively (Das 2013, Chapter 2). Furthermore, the Central government itself has not been particularly supportive of the Act, both during the UPA terms, when it tried to dilute the Act (EPW 2006; 2012), and after the 2014 elections, since when the government has tried to 'strangle to death' the RTI (EPW 2015).

However, an early analysis found that, overall, 68 per cent of those seeking information do obtain access to it and in no state is the rate lower than 50 per cent (PRIA 2009). Experimental research also found the usage of the RTI to be almost as effective as paying a bribe to obtain access to basic public services (Peisakhin and Pinto 2010). These are not trivial achievements. The threat that the RTI constitutes for corrupt bureaucrats and politicians can also be inferred by the high number of cases where RTI activists have been threatened, beaten up or even murdered—since the mid-2000s, 69 RTI activists have been killed (Jaffrelot and Nissa 2018).

A second major policy initiative of the UPA governments that we do not cover in this book was the National Rural Health Mission (NRHM), launched by the prime minister in April 2005. The health sector, long neglected by successive Indian governments, was one of the top priorities of the CMP, which pledged: to increase public spending on health to 2–3 per cent of the GDP (which did not materialise); to introduce a national health insurance scheme for poor families (the Rashtriya Swasthya Bima Yojana (RSBY), launched in 2008); and to step up efforts to control communicable diseases (Rao 2017, Chapter 5). The NRHM was the pillar of the government's strategy to address what was increasingly recognised as a health emergency, which was not only seen as a major cause of poverty—India has an exceptionally high figure of 'out-of-pocket' expenditure, which is a major source of poverty and a leading cause for falling back into poverty (Krishna 2011)—but also as a constraint on economic growth. According to a World Bank study, malnutrition alone costs India between 2 and 3 percentage points of GDP each year (Gragnolati et al. 2006).

In fact, India's health indicators were—and still are, despite relatively rapid progress, as we shall see in the conclusion of this book—terribly poor and on par with much poorer countries in Sub-Saharan Africa, lower than neighbouring (and poorer) countries like Sri Lanka and Bangladesh, and much lower than other emerging economies. The main objective of the NRHM was to rapidly improve health indicators (also in light of India's targets in the context of the Millennium Development Goals) through the strengthening of the public health system.

The NRHM consisted, on the one hand, of a series of governance reforms, including increased (and more flexible) funding, especially for primary health care; decentralisation of health management at the village level to facilitate coordination with other schemes impacting on health such as drinking water, sanitation and child development; promotion of the non-profit sector to increase community participation and ownership; and the strengthening of monitoring systems against targets. On the other hand, the Mission involved specific policy actions. These included the streamlining of the accredited social health activist (ASHA) at the village level to promote the usage of public health services and to increase immunisation rates and a cash-transfer programme (called the Janani Suraksha Yojana) to incentivise institutional deliveries.

A major problem of the NRHM was insufficient funding. During the first five years, expenditure was less than 0.2 per cent of GDP (Drèze and Sen 2013: 317), even though, during the *Eleventh Five Year Plan* period (2007–12) the total expenditure on the programme represented a threefold increase in rural health expenditure as compared to the previous Plan period (Rao 2017: 356). Insufficient administrative capacity and design problems—particularly the split of implementation responsibility across two different line ministries—also limited the impact of the Mission.

However, studies have found that NRHM had a substantive and positive impact on the number of institutional deliveries, a decline in neonatal mortality, improved immunisation rates, promotion of exclusive breastfeeding and reduced inequalities in access to health care facilities (Vellakkal et al. 2017; Sinha 2012).

These far from trivial achievements, while certainly not signifying that the NRHM is the solution to India's health care problems which remain huge, are a clear confirmation that the public health sector is not irremediably doomed and that it can actually serve as a way to provide quality care at low cost (Drèze and Sen 2013: 379).

A third area that we do not cover is education. The UPA government enacted the Right to Education (RTE) Act, 2009, which sought to—at last—fulfil the commitment of Article 45 of the Constitution which stipulated that: 'the State shall endeavour to provide, within a period of ten years from the commencement of this Constitution, for free and compulsory education for all children until they complete the age of fourteen years'.

The delay in enacting legislation for the provision of free and compulsory education by itself shows how low on the agenda education has been for successive Indian governments since Independence. Low prioritisation translated into disastrous educational achievement. Suffice it to say that literacy rates in India today are lower than in China in 1982 (Maiorano and Manor 2017).

The RTE established a set of principles and standards that educational policies had to conform to, such as maximum teacher–pupil ratios (1:30), minimum qualifications for teachers, and the provision of free and compulsory education for all Indian children. Considering that high out-of-pocket expenditure for education (even in government schools) had been indicated as a major reason for low enrolment and high dropout rates (Das 2013: 262), the RTE was an important (and long overdue) step in the right direction.

An important element of the RTE was Section 12 of the Act which stipulated that special category schools (Kendriya Vidyalaya, Navodaya Vidyalaya, Sainik School etc.) and private schools had to reserve 25 per cent of the seats to children from disadvantaged communities from the neighbourhood. This was a quite radical provision as it sought to temper the elitist nature of many private and special category schools by mixing children from different backgrounds (both in terms of caste and class). This is important as research shows that everyday contact between ethnically segregated communities contributes to behavioural change and a reduction of discriminatory practices (Scacco and Warren 2018; Lowe 2018). Section 12 of the RTE Act also resonates with a provision included in the Midday Meal Scheme—scaled up nationally by the UPA—whereby children share the same food irrespective of caste and by which preference in hiring cooks should be given to SCs/STs, again with the intention of contributing towards eroding rigid forms of caste segregation and discrimination.

However, Section 12 of the Act was very poorly and unevenly implemented across the country. According to a recent report the share of seats actually allocated (in the school year 2014–15) to disadvantaged groups in private schools varied widely: 0 per cent in Andhra Pradesh, less than 1 per cent in Odisha and Uttar Pradesh, 4 per cent Punjab and Kerala, 7 per cent in Gujarat. In other states, however, the percentage of seats allocated was much higher: 31 per cent in Bihar, 32 per cent in Karnataka and Uttarakhand, 38 per cent in Tamil Nadu and 45 per cent in New Delhi (*State of the Nation* 2015).

Nevertheless, the UPA's educational initiatives seem to have had a positive impact at least in terms of enrolment rates, which increased by 9 percentage points between 2003 and 2013 to 92.3 per cent of the children in primary school age. The impact seems to have been particularly significant for female students, who were lagging behind males in 2003 but have now closed the gap. This does not mean, however, that the Sarva Shiksha Abhiyan (SSA) or the establishment of the right to education will address India's educational challenges. In fact, the quality of education remains abysmal, especially in rural areas (ASER 2019).

THE STRUCTURE OF THE BOOK

The second chapter places the UPA's initiatives in historical context by examining the Congress Party's discourse on poverty over time, its rhetoric on the issue, and the impact of the policies it pursued in government on the mass poverty that persists in the rapidly expanding Indian economy of the early twenty-first century. It emphasises the profound ambivalence that characterises both the rhetoric and the practice of the politics of poverty in India.

Chapter 3 focuses on the MGNREGA which is India's (and arguably the world's) largest poverty programme. It sought to provide—as a right—100 days' employment on public works projects to every rural household as a safety net in a context of marked income insecurity and the widespread lack of employment opportunities. The chapter seeks to explain why this programme was more successful than the other initiatives considered in this collection.

In absolute terms, more undernourished people live in India than any other country—as many as 217 million people or 17.5 per cent of the population in 2010–12. Chapter 4 addresses one of the final initiatives of UPA-II, a long-negotiated NFSA. This legislation sought to provide statutory underpinning for a 'right to food', but opened up a much wider debate about the role of the state in reducing poverty.

Chapter 5 is devoted to the FRA, which was intended to improve the material well-being of people who reside in India's forested areas—the great majority of whom are poor. Chapter 6 analyses the political and policy processes that led to the restructuring of India's main instrument to tackle child malnutrition, the ICDS. India suffers from child poverty and malnutrition rates higher than those of most lower-income Sub-Saharan African countries, making this a crucial policy initiative to consider.

Lastly, Chapter 7 considers how the JNNURM, while not entirely designed as an anti-poverty programme, included one initiative which sought to tackle the mass poverty that is an inescapable feature of the urban Indian landscape. This was arguably the missing element of the UPA's anti-poverty agenda, which did not include a specific focus on urban poverty—although some of the other programmes that we analyse, like the ICDS and the NFSA, cover urban areas as well.

The chapters in the book were written individually by the four authors, who then commented extensively on each other's drafts and jointly developed the overarching analytical framework. The analyses of individual policies are based on semi-structured interviews with members of a policy community that, as we have noted, was rather broad, especially in comparative perspective (Tillin and Duckett 2017), and included politicians, civil servants, civil society activists, academics and representatives of various interest groups.

While majority of the research was conducted in New Delhi, the chapters on the MGNREGA, the ICDS and the NFSA also draw on extensive fieldwork in rural areas and several state capitals conducted by each of us individually. Collectively, we conducted over 100 interviews, which were based around a common core of key questions agreed by all team members before fieldwork. The interviews covered four broad areas: policy-makers' political perceptions, calculations, machinations, and 'presentations' of themselves and their policies; their ideological commitments (if any); plus, their assessments of the political, financial and administrative feasibility of potential programmes; and of what was conceived as politically necessary and/or advantageous. The interviews were used to develop case studies of the interplay of political and policy processes that led to the expansion of India's welfare regime via 'process tracing' (George and Bennett 2005; Checkel 2006). This had the intent of identifying small sets of key causal mechanisms, and charting the interplay between them, to characterise the larger processes at work. The research for the book was conducted as part of a larger comparative project looking at the politics of anti-poverty policies across Brazil, China, India and South Africa (see Tillin and Duckett 2017 for an overview). Our analysis of the politics of the policy processes in India is thus implicitly informed by a wider comparative frame.

26 October 2019
London

James Chiriyankandath
Diego Maiorano
James Manor
Louise Tillin

NOTES AND REFERENCES

1. On the significance of these new approaches to social security, see Drèze and Khera 2017a.

2. The research for this book was funded by a major grant from the Economic and Social Research Council, United Kingdom.

3. For a summary of the main approaches to understand welfare state expansion in both industrialised and developing countries, see Tillin and Duckett 2017.

4. This is discussed further in Chapter 4.

5. Maiorano's direct observation, Medak district, 12 December 2012.

one

The Congress Party, the Politics of Poverty and Policies of the UPA Government

POVERTY IN INDIA

It needs to be stressed that the measurement of poverty is a question that has long bedeviled economists and politicians and remains the subject of intense controversy. Historically, poverty has been measured in India in terms of income and consumption. If we use this method, the percentage of those below the official poverty line has gone down from well over half the total population—57.3 per cent of the rural and 45.9 per cent of urban dwellers (Drèze and Sen 1995: 224)—in 1970–71, the year of *Garibi Hatao*, to the Planning Commission's controversial 2012 estimate of 29.8 per cent: 33.8 per cent in rural areas (where 68.8 per cent of Indians still live (Census of India 2011)) and 20.9 per cent in urban India (Balchand 2012).

The basis for these estimates has always been vigorously disputed. Even Planning Commission Deputy Chairman Montek Singh Ahluwalia admitted to persistent serious discrepancies between the National Sample Survey Office (NSSO) and national accounts based on data from the Central Statistical Organisation (CSO) in the pegging of the daily per capita consumption at Rs 28.65 in urban areas and Rs 22.42 in rural areas. Those figures amount respectively to US$ 192 and 151 per year, compared to US$ 10,980 in the United States.[1] Looking beyond debates over the statistical basis of poverty measurements, Amartya Sen has persuasively argued that 'poverty must be seen as the deprivation of basic capabilities rather than merely as lowness of income' (Sen 2000: 87). The United Nations Development Programme (UNDP) Human Poverty Index, based on health, education and living standards, finds that over half of all Indians (51.1 per cent) still live in multidimensional poverty. Nearly a third (32.68 per cent) are under the international poverty line of a purchasing power parity (PPP) of US$ 1.25 a day.[2]

Besides, there is little difference in consumption levels between the official category of the poor and a large section of the so-called middle class, especially in rural areas (World Bank 2011: 3). N. C. Saxena, a member of the National Advisory Council (NAC) and a former secretary of the Planning Commission, estimates that around 70 per cent of India's population can be said to be poor.[3] But many Indians who remain by globally applicable criteria, poor, see themselves as middle class (Venkataramakrishnan 2015). That helps to explain the conundrum of why poverty has not, as we shall see, been politically salient.

The 'Politics of Poverty'

Addressing the ninth session of the Indian National Congress at Lahore in 1893, Dadabhai Naoroji proclaimed the poverty of India to be the greatest question for the assembled delegates of the early Congress (Naoroji 1893, in Batabyal 2007: 38). More than half a century later, Jawaharlal Nehru, soon to be independent India's first prime minister, told the Constituent Assembly that its first task was:

> to free India through a new Constitution, to feed the starving people, and to clothe the naked masses, and to give every Indian the fullest opportunity to develop himself according to his capacity.[4]

Seventy years after independence, it arguably ought to remain so both for the Congress Party and for India. Yet a disenchanted prominent former Congress minister, Mani Shankar Aiyar, wrote as the Congress-led UPA began its second term of office in 2009:

> Our politics of poverty is characterised by our poverty of politics. Although poverty is the overwhelming fact of our national life, it is hardly the theme of our politics. (Aiyar 2009)

Even Sonia Gandhi, the Congress president, has remarked on how 'India has long presented the paradox of a democracy where the poor majority, despite its voting power, has not always commanded its due' (Gandhi 2010a). For the pre-independence Congress leaders engaged in the struggle for Indian self-government, from Naoroji and Romesh Chandra Dutt to Jawaharlal Nehru and Subhas Chandra Bose, the causes of India's poverty were directly related to the ills of the British colonial government. Naoroji (1901: 33–56) and Dutt (Dutt 1901, in Batabyal 2007: 52–55) forensically detailed the crippling drain of Indian revenues to Britain.

Nehru and Bose's concern with poverty drew them towards what they saw as its antidote—modern economic development based on planning and the ideal of socialism. When in 1938 Bose, as Congress president, appointed a National Planning Committee, chaired by Nehru, it declared its aim to be to ensure an adequate standard of living for the masses and to rid India of the appalling poverty of its people (Nehru 1961: 397). Prefigured in the resolution on fundamental rights introduced by Nehru at the 1931 Karachi Congress, the Congress' policy found formal post-independence expression at its Avadi session in 1955. It resolved that:

> planning should take place with a view to the establishment of a socialistic pattern of society, where the principal means of production are under social ownership or control, production is progressively speeded up and there is equitable distribution of the national wealth. (Brecher 1959: 528)

Yet Nehru's speech moving the motion revealed the tension between addressing poverty and a commitment to equity that continues to characterise the party's economic policies. He noted that:

> Socialism or communism might help you to divide your existing wealth, if you like, but in India, there is no existing wealth for you to divide; there is only poverty to divide ... We must produce wealth, and then divide it equitably. How can we have a Welfare State without wealth? ... Our economic policy must therefore aim at plenty. (Nehru 1955, in Batabyal 2007: 501)

Thirty-seven years later, Manmohan Singh, then finance minister in P. V. Narasimha Rao's minority Congress government, while expressing eternal gratitude to Nehru's vision, sought to square the circle by introducing the landmark 1992–93 liberalising budget as a contribution to building 'an India free of war, want and exploitation' (Singh 1992a). Communist leader Somnath Chatterjee decried the same budget as 'the final nail in the coffin of the principle of self-reliance and mixed economy which was the dream of Pandit Jawaharlal Nehru' (Chatterjee 1992).

Garibi Hatao

The obscure origin of the slogan *Garibi Hatao* (End Poverty) reflects the ambiguity of the Congress Party in confronting the problem of poverty. It became the catchphrase of Prime Minister Indira Gandhi's triumphant general election campaign in 1971 in the wake of her break with the conservative old Congress bosses in 1969 and measures such as the nationalisation of banks and the abolition of princes' privy purses. Coined as a remarkably successful riposte to the short-sighted and negative personal slogan of 'Indira *hatao*' of the coalition of parties opposed to her—'They demand the removal of Indira, we demand the removal of poverty'—it scarcely expressed a coherent programme focused on eliminating poverty. It reflected the leftwing sympathies harboured by many of Mrs. Gandhi's coterie of advisors in this period including P. N. Haksar, her principal private secretary, D. P. Dhar and I. K. Gujral (both of whom served as ministers in her cabinet), and the journalist Romesh Thapar.

P. V. Narasimha Rao, an Indira loyalist promoted to the chief ministership of Andhra Pradesh shortly after the 1971 election, described *Garibi Hatao* as fantastic in its impact, almost matching Congress' call in 1942 for the British to 'Quit India' in 'its brevity, its exquisite simplicity' (Rao 1998: 622). Unlike 'Quit India', however, '*Garibi Hatao*' remained merely a populist slogan as successive droughts and the global hike in oil prices contributed to severe food shortages and spiraling inflation in the years following the polls. Recounting her experience of travelling across India during the 1971 campaign, Indira Gandhi revealingly remarked:

> nowhere did I see the sort of poverty which was so prevalent twenty years ago. *Whether they had proper shelter or clothing or not* [italics added], almost everywhere the children were healthy and bright-eyed. (Norman 1985: 132)

While *Garibi Hatao* was strikingly successful as a political slogan, the political strategy and economic policies that followed in its wake were not. The latter included a renewed effort at land reform—enforcing ceilings on ownership and redistributing land—as well as anti-poverty programmes such as the Small Farmer Development Agency, the Marginal Farmer and Agricultural Labour Programme, the Crash Scheme for Rural Employment, the Drought-Prone Areas Programme, the Pilot Intensive Rural Employment Programme, and the National Rural Employment Programme (NREP) (the last four sought to provide temporary wage employment for the rural poor). With implementation centralised in New Delhi, they sought to reduce rural inequality and erode the influence of the dominant landed castes so that Mrs. Gandhi's reconstituted Congress Party could establish a national power base independent of the state-level party bosses, many of whom she distrusted (Brass 1990: 266–267).

However, especially after her more leftwing advisors were sidelined and the introduction of authoritarian Emergency rule in 1975, it became obvious that *Garibi Hatao* did not represent a break with Congress' continued reliance on growth and development as the solution to the problem of mass poverty. A sweepingly ambitious Twenty-Point Programme announced shortly after the declaration of Emergency rule was virtually superseded within a year by a simplistic Four-Point Programme of social reform advanced by the Youth Congress, led by Indira's notorious younger son Sanjay Gandhi: 'each one teach one [to read and write]', 'plant a tree', abolish dowries, and family planning (Wallace 1978: 13).

The echo of *Garibi Hatao* grew even fainter when Mrs. Gandhi returned to power in 1980. Conscious of the negative impact that her earlier populist anti-capitalist stance had on economic growth and how it had served to alienate business, Mrs. Gandhi initiated a political realignment that created a ruling alliance between the Indian State and capital (Kohli 2012: 27). In her second period in office Mrs. Gandhi also saw middle-class Indians as a key element in consolidating her power (Maiorano 2015: 95–99, 121–135). In the general election following her assassination in 1984, her elder son and successor, Rajiv Gandhi, adopted the rhetoric of economic liberalisation and technological change propelling a youthful India into the twenty-first century (Frankel 2005: 677). Under growing pressure from a diverse Opposition that eventually defeated Congress in the 1989 polls, he reverted, partially and unsuccessfully, to the rhetoric of populist socialism (Kohli 1990: 337). A notable tangible legacy of the Rajiv government (1984–89) that reflected this was the Jawahar Rozgar Yojana, launched just months before the elections to mark the centenary of Jawaharlal Nehru's birth. This merged the erstwhile NREP and the Rural Landless Employment Guarantee Programme (introduced by Indira Gandhi's government in 1983) and was targeted at people below the poverty line, particularly those belonging to Scheduled Castes and Tribes, and women.

Liberalisation, Poverty and Electoral Politics

In his first budget speech as finance minister in July 1991, Manmohan Singh ushered in the liberalising reforms introduced by Prime Minister P. V. Narasimha Rao's minority Congress government. He dedicated it to the memory of Rajiv Gandhi, assassinated during the 1991 election campaign. Narasimha Rao saw encouraging the expansion of the private sector as a way to spur growth that would yield revenues that the government could more effectively invest in welfare (Manor 2005a: 100). Singh set out, less ambiguously than any Congress minister had previously done, the logic of the position that Nehru had taken at Avadi in 1955:

> In India, we launched an experiment under the leadership of Pandit Jawaharlal Nehru, an experiment which sought to unite the strengths and merits of different approaches to accelerated development of our backward economy. We have achieved considerable success in the field of development, modernisation and greater social equity. However, we are yet far from realising our full potential in all these areas. We have to accomplish the unfinished task
>
> ... we must restore to the creation of wealth its proper place in the development process. For, without it, we cannot remove the stigma of abject poverty, ignorance and disease. But we cannot accept social misery and inequity as unavoidable in the process of creation of wealth. The basic challenge of our times is to ensure that wealth creation is not only tempered by equity and justice but is harnessed to the goal of removal of poverty and development for all....
>
> In highlighting the significance of reform, my purpose is not to give a fillip to mindless and heartless consumerism we have borrowed from the affluent societies of the West.... Our approach to development has to combine efficiency with austerity... austerity is a way of holding our society together in pursuit of the noble goal of banishing poverty, hunger and disease... (Singh 1992b: 281–282)

In the next decade and a half, both India and the Congress Party underwent significant change. Congress returned to power in 2004 after eight years in Opposition with a Gandhi back at the helm—Rajiv Gandhi's widow, Sonia, was elected party president in 1998. In its first election manifesto under her leadership in 1999 there were almost fifty references made to poverty and the poor. The eradication of poverty was highlighted as 'the single most important objective of national development' (Indian National Congress 1999). In 2004 Congress leaders found it expedient to play along with the useful media (urban) myth that its unexpected triumph had resulted from a backlash of the rural poor against the 'India Shining' slogan of its main opponent, the Hindu nationalist Bharatiya Janata Party (BJP) that had headed the government since 1998 (Manor 2011c: 217).

In his first address to the nation, after unexpectedly becoming prime minister of the first UPA government in 2004, Manmohan Singh recalled Mahatma Gandhi's injunction to think of the poorest person you had ever seen, 'and ask if your next act will be of any use to him'. Noting the chronic poverty still afflicting millions, he then added:

> Much of the focus of economic reforms in the past decade has been on reducing the role of the government in controlling the Private Sector; controls that hampered entrepreneurial dynamism and often bred corruption. This was necessary. Yet, there are many areas, critical areas, that directly affect the quality of life of every citizen, where the government has a role, and is expected by every citizen to have a role. (Singh 2004)

Yet the Congress manifesto foregrounded its appeal to the *aam aadmi* [common man] and not the *garib* [poor] and made a point of acknowledging the country's burgeoning middle class—the face of 'India Shining'—acclaiming them as 'the proud creation of the Congress' and identifying as a priority of governance 'Arthik Navotthan [economic resurgence] to unleash the creative energies of our professionals and entrepreneurs, the cutting edge of our middle class' (Indian National Congress 2004).

The National Advisory Council: Keeper of Congress' Social Conscience

In government a lot of the thinking behind the role of the State in addressing poverty, sometimes seen as advancing a new 'rights agenda' (Ruparelia 2013), came not from within Manmohan Singh's cabinet but from the NAC, politically significant in linking the UPA to the Left Front which extended support to it from outside government. Set up by the government in 2004, the

NAC was chaired by Sonia Gandhi (also the UPA chairperson) until 2006 when she resigned. Though the Council was wound up in 2008, it was reconstituted in 2010, with Sonia Gandhi again assuming the chair until its demise with the defeat of the UPA government in 2014. Including social activists, scientists, economists, ex-civil servants and prominent figures from the non-governmental organisation (NGO) sector, the NAC became the main focus of the 'policy community' (Manor 2014) behind the UPA's major initiatives to tackle mass poverty and was widely regarded as more leftwing than the PMO, the Planning Commission and the government. Like Indira Gandhi's radical confidantes at the time of *Garibi Hatao*, the majority (eight of the twelve in May 2012) held degrees from leading US or British universities (National Advisory Council 2012a). However, the ways in which the NAC was unlike Indira's coterie are far more significant: while temporary, it was institutionalised and formally subject to government authority; and it had, as Right to Information activist Ruchi Gupta says,

> partly through the kind of members chosen, and the norms of functioning ... evolved, ... opened up the otherwise closed and secretive processes of formulation of law and policy, beyond its own membership to citizens groups and people with expertise. (Gupta 2011)

While deriving its distinctive character from the sorts of people included, the pivot of the NAC was Sonia Gandhi. She revealed the thinking that lay behind its creation in a speech to a *Hindustan Times* Conclave in 2005. After acknowledging the contribution of entrepreneurs, scientists, technologists, academics and researchers, she added, 'But if our concern is with people at large and their day-to-day lives, particularly of the weaker sections, then we need a new paradigm for sustained cooperation between the government and civil society'. It was to make this happen that the government had 'to create an institutional framework for the involvement of a diverse array of civil society groups and organizations in both the democratic and developmental process' (Gandhi 2005).

As the NAC chair, Sonia Gandhi played a crucial role, conveying the sometimes stridently expressed ideas of members in tempered language in letters to the prime minister and subtly bringing her influence to bear in trying to limit the degree to which the resulting legislation was diluted (Singh 2011: 202–204). This was the case with the two major pieces of legislation under the first UPA government, in the drafting of which the NAC played a vital role. Both were enacted in 2005 with two key NAC members, Aruna Roy and Jean Drèze, acting in tandem. Roy, a former Indian Administrative Service (IAS) officer-turned-rights activist, was a driving force behind the Right to Information Act mandating timely response to citizens' requests for government information (Government of India 2005a). Drèze, a Belgian-born Indian national, a development economist who had collaborated with Amartya Sen, was particularly involved with the National Rural Employment Guarantee Act (renamed the Mahatma Gandhi NREGA on the 140th birth anniversary of the 'father of the nation' in 2009).

Linking MGNREGA's introduction to the old slogan of *Garibi Hatao*, Prime Minister Singh in his Independence Day address at the Red Fort in Delhi in 2005 recalled that:

> Smt. Indira Gandhi had given the nation the goal of "Garibi Hatao". Today, if we need to remove poverty, we need to create employment "Rozgar Badhao". (Singh 2005)

Aimed 'at enhancing the livelihood security of people in rural areas by guaranteeing hundred days of wage-employment in a financial year to a rural household whose adult members volunteer to do unskilled manual work' (Government of India 2005b), by 2017 MGNREGA had cost Rs 420,744.76 crore (c. US$ 64 billion).[5] While large, this was still a modest figure when set against the national GDP, amounting to an average annual expenditure of merely 0.3 per cent. Two other programmes initiated by the first UPA government were the Aam Aadmi Bima Yojana (to provide life insurance cover for the rural landless) in 2007 and the Rashtriya Swasthya Bima Yojana (to provide health insurance for people below the poverty line) in 2008. Like MGNREGA, the cost of these schemes was shared between the

Centre and state governments with the former bearing the larger share.

After the UPA's return to power in the 2009 general election, the reconstituted NAC's major focus was the drafting of a National Food Security Bill (NFSB), a commitment made in Congress' 2009 election manifesto. However, it took four years for the bill to be passed. It was only laid before Parliament at the end of 2011 and received Parliamentary approval in late 2013, but only after being introduced via a Presidential Ordinance. There were differences between the government and NAC members, most notably Jean Drèze, a prominent advocate of the right to food (Drèze 2004), on how wide its scope should be. At one point a frustrated Drèze said he felt that the Indian middle class living 'in a make-believe world that exists only on television and small islands of privilege' had 'completely lost track of how poor this country is' (Drèze 2010a). Having at one point left the working group on the bill, in March 2012 Drèze joined 35 other leading Indian development economists in addressing an open letter to Prime Minister Manmohan Singh calling for a simplification of the bill, building on providing subsidised food grains to around two-thirds of the population (Abreu et al. 2012).

Sonia Gandhi, the Congress Party's longest serving president, was certainly not oblivious of the danger for Congress in appearing to flaunt the embrace of wealth. In a speech concluding celebrations of the 125th anniversary of the party's foundation in 2010, she warned:

> It ill becomes representatives of a Party claiming to speak for the poor to indulge in greed, extravagance and luxury. Simplicity, restraint and austerity must be our chosen way. We cannot make this a law. But in a country where poverty is still widespread, let us at least have the moral sensibility to avoid vulgar displays of wealth and waste. (Gandhi 2010b)

The Politics of the Poor, the Politics of Poverty and the Politics of Congress

India is a country the majority of whose people are, by most international measures, poor. So why has poverty not been a dominant theme in politics? Is it because 'Indian democracy is trapped in a vicious circle of exclusion and elitism' with the majority effectively disempowered by economic insecurity, lack of education and social discrimination (Drèze 2004: 1725)? There is more to the supposed lack of political will to address hunger than simply the powerlessness of the hungry. There is the way in which poverty is both perceived and experienced. For people belonging to different social categories, whether Scheduled Castes and Tribes, backward castes, or marginalised religious or ethnic minorities, poverty is not simply material want but it is bound up with historically embedded practices of social discrimination that deny human dignity (Ahmed and Varshney 2008: 20–21). This substantial correspondence between caste-based disadvantage and material deprivation has produced a peculiar pattern of poverty and social inequality. In the context of the spread of mass democracy the correlation has caused the politics of the poor to be predominantly expressed through varied idioms of identity politics while the discussion of anti-poverty policy takes the form of elite debates on poverty alleviation.

Against this backdrop the rationale behind the Congress Party's changing approach to poverty can be grasped. By mixing populist rhetoric, appeals to identity politics and elite policy debate, it was able to transcend the politics of the poor and the politics (global as well as national) of anti-poverty policy-making. It has always been a changing mix. The mid-twentieth century promise of directive State planning under Nehru and Indira Gandhi gave way to the view in the early twenty-first century that, as the Planning Commission's website put it in 2012, planning 'should increasingly be of an indicative nature' (Planning Commission 2012). In the intervening years the stewards of the Indian State, whether belonging to the Congress or the BJP which returned to power under Narendra Modi in 2014 or a variety of regional parties, came to share a consensus on prioritising private sector-led growth.

The key to understanding the Congress' attitude to particular anti-poverty initiatives is the prevailing array of forces and ideas within and beyond the party as well as in the broader society.

During the first UPA government the attitude taken by many of the leading actors, the role of the Left (Communist and allied) parties in extending it support, as well as pressure from radical civil society movements (a few of whose leading activists were included in the NAC), helped to enact anti-poverty legislation such as MGNREGA (Chopra 2011b: 162; Hasan 2009: 16). The parting of ways between Congress and the Left in 2008 over the agreement on nuclear cooperation reached with the United States, and the ill-health of Congress president Sonia Gandhi, were among factors that affected the policy mix in the UPA's second term, contributing to a sense of drift in this as in other policy areas. The reconstituted NAC was also given a weaker mandate: in 2004 it was mandated to oversee the implementation of the UPA's National Common Minimum Programme (Government of India 2004), while in 2010 it was merely asked to 'give attention to the priorities stated in the address of the President of India to Parliament on 4 June, 2009 .... [and] review the flagship programmes of the Government and suggest measures to address any constraints in their implementation and delivery' (National Advisory Council 2012b).

Consider the references to 'poverty' and the 'poor' in the speeches made by finance ministers introducing their annual budgets in Parliament. They might have amounted to mere lip service, but it was striking to see the decline from 21 references by P. Chidambaram in 2004 to 12 in the post-election budget of 2009, and then to just two in each of Pranab Mukherjee's last three budget speeches.[6] If budget speeches are crudely reflective of the themes that loom largest in policy-making, it is noteworthy that on those same occasions, references to 'growth' occurred between 21 and 35 times.

Six months before the *Garibi Hatao* campaign, Indira Gandhi had this to say about the Fourth Five Year Plan:

> Our planning should result not only in an integrated process of increased production, but rational distribution of the added wealth. The overriding inspiration must be a burning sense of social justice. While increased production is of the utmost importance it is equally important to

> remove or reduce, and prevent the concentration of wealth and economic power... There can be no doubt that the responsibilities devolving upon the public sector—without diminishing those of the private sector, in our mixed economy—will grow in range and volume. Socialism involves a reordering of society on a rational and equitable basis and this can only be achieved by assigning an expanding role to the public sector ... [which] can be expected more and more to occupy the commanding heights of the economy. (Planning Commission 1970)

Contrast this with what her daughter-in-law had to say about the role of the State four decades later. Addressing a *Hindustan Times* conference on the peace dividend in South Asia in 2003, Sonia Gandhi made clear there would be no departure from the new orthodoxy of high growth being the main purpose of economic policy:

> Our nation-states have been far too centralized. That had a logic [*sic*] at a particular point of time over half a century ago... Our economies have performed well in recent times. But not well enough to deal with the huge backlog of poverty, malnutrition, disease and unemployment. There is no alternative to faster economic growth. There is no alternative to an effective role for the state in this transformation. (Gandhi 2003)

Five years on, in his 'Foreword' to the Eleventh Plan, Prime Minister Manmohan Singh sought to explain Congress' commitment to combating mass poverty with its endorsement of the State's embrace of the private sector:

> The transition to high growth is an impressive achievement, but we must not forget that growth is not the only measure of development. We also need to ensure that growth is widely spread so that its benefits, in terms of income and employment, are adequately shared by the poor and weaker sections of our society ... Planning in a market economy which is becoming increasingly integrated with the world is bound to be different from what it used to be in earlier years. Much of what used to be done by governments ... is

> now being done by the private sector. India is blessed in having a long tradition of private entrepreneurship and the private sector has responded magnificently to the new opportunities opened up by economic reforms. However, this does not mean that the role of the government must shrink. On the contrary, the government must play a much larger role in some areas even while shifting out of others. (Planning Commission 2008a)

After ten years in power, the evidence suggested that the increased spending on poverty alleviation programmes such as MGNREGA, estimated to amount to as much as US$ 57 billion during the first term of the UPA government (Manor 2011c: 215), had made growth more inclusive. But since India still spent relatively little on poverty reduction, health and education, the poor could not be said to have fully shared in the benefits of growth (Maiorano and Manor 2017: 282–286). While surveys suggest some progress in addressing gross inequality, welfare schemes like MGNREGA or the Food Security Act have still been criticised as doing 'little to address the problems of human capital formation in India that are the outcome of decades of under-investment in the public sector in education and health' (Harriss 2011: 22). Growth in the country's agricultural sector, on which a majority of the population still depends for their livelihood, remains stubbornly stuck at 2–3 per cent. The sector's contribution to national GDP has shrunk from over 60 per cent in 1950–51 to under 20 per cent today (Harriss 2011). Elsewhere the impressive 6–9 per cent growth figures of the past decade have not delivered commensurate job growth, with the vaunted information technology (IT) sector a case in point. By 2011–12, it accounted for 7.5 per cent of GDP but provided employment (direct or indirect) for less than one per cent of the population (Government of India 2011: 241).

Although the politics of poverty eradication in India can still be said to remain at an impasse, this book shows that significant progress was made under the UPA in advancing human development. Four decades ago Atul Kohli pointed out that lending substance to *Garibi Hatao*

> would have required high rates of economic growth, some effective redistribution, and the capacity to penetrate and reorganize rural society. This ... would have required a cohesive political party and bureaucracy. Indira Gandhi, however, achieved nearly the opposite... (Kohli 2012: 88)

Since then the Indian State has abandoned any thought of the public sector occupying the commanding heights of the economy and opted for an alliance with the private sector, especially big business, in pursuit of the goal of rapid economic growth. This has resulted in what has been variously characterised as a 'two-track polity' (Kohli 2012: 65) or a 'two-track democracy' (Kumar 2008: 59). The former highlighted how economic decision-making has become disconnected from democratic politics and been delegated to a technocratic elite, exemplified by Manmohan Singh, economist turned prime minister. The latter argument draws attention to how India's ruling politicians, no longer able to claim the moral legitimacy of pursuing the well-being of society through planning or to rely on an alliance of the bourgeoisie and the rich peasantry, seek to create a hiatus between the 'polity' and 'economy' in order to achieve market economic transformation by stealth. However, the notable achievements of the UPA in enhancing human development in its decade in power indicate that this does not provide us with the whole picture. The UPA was by no means a radical transformative government, but our study indicates that its various programmes made an appreciable impact in diminishing poverty.

NOTES AND REFERENCES

1. 'Bad data led to fall in poverty: Montek', *Indian Express*, 21 March 2012.
2. http://hdr.undp.org/en/content/population-living-below-125-ppp-day (accessed 30 August 2019).
3. 'About 70 percent of India is poor: N. C. Saxena', *The Bihar Times*, 25 March 2012.
4. https://www.constitutionofindia.net/constitution_assembly_debates/volume/2/1947-01-22 (accessed 30 August 2019).

5. http://mnregaweb4.nic.in/netnrega/all_lvl_details_dashboard_new.aspx (accessed 29 September 2017).

6. The budget speeches are available here: https://www.indiabudget.gov.in/bspeech.php (accessed 30 August 2019).

two

The Mahatma Gandhi National Rural Employment Guarantee Act

In 2005, the Indian Parliament passed a rural employment guarantee act which was implemented the following year in the poorest one-third of districts in the country, and by 2008 extended to all districts. After 2009, it was officially renamed the 'Mahatma Gandhi National Rural Employment Guarantee Act' or MGNREGA.

It seeks to give every rural household the right to demand 100 days' employment per year (unskilled manual labour) on public works sites, at a modest but non-trivial wage, as a hedge against destitution. Unlike many Indian programmes, it is not targeted at people holding 'Below Poverty Line' cards, which is an advantage because many very poor people have not been able to obtain them. Nor is it targeted at any special social category such as the severely disadvantaged Scheduled Castes (Dalits) or Scheduled Tribes (Adivasis). It is self-targeting: anyone willing to work should be able to access it.

Vast numbers have done so. So far, over 25 billion person-days were worked under the programme. On any given day, over 11.5 million workers are expected at over 1 million worksites throughout the country.

Powerful transparency mechanisms were built into the programme, linking IT records of every step in a worker's engagement with the scheme to notations on paper job cards for each worker—to enable cross-checking to detect and deter corruption. Early on, this was reinforced by a requirement that every worker be paid through a bank or postal account. This combination of devices makes it exceedingly difficult to steal from workers' wages, on which at least 60 per cent of the programme's budget is spent.

As we shall see, many painful ambiguities attend the MGNREGA, and in some of India's 29 states it has not worked well (see Table 2.1). But for the most part, its impact on poverty has been substantial.[1] For example, a poor villager who works for just one day (out of the billions) is paid enough to purchase sufficient subsidised food in most states to provide a family with two meals per day for over a month. The programme has also helped to erode bonds of dependency which have long tied poor villagers to prosperous neighbours (Jenkins and Manor 2017).

The MGNREGA helped the ruling alliance in New Delhi which introduced it to win the re-election in 2009. Contrary to lazy media reports on that election, the role of the MGNREGA was not decisive. But reliable polling data clearly shows that beneficiaries of the MGNREGA voted in greater numbers for parties in that alliance than for rival parties. This almost certainly enabled the ruling alliance to win between 12 to 15 extra seats in Parliament—in close contests, in a House of 542—which gave it a firmer grip on power after the election (Manor 2011a).

ORIGINS

After the surprise victory of the UPA in the 2004 general elections, a 'consensus' emerged in the Indian and international media, attributing this victory to a revolt of the rural poor against globalisation and economic liberalisation. This was inaccurate. The UPA did better in urban areas than in rural and among prosperous groups than among the poor (Manor 2011a). Congress leaders knew that the explanation for their victory was a myth,[2] but they carefully avoided challenging it because it made them look more progressive and humane. They then set out to reinforce that image in ways that might benefit the party at the next general election in 2009. They did this by providing more generous funding to existing programmes to benefit the poor (rural and urban) and by introducing new initiatives for them. Of these, the MGNREGA was by far the largest—the centrepiece.

The leader of the Congress, Sonia Gandhi, declined to become prime minister, choosing the economist Dr. Manmohan Singh for that role. To generate ideas for initiatives that would address poverty and inequality, she invited a small group of distinguished and progressive civil society leaders, retired civil servants and intellectuals to join a small NAC which she chaired. It would propose new programmes, most of which were consistent with pledges in the CMP or manifesto of the Congress-led UPA, and the revamping and expansion of existing programmes—and where necessary, fresh legislation. It would then develop detailed proposals for initiatives that seemed promising, before they went to government ministries and then to Parliament for consideration and action.

Only a limited agenda had been fixed for the initial meeting of the NAC, but two of its members—the civil society leader Aruna Roy and the economist Jean Drèze—arrived with elaborately detailed plans for two new initiatives: a Right to Information Act and an ambitious employment guarantee programme for the rural poor.[3] Since these gave NAC members something to get their teeth into at the outset, they became the first two initiatives to be developed by it. The initial draft of a law for what we now call the MGNREGA emerged from the NAC on 19 August 2004, only a month after its first meeting.[4]

Its antecedents included an Employment Guarantee Scheme that had long existed in the state of Maharashtra, but more crucial was the work in the state of Rajasthan by a civil society organisation called the Mazdoor Kisan Shakti Sangathan (MKSS, or Association for the Empowerment of Workers and Peasants).[5] Since 1990, it had worked among the rural poor there in efforts to raise their awareness and political capabilities, and to forge them into a force capable of persuading the government to respond to their needs—with information, action and resources. It had done so through impressive campaigns stressing poor people's right to information, and their need for employment on public works schemes which were often developed in that arid state to cope with droughts. These were the two themes—the right to information and the right to work—that were addressed at that first NAC meeting.

Aruna Roy was the leader of the MKSS. She brought to the NAC not just a knowledge of how drought relief efforts worked and sometimes went awry, but of how public works programmes might be structured in ways that would genuinely benefit poor people. Jean Drèze, an activist as well as a distinguished economist, also made an important contribution to the initial push in the NAC that led to the MGNREGA. He had co-authored books with the Nobel laureates Amartya Sen and Angus Deaton and, having worked closely with Aruna Roy and other like-minded civil society leaders, was, despite his Belgian origins, widely respected and accepted as an Indian of note. Drèze brought ideas that he and Sen had developed into NAC discussions. Notable among them was a broad definition of 'poverty': as not just a severe shortage of incomes and assets, but also a severe shortage of opportunities, rights and capabilities. The MGNREGA was clearly intended to tackle the latter problems, along with the former.

It should be stressed that their advocacy for a rural employment guarantee resonated with themes that had previously been emphasised by Sonia Gandhi, leader of the Congress and chairperson of the NAC. She had been involved with problems of rural distress since 2002,[6] although she had begun to refer specifically to the right to work for the rural poor only during the national election campaign of 2004, when she had spoken of the agrarian crisis and the failure of rival parties to address it adequately. The Congress leadership had fixed on these themes well before it developed an understanding with India's two main Communist parties after the 2004 election. Contrary to claims, this did not occur because of a groundswell of pressure from rural areas. Party leaders took up these ideas from civil society organisations—most notably, MKSS—that had worked among the rural poor, but they faced little pressure from the villages to create this new programme.

Nor (despite claims to the contrary) were they responding to lobbying or to competition from the Left parties—although the latter were helpful in getting a strong version of the MGNREG Act passed in Parliament. The Left had won more seats in the 2004 election (61 in a House of 542) than ever before, but it was rightly understood that they had little prospect of winning many more at later elections (as their losses in 2009 confirmed). Congress leaders were more concerned with competition from the BJP or the Hindu nationalist right. An employment guarantee act would broaden the base of Congress and its allies, and attract more votes from the rural poor, from whom they were wrongly reported to have reaped mighty rewards in 2004.

Sonia Gandhi's sympathy with proposals for an employment guarantee was important in swaying sceptics both within the Congress and within the government that it led. In fact, Jean Drèze recalls that the MGNREGA 'entered national policy debates like a wet dog at a glamorous party' (Drèze 2011). However, it is next to impossible within 'Congress culture' to differ with the supreme leader. (She had been urged to create such a guarantee by certain key advisors—notably Jairam Ramesh, a future minister who was a member of her circle—and others.) So, Congress leaders who had doubts about the programme felt the pressure to restrain themselves owing to worries about disapproval not from the rural poor, but from 'Madam'.[7] However, the creation of the MGNREGA was not entirely the result of decisions made at the apex of power within the Congress. Sonia Gandhi and other party leaders drew ideas—before and after creation of the NAC—from lessons learned and strategies developed by grassroots civil society activists, most importantly in Rajasthan. They may also have drawn on ideas contained in certain progressive Supreme Court rulings. When we consider both the 'Origins' and the 'Formulation' of the MGNREGA, we see 'an iterative blending of top-down and bottom-up approaches to policymaking'.

One last, curious theme is worth noting. It might be argued that the origins of these efforts to tackle poverty and inequality can also be traced to the social democratic traditions of the Congress Party. There is some truth in that, but it is more accurate to say, as argued in Chapter 1, that they can be traced to the social democratic *aspirations* of the Jawaharlal Nehru era (1947–64), and to the *empty promises* of the Indira/Rajiv Gandhi era (1967–1989).

As that chapter established, Nehru focused heavily on State-led industrialisation, and on expanding the role and size of the state sector. He wished to redistribute wealth and to provide the poor with programmes that delivered concrete benefits. But he was largely thwarted in those efforts by the landowning castes that dominated his party in that era—and he was enough of a democrat to yield to their views. So in his era, social protection was largely an *aspiration*. Indira Gandhi won a landslide election victory in 1971 by promising to 'abolish poverty', but she then did little to follow through on that slogan. Instead, she concentrated on centralising power in the interests of personal (and eventually, dynastic) rule. This resulted in severe damage to the strength of most political institutions, including her party. Rajiv Gandhi succeeded her in 1984, but his premiership (1984–89) was marked by great confusion. He reversed direction on most major policy issues. So, in the Indira/Rajiv Gandhi years, social protection remained an *empty promise*.

The Congress-led government of 2004–14—especially in its first five years, before drift overtook it—began to make good on that aspiration and promise. In its first five years, it spent over US$ 57 billion on poverty programmes—a greater sum than any previous Indian government (Manor 2011a). This was made possible, as mentioned in the introduction, by a surge in tax revenues after 2003 by over 300 per cent over the next decade, which gave that government far more resources than any predecessor. It should be stressed that those revenues also enabled the ruling alliance to spend heavily on initiatives for *prosperous* groups. The Congress was sticking to its traditional strategy of seeking to please a broad array of interest groups. This was an important element of the UPA's poverty reduction strategy as even relatively modest expenditure on social policy—the MGNREGA cost around 0.3 per cent of GDP, for instance—is met with substantial and sustained opposition from business circles and the upper middle class, who tend to scorn expenditure on the poor as 'populism'. The Congress' efforts to address poverty and inequality can also be traced in part to the emergence in unprecedented strength of civil society organisations and researchers with progressive ideas—and to a willingness among senior politicians to *listen* far more to these emerging groups than any previous set of senior leaders.

FORMULATION

The members of the NAC responded to the proposal for a rural employment guarantee scheme sympathetically and proceeded to hammer out the details. A sophisticated IT system would be created to record every step in a villager's engagement with the programme—from registration, to the first attempt to seek work, to the provision of work, to each day's labour at work sites, to payments of wages earned. Each worker would have a registration number that would lead to an electronic file containing the record. Each would also be given a paper 'job card' containing a photo, and on it would be written the dates and numbers of days worked, wages earned, etc. This would enable checks to be made against the electronic record, to detect malfeasance. A worker who did not receive work within 15 days of seeking it would be entitled to compensation payments (a provision which has scarcely become a reality in practice).

Other transparency mechanisms were also built into the design of the programme. State governments in India's federal system (which would implement the programme) were legally required to channel at least half of the scheme's very substantial funds to elected local councils (gram panchayats) which would decide on and undertake local works projects. They were legally required to hold periodic village-level mass meetings to discuss priorities for MGNREGA works projects and the functioning of the programme—and to conduct social audits. 'Muster rolls' (lists of workers on any site) were to be posted publicly to avoid padding. Contractors and the use of machines in works projects were banned.

One flaw in the design of these transparency mechanisms was to become evident once the implementation of the programme got underway. They were targeted almost entirely at the local level and on elected councils there, and not on bureaucrats who dominate at the next level up in the administrative hierarchy: the sub-district or *block* level. Elected councils exist at the block level, but in all Indian states, they are very weak—unlike elected councils lower down at the local level and higher up at the district level. This helps preserve the dominance of block-level bureaucrats. Those bureaucrats, like elected local councils, were given significant new powers under the MGNREGA—to measure and approve local councils' public works projects, and thus to determine levels of payment for them. But their exclusion from the purview of the transparency mechanisms has enabled them to bully local councils and to extort bribes from them—with considerable impunity. (See the section below on 'implementation'.)

Despite their excessively localised focus, the transparency mechanisms in the MGNREGA are more elaborate and formidable than those found in any other poverty programme in the world. They have two purposes. First, they are intended to impede corrupt diversions of funds. Since the introduction in 2008 of a requirement that all payments to workers should pass through bank or postal accounts (rather than being handed over by local officials)—a further transparency provision—these mechanisms have succeeded very substantially in preventing theft from workers' wages. Second, the transparency mechanisms are intended to reveal attempts to steal wages from poor workers—and in this they have again largely succeeded since the introduction of bank accounts. Needless to say, corruption still affects programme implementation, mainly in the expenditure component for the procurement of materials needed for executing the works (Afridi and Iversen 2014). However, research shows that this is much less of a problem than with previous employment programmes, and it has been declining over the years (Khera 2017).

Members of the NAC sought to achieve such revelations because they would discomfit poor workers, and thus make them more aware and more proactive politically in pursuit of their own interests. In other words, they sought to *cultivate discontent* among poor villagers,[8] to strengthen what we call their 'political capacity' (their political *awareness*, their *confidence* as political actors, their political *skills*, and their political *connections* to other poor people and to allies among the non-poor). NAC members sought this because they regarded poor people's political *in*capacity as one important dimension of their 'poverty'.

As Roy, Drèze and a colleague put it, the programme offered 'a wage entitlement that would give people a measure of dignity and *create space for their political mobilisation*' (Roy, Drèze and Dey 2011: 410; emphasis added). The transparency mechanisms would offer new opportunities 'for social movements to build campaigns for people's empowerment' (ibid.: 410). Other NAC members have stated plainly in numerous interviews[9] that the cultivation of discontent was well understood by Sonia Gandhi and all (or nearly all[10]) NAC members—although not all officials in New Delhi and Members of Parliament who were involved in the passage of the MGNREG Act fully grasped this. We know of no other government in Asia, Africa or Latin America that is progressive enough and self-confident enough to cultivate discontent among the poor—not even the Brazilians.

As the NAC's planning proceeded, the prime minister met several members to discuss his concerns about the burden that the programme would impose on the exchequer. This occurred before it became entirely clear that a marked surge in government revenues, which began in 2003, was going to continue for several years. At the meeting, an NAC member—Dr. N. C. Saxena, an eminent retired civil servant who had served as the senior official in both the Ministry of Rural Development and India's Planning Commission—presented calculations showing that the MGNREGA would not entail a huge spending increase over pre-existing rural development programmes which it was to replace (with mechanisms to overcome problems that had impeded their implementation).[11] The prime minister was reassured and raised few objections to the programme thereafter.

Before long, a draft bill to create the MGNREGA was sent to the PMO. Several issues triggered opposition within certain government ministries. Some officials—despite the reassurances to the prime minister—were concerned about the possible costs of the programme. The right of any rural household to demand work made it, in theory at least, impossible to place an upper limit on expenditures. Its demand-driven character made it appear to be a 'blank cheque', as one Finance Ministry official said to an NAC member.[12] People in other ministries worried that its cost would force the government to reduce funds for *their* programmes. Some powerful figures in the executive had hesitations about devolving massive MGNREGA funds onto elected local councils. Others were anxious about the possibility of corruption, and still others (paradoxically) wanted the transparency mechanisms which would combat corruption to be weakened.

The bill which was sent to Parliament deviated greatly from the NAC draft. A provision calling for the extension of the employment guarantee to the entire country within three years had been removed. The government was given the power to opt out of the Act's requirements so that it was, in effect, no longer a guarantee. The universal (self-targeting) nature of the programme—rooted in a deep suspicion of discretionary authority in the hands of junior officials—had been replaced with a means-tested approach, in which only families officially designated as living 'Below the Poverty Line' could participate. The main responsibility for implementing the programme had been given to bureaucrats—undermining downward accountability to elected local councils and village mass meetings. Penalties for non-compliant bureaucrats had been weakened. Poor villagers now had to apply for work not as individuals but in groups of 50. The excision of the NAC draft's minimum-wage requirement was seen by activists for a rights-based approach to social protection as particularly brazen backsliding on earlier commitments. References to labourers' entitlements had been shifted out of the main body of the bill into 'Schedules' (appendices) which made them easier to ignore. In sum, it no longer represented a rights-based approach in any meaningful sense.

This alarmed several key NAC members. Even Opposition leaders in the BJP professed unhappiness—opportunistically. One called the government's bill a 'betrayal'. As the Parliamentary Standing Committee on Rural Development took up the bill for consideration, civil society organisations mounted demonstrations in New Delhi and elsewhere, calling for the bill to be strengthened. Several advocates of the original draft—including the NAC's Aruna Roy and Jean Drèze—appeared before the Committee to argue that the teeth that had been removed should be reinserted. Activists grouped around the 'Right to Food Campaign' (RTF)—a collective of committed citizens that fought for the adoption of rights-based legislation, which included several members of the NAC[13]—visited numerous members of the committee at their residences seeking to persuade them about the importance of a meaningful right to work.

The committee included several progressive members of the Congress and of the two Communist parties sympathetic to these arguments. (Those two parties did not join the ruling UPA, but they gave it issue-based support from outside until mid-2008.) Some committee members from the BJP and other parties were also sympathetic. Congress leaders had seized upon and begun developing the idea for an employment guarantee scheme before their links to the Left were forged. Support from the Communists for a strong MGNREGA was especially helpful during the final stage of negotiations within the committee, but the main force driving the creation of this and other poverty programmes was not pressure from the Left, but competition between the Congress and the BJP.[14] The committee eventually recommended that most of the original provisions of the bill be restored, and returned it to government ministries. It is customary for governments to accede to the views of parliamentary committees. They did so in this case, and the Parliament then (in September 2005) passed the bill—unanimously.

The Act which emerged was very complex. Both the original architects of the MGNREGA and the members of that parliamentary committee were particularly concerned to include carefully detailed provisions relating to the scope of the entitlement to work, the methods by which it would be fulfilled, eligibility requirements, administrative procedures to be followed, etc. They adopted this painstaking approach because they had seen many previous programmes to address poverty and inequality subverted in practice, and they were fiercely determined to avoid that in this case.

One last (and important) comment on 'formulation' needs to be added. Under the MGNREGA, the 'formulation' of policy takes place not just in New Delhi and Indian state capitals, but also at the grassroots. The Act assigns ordinary villagers tasks (which are also opportunities) in the 'formulation' of plans for local works projects which will be executed. This entails exercises in both representative democracy and direct democracy. Elected local councils are to play the former role while village-level mass meetings (*gram sabhas*) are to play the latter. In other words, the MGNREGA seeks to include ordinary (and poor) people in the 'policy community' at 'formulation' stage.

In the real world, it is not that simple. Problems have afflicted both the representative and the direct dimensions of democracy in this programme. Elected local councils have had their influence reduced in two ways. Council chairpersons have been able to centralise power in a great many localities so that other elected councillors have little or no influence (Manor 2013a). And local councils, including their chairpersons, have often been bullied by bureaucrats at the next level up in the administrative structure—the sub-district or block level—into executing works projects that are imposed from above.

Mass meetings of villagers, to influence and then audit local MGNREGA works, seldom have much substance. This is mainly explained as an acute 'allergy' to transparency and downward accountability which elected leaders of local councils share with politicians and bureaucrats at higher levels in the Indian system. They often neglect to summon mass meetings—and when such meetings occur, they are often held in a perfunctory manner, with little prior notice and at times when many villagers cannot attend. One of us attended a 'mass meeting' in Rajasthan where the chairperson sent some of his associates door to door to convince some villagers to attend the gram sabha in order to have the legally required minimum number of people present. In another case, in Uttar Pradesh we could not find a single Dalit villager who had ever heard of a gram sabha being held in their locality.

Despite this, India's record on such mass meetings is less dismal than the international norm. In the late 1990s, a World Bank study by people with little knowledge of democratic decentralisation in developing nations condemned the government of one Indian state for managing to hold such mass meetings only 17 per cent of the time; 17 per cent seemed low, so that team regarded this case as a failure. What they did not realise was that the international norm for mass meetings is zero—against which 17 per cent represented a non-trivial achievement.

Genuine mass meetings under the MGNREGA have actually occurred more often than those across India. In a survey that one of us conducted in Rajasthan and Andhra Pradesh in 2013, among 1,237 MGNREGA workers, as many as 39.72 per cent of the respondents had discussed the programme in gram sabhas. Significantly, 71.3 per cent of them said that they had never attended a gram sabha before the introduction of the programme, signaling that the MGNREGA can promote democracy at the grassroots, exactly as the designers of the policy had hoped. We attended several meetings where villagers contested the decisions taken by the council. In some cases, this did not produce any result. But in one of these meetings, Dalit villagers eventually managed to remove the construction of (yet another) farm pond from the list—one of the 'priority works' decided at the state level—and to include additional land development works on the private land of Dalits. So, this is not a total disaster, but the record is still uninspiring.

Despite these problems, the intention of the MGNREGA to bring villagers into the 'policy community'—which actually happens in many, though, not most localities—is worth noting.

IMPLEMENTATION

The story of the implementation of the MGNREGA is complex in the extreme—partly because the Act is so complicated, and partly because state governments' attitudes, capabilities and administrative strategies have varied. What follows is thus an inevitably over-simplified account, but it focuses on what abundant evidence has shown to be the predominant trends.[15]

At the national level, the government selected dynamic, committed and meticulous civil servants to manage the programme, although the resources provided to the core team were rather limited. The key administrator had highly relevant experience in designing and then overseeing a successful rights-based programme in Madhya Pradesh. She and her colleagues carefully sifted evidence of problems with the implementation of the MGNREGA and made several telling, constructive adjustments as events unfolded.

State governments in India's federal system were to decide on certain key details, including the minimum wages to be paid to workers and the proportion of the programme's funds which would pass to elected local councils. Many state governments have stuck to the legal requirement that 50 per cent of the funds should go to the local councils, giving the rest to line ministries. But a few have transferred 90 per cent or more—because they knew that local councils were far more transparent than the ministries.

Most of the 29 state governments sought to make the programme work well—for the most part. In a very small number, feckless senior politicians took little interest. In a similarly small number of other states, energetic efforts by politicians and civil servants at the state level were undermined by bureaucratic incapacity. The most striking example is Bihar where an incoming state government discovered that roughly half of the key administrative posts (Block Development Officers or BDOs) at the sub-district or block level stood vacant. BDOs have often created problems for the MGNREGA, squeezing local councils for kickbacks, but if they are absent, the programme cannot operate effectively. Efforts were made to fill those posts, but the state's archaic hiring procedures made it a painfully slow process. In one state, Andhra Pradesh, the centralising government which (unusually) sought rigorous top-down control broke the law by giving no funds to elected local councils—and got away with it because the Congress then held power there. In several states, senior politicians identified tiny numbers of districts where systematic efforts would be made to loot funds from the programme—'worst case' districts that tended to be remote and devoid of much civil society activism, and thus less visible. But those same leaders ensured that the MGNREGA functioned effectively in most districts, because they anticipated (accurately, as it turned out) a political payoff from that—not just for the Congress-led government at the national level, but for state governments led by parties not aligned with the Congress.

In sum, most state governments made serious efforts to make the programme work tolerably well. Table 2.1 provides an overview of the implementation performance of the MGNREGA in India's major states. These figures, while showing the quite significant variation in implementation across states, conceal variation within states, which can be quite striking—across districts, sub-districts and even gram panchayats.

At the sub-district level which bureaucrats dominate, BDOs and junior engineers have often imposed their priorities on local councils, in violation of the Act which seeks to give those councils the initiative. They have also often extorted bribes from local councils in exchange for measurements and approvals of works, both of which are crucial to the release of full funding. Administrators at the national level curbed the powers of these bureaucrats somewhat after learning of these practices, but problems have nonetheless persisted. In places where senior politicians want the programme to work well, block-level bureaucrats have often been pressed by superiors at the district level to avoid such activities, but since MGNREGA transparency mechanisms do little to affect the block level, abuses have sometimes continued even there.

TABLE 2.1: Average person-days per household in selected states, 2008–2017

State	*Average person-days 2008/09–2016/17*
All India	46.35
Andhra Pradesh	54.15
Bihar	36.33
Chhattisgarh	45.78
Gujarat	37.71
Karnataka	46.09
Kerala	43.75
Madhya Pradesh	45.66
Maharashtra	49.91
Odisha	39.15
Rajasthan	55.89
Tamil Nadu	53.42
Telangana	52.55
Uttar Pradesh	40.84
West Bengal	35.52

Source: Authors' calculations, aggregating data from the MGNREGA website (http://www.nrega.nic.in).

At the local level, leaders of elected councils have often found it difficult to escape demands from block-level bureaucrats for illicit payments. This is true even of local leaders with connections in the states' ruling parties. However, in numerous areas where strong civil society organisations work to bolster local councils and engage with block-level bureaucrats to ensure that the MGNREGA is appropriately managed—or where district-level bureaucrats have pursued that goal—this problem has been substantially mitigated. Transparency mechanisms have created acute problems for local council leaders who seek to divert funds for bribes from workers' wages—especially since bank accounts have been used to deliver those wages to workers. Local leaders have often sought to obtain such funds by concocting false invoices for the purchase and transport of materials for works projects. But canny block-level bureaucrats, who understand how difficult it is to steal from workers' wages, have sometimes centralised the management of materials because they also see the opportunity that it offers.

That leaves local council leaders in severe difficulty, but many have taken some comfort from one other (unintended) consequence of the MGNREGA. In many local councils, power has been centralised in the hands of the elected chairperson—partly because s/he is the sole gatekeeper to crucial negotiations with the block level. This has enabled council chairpersons to restrict the flow of information about the process surrounding works projects even to other elected councillors, and thus to villagers more generally. It has also strengthened (somewhat) the chairpersons' capacity to ration work opportunities for the poor. It has also allowed them to use the allocation of work as a clientelistic mechanism to reward their supporters (Maiorano, Das and Masiero 2018). But it has not done great damage to the operation of the programme.

Poor people's awareness of the rights-based, demand-driven character of the MGNREGA, and of several key features of the scheme, has been very slow to develop. This is mainly the result of the strong allergy to transparency and downward accountability shared by political actors at all levels in the system—from state capitals down to the villages—and thus of their efforts to keep poor people in the dark. Awareness-raising campaigns, when they are actually mounted, have often been deliberately ineffective. Genuine (as opposed to phoney) village-level mass meetings and social audits have occurred more often than is common, globally, in decentralised systems (where the norm is near-total failure), but not often enough to enable poor people's awareness, voice and influence to acquire much strength. However, in a minority of villages, civil society organisations have assisted in building these things. Across Madhya Pradesh, for example, Samarthan and other enlightened civic associations estimate that approximately 17 per cent of mass meetings have been genuine—which is quite a high proportion by international standards.

Even where such organisations have had no impact, poor people have made gains in awareness and political capacity on two fronts. They have gradually become aware of how the programme works—and is intended to work—and have been able, proactively, to seize at least some of the opportunities that it offers, often by pressing elected councillors (who will need their votes at the next local election) for some assistance. They have also become aware of (often unsuccessful) attempts to siphon funds from their wages, thanks in large measure to the requirement that they be paid through bank accounts. Those accounts also enable them to access other government benefits—insurance provisions, pensions, etc.—often for the first time. In some cases, MGNREGA workers have also started colluding with local level implementers to get a share of the illicit profits made by them (Veeraraghavan 2015). While this is not a welcome development, it also shows how poor villagers are using the transparency mechanisms built into the MGNREGA to their advantage instead of either passively accepting corruption or being completely unaware of it.

In sum, despite many disappointments and ambiguities, the MGNREGA has in most localities worked well enough to provide poor people with significant extra earnings. These often provide them not merely with a hedge against destitution, but also the capacity to feed their families more adequately, to make modest investments in assets like livestock or in agricultural inputs on small plots of land which roughly half of them possess, etc. (see the discussion on 'Impact and Implications' below). These have eroded the bonds of dependency which have long subordinated poor villagers to their prosperous neighbours, thus enhancing their autonomy. One Dalit MGNREGA worker from a village in Andhra Pradesh told us how crucial the scheme was in changing their relationship with the local dominant landowning caste (the Reddys):

> The relation with the Reddys is often marked by confrontation. A few years back they decided that they would not give us any work in their fields as they claimed we had to be punished for our insolence. The Reddys brought

> labourers from outside the village. It was very hard for us. But something like this cannot happen anymore. We have guaranteed employment with MGNREGA now. We are less dependent. We are confident now.[16]

The programme has also drawn many poor people—including women who have performed nearly half of the labour under the programme—into the public sphere, in many cases for the first time. In the process, their 'political capacity' has often been strengthened—usually modestly but sometimes substantially.

Let us now shift our focus from the various levels in the system to a more general theme of great importance. The MGNREGA is intended to be a 'post-clientelist' programme—in that safeguards have been incorporated into it to prevent those who wish to divert resources from it for use in patronage distribution (or clientelism), which has until recently been the very life blood of Indian politics. In other words, it is intended to operate according to Weberian norms, and not to be bled to fortify patronage networks that serve partisan purposes. This and numerous other 'post-clientelist' initiatives have emerged in India in recent years, in large measure because politicians have rightly concluded that patronage distribution is insufficient to achieve re-election. It must be supplemented by such initiatives (see Manor 2013b).

Two things have ensured that the MGNREGA is—to a considerable extent—a successful 'post-clientelist' initiative. First, Congress chief ministers at the state level were firmly told by the party's 'high command' to instruct party operatives at lower levels to follow a 'hands off' policy—to minimise possible diversions of programme funds to patronage networks (Maiorano 2014). The party's national leaders hoped, paradoxically, that the party would be rewarded by voters for launching a programme that was unexploitable by party activists.[17] The leaders of non-Congress parties in many Indian states took similar action, partly for the same reason: because they believed, correctly as it turned out, that state governments would reap much of the political reward for administering the programme well. But they also recognised that the formidable transparency mechanisms built into the programme made it extremely difficult to milk the MGNREGA for substantial resources. There were easier ways to obtain far more massive illicit sums.

Second, those transparency mechanisms have impeded many other actors (mostly bureaucrats) who are not involved in clientelism from siphoning funds from the programme. So, while the MGNREGA has indeed been—to a considerable extent—a successful 'post-clientelist' initiative, it is not entirely immune to clientelism. That problem arises mainly at the local level (Maiorano, Das and Masiero 2018). The rationing of work opportunities by powerful people in elected councils in some villages enables those leaders to strengthen very localised patronage networks. But because it is extremely difficult even at village level to steal from workers' wages, the MGNREGA is substantially protected. (The main way to divert funds illicitly is to prepare phoney invoices for the purchase and transport of materials for works under the programme; over 30 per cent of the budget is spent on that. However, very few of those stolen resources go into clientelist networks. They are mainly used by local leaders to pay bribes to bureaucrats who dominate the next higher level in the system—the sub-district or block. And those bureaucrats engage far more in self-enrichment, and in illicit payments to their superiors, than in running patronage networks of their own.)

IMPACT AND IMPLICATIONS

The impact of the MGNREGA has been widely analysed. Most analysts concur that it has had a positive contribution in a number of spheres. These include impact on poverty levels, education, the empowerment of women, dietary intake, infant nutrition, and reduction in violence and distress-led migration (Afridi, Iversen and Sharan n.d.; Das 2015a, 2018; Dasgupta, Gawande and Kapur 2017; Deininger and Liu 2013; Imbert and Papp 2015; Li and Sekhri 2013; MORD 2012; Nair et al. 2013; Nayak and Khera 2009). A study based on panel surveys covering more than 45,000 households throughout the country concluded that the MGNREGA alone is responsible for 32 per cent of poverty reduction since 2004 and for preventing 14 million families from falling into poverty (Desai, Vashishtha and Joshi 2015). There are also a number of studies that show how—contrary to a widespread myth common among the urban middle classes—the MGNREGA is far from being a programme where people are paid to 'dig a hole and then fill it up again'. In fact, although there is great variation even within single villages, assets created under the programme are usually useful and are contributing to the rural economy (MORD 2012). The World Bank called the MGNREGA a 'stellar example of rural development' (World Bank 2013) which contributes significantly to poverty reduction and provides an important safety net for India's rural poor.

The MGNREGA has yielded crucial insights into the character of the Indian State. It shows us the State at its best—as we saw above, in the willingness of senior leaders to cultivate discontent among the rural poor—but it also reveals it at its *worst*. There is a great mass of evidence to indicate that political actors (especially bureaucrats, but also politicians) at all levels, from state capitals down to villages, have an acute allergy to transparency and downward accountability. That makes State institutions sclerotic, unresponsive and at times callous. That allergy may do as much damage as corruption, although it has received far less attention from analysts. The MGNREG Act is intended to create counter-pressures to combat it, from two sources: from the legal force of the Act itself, and from poor people and their allies operating at the grassroots. That latter type of counter-pressure is taking time to gather force, but there is also evidence to show that it has begun to develop, and that it has, to varying but often non-trivial degrees, deepened the democratic process across much of rural India—as the architects of the MGNREGA intended.

NOTES AND REFERENCES

1. Much of the material in this report is drawn from extensive field research in two Indian states and investigations of other states by Rob Jenkins and James Manor (see also Jenkins and Manor 2017).

2. Interviews with three Congress Party strategists, New Delhi, August 2004. All interviews cited in this chapter were conducted by James Manor and Diego Maiorano.

3. The proposed Right to Information Act resonated powerfully with the proposed rural employment guarantee programme. It was intended to close many loopholes in the Freedom of Information Act passed in 2002 by the previous Indian government, and to create substantial new opportunities for ordinary (and poor) people to seek important information from State actors. (It also brought greater pressure on State actors by creating an institutional structure to achieve government compliance, and by introducing penalties for officials who refused to divulge information.) Opportunities were thus created for ordinary folk to engage proactively with an opaque system—similar to the opportunities that were to emerge out of the MGNREGA.

4. It was originally called the National Rural Employment Guarantee Act or NREGA. The name of Mahatma Gandhi was attached to it five years later. Senior politicians carefully avoided attaching the name of a Congress Party leader to this programme—as they did to the Jawaharlal Nehru National Urban Renewal Mission, one of the other initiatives being analysed by the India team—because they wanted it to be acceptable to rival political parties. Rival parties would need to administer it in many Indian states, and they might capture power at the national level in future elections. Mahatma Gandhi is not perceived as a partisan figure.

5. The chain of procedural rights built into the MGNREGA was derived in substantial measure from the Maharashtra Employment Guarantee Scheme, but in that programme the state government enforced compliance with the Scheme in a top-down manner, from above. By contrast, the MGNREGA drew upon civil society organisations' strategies in Rajasthan by creating processes that were intended to enable poor people to enforce downward accountability, from below—as this analysis will explain. Maharashtra can thus claim partial parentage, but Rajasthan had a more important influence on the MGNREGA.

6. See for example, 'Rajasthan to set up commission to probe starvation deaths: Sonia', *Press Trust of India*, 9 November 2002. We share the views on this set out by Gonsalves et al. 2004. See also the discussion of the RTF movement or network in the next chapter.

7. Congress leaders were weighing their options in an atmosphere in which rights-based approaches to development and poverty reduction

had been strengthened by a Supreme Court ruling on the right to food—although that made no mention of a right to work which the MGNREGA addressed.

8. This comment is based on interviews with three members of the NAC.

9. These were conducted in New Delhi by Rob Jenkins and James Manor in 2008 and 2009.

10. An interview in 2012 by Manor with one NAC member indicated less than complete awareness of this.

11. Those programmes included the Employment Assurance Scheme and the Jawahar Rozgar Yojana.

12. The NAC had estimated that the cost of the programme, if fully implemented (which would, inevitably, not occur), would be 1.3% of the GDP. An independent assessment used by sceptics came up with a figure of 1.7% (Ravallion and Murgai 2005).

13. See Chapters 3 and 5 for further details on the RTF Campaign.

14. We agree on this point (despite several disagreements on other details) with the study by Shankar and Gaiha 2013: 8. They draw a useful parallel between the creation of the MGNREGA and Theda Skocpol's argument that in the American case, intense competition between Republicans and Democrats led to a 'ratcheting up' of pension coverage for veterans of the Civil War in the late nineteenth and early twentieth centuries (Skocpol 1992).

15. A more detailed and complex assessment appears in Jenkins and Manor 2017.

16. In an interview by Maiorano, Chittoor district of Andhra Pradesh, 19 October 2013.

17. We are grateful to Yogendra Yadav for stressing this point.

three

The 'Right to Food' and the National Food Security Act

This chapter reports on the long-negotiated National Food Security Act (NFSA) which sought to provide statutory underpinning for a 'right to food'. The origins of the legislation lie in the recognition that India's rates of hunger and undernutrition were among the highest of any country in the world, and that existing food safety nets—such as the Public Distribution System (PDS), and Integrated Child Development Services (ICDS)—were failing to address a problem which remained stubbornly persistent even in the face of rising incomes. In absolute terms, when the NFS Act was being debated, more undernourished people lived in India than any other country in the world—as many as 217 million people or 17.5 per cent of the population.[1]

The stated goal of the NFS Act, passed eventually in late 2013, was 'to provide for food and nutritional security in human life cycle[2] approach, by ensuring access to adequate quantity of quality food at affordable prices to people to live a life of dignity' (Ministry of Law and Justice 2013). The major thrust of the legislation was to provide a legal minimum entitlement to food through an expansion in the size of the population entitled to receive subsidised food grains through the PDS—a nationwide architecture for the distribution of food procured by the Indian government from farmers to poor people via a network of 'fair price' or 'ration' shops. The legislation also mandated a further reduction in the price at which food grains are sold, and the encouragement of reforms to improve performance of the PDS, which had long had a reputation for being leaky and failing to reach intended beneficiaries. Additionally, it also encompassed one element of the ICDS—the provision of cooked meals at *anganwadi* centres for pregnant women and lactating mothers, and children under the age of six;[3] the provision of meals to school children under the Midday Meals scheme, and a maternity benefit of Rs 6,000 for every pregnant woman.

In legislating in these areas, the National Food Security Bill (NFSB) underlined what had already become legal entitlements because of Supreme Court orders since 2001 acting on a Public Interest Litigation (PIL) filed by civil society organisations. But the bill also went further than the Court orders by reducing and stipulating the price at which food grains should be supplied via the PDS. The Congress appeared keen to make the promise of Rs 3/kg rice and Rs 2/kg wheat a central campaign plank in the 2014 general elections following their 2009 manifesto commitment to legislate on a right to food.

M. S. Swaminathan, agricultural scientist and a leading light of India's Green Revolution, described the significance of the national legislation thus: 'India is on the threshold of a historic transition from a ship-to-mouth existence to implementing the world's largest social protection programme against hunger with home-grown food'.[4]

The provision of subsidised food is a well-tried electoral strategy at the state level. This has been attested to in numerous states over time from the Midday Meals programme launched in Tamil Nadu in the 1960s, to the Telugu Desam's N. T. Rama Rao in Andhra Pradesh who introduced Rs 2/kg rice in the 1980s, to Chhattisgarh's Chief Minister Raman Singh in the late 2000s who is popularly known as '*Chawal wale Baba*' (rice man) (Tillin, Saxena, and Sisodia 2015). Yet, negotiating a major food security initiative at the national level was considerably more challenging. For a start, reform efforts within the Central government took place within a landscape in which the Supreme Court had already established a set of legal rights, and in which India's state governments operated a variety of different approaches to implementing these. The architects of the new legislation effectively had to work within the existing architecture of food security policies.

But perhaps more profoundly, the legislation provided the platform for a much wider debate about the extent, and modalities, of public provision for welfare in India. Crystallising in the second half of the UPA's second term, in the context of a slowdown in the dizzying rates of economic growth seen between 2003–04 and 2011–12 and against the waning legitimacy of the Congress-led government in the wake of numerous corruption scandals, debate around the NFSB was heavily polarised. The 'right to food' debates were thus drawn into newly crystallising political fissures over how to align or balance the expanding welfare commitments that had been symbolised by new programmes such as the MGNREGA in the UPA's first term with the pro-market sensibilities of a reform lobby which sought to reduce rather than entrench what they saw as the price distortions entailed by food and agricultural subsidies.

The bill therefore initiated a wider debate about the role of the State in welfare provision, and revealed the absence of effective agreement—either within the Congress or among other parties—about public investment in anti-poverty initiatives. A slowdown in economic growth after 2011 affected perceptions (if not quite the reality) of revenue availability for an expansion of the food subsidy regime. This led to the pursuit of more conservative policy proposals from the PMO. Meanwhile, other critics questioned the desirability of bolstering State-led delivery mechanisms which had proved inefficient and wasteful in the past. A widely cited Planning Commission report in 2004, for instance, estimated that 58 per cent of subsidised food grains did not reach their intended beneficiaries, with 36 per cent being sold on the black market (Saxena 2012). Strong voices within and beyond government increasingly advocated the replacement of in-kind food subsidies with cash transfers (see, for example, Kapur, Mukhopadhyay and Subramanian 2008; Bardhan 2011; Svedberg 2012).

More than any of the other initiatives discussed in this book, the NFSB therefore had a very rocky journey through its pre-legislative phase and after its introduction to Parliament. In the short term, Opposition parties wanted to prevent Congress from taking the political credit from leading on food security measures. They sought to walk a delicate line between dragging their feet over the legislation, without appearing to oppose the food security measures themselves—especially when several Opposition parties had overseen their own, sometimes more extensive, subsidised food programmes and reforms to the PDS at the state level. As Baijayant 'Jay' Panda, a Biju Janata Dal Member of Parliament (MP) from Orissa, explained: 'Whenever a party in government takes a populist stand like this, there are huge pressures on other parties to fall in line. This is not the first time it has happened—the same thing was there with MGNREGA'.[5]

But the Congress also faced opposition on the bill from its own allies within the UPA, as well as more tentative support within the PMO and Ministry of Finance. The bill had both the strength and the weakness of being clearly seen as Congress president Sonia Gandhi's personal priority, but there was exceedingly little political leadership or vocal public support on the right to food by others within the Congress. Many within the party appeared sympathetic to calls for cash transfers, or concerns about the fiscal implications of legislating on a right to food. Furthermore, unlike the first term of the UPA, the Congress did not have the support of the Left parties in Parliament, and opposition to the government was growing as a series of large corruption cases took their toll on governmental legitimacy. When the NFSA was eventually passed by the Parliament in late 2013, it only did so after first being introduced as an ordinance in the face of parliamentary paralysis. The case for the new measures was not made convincingly, or won, in the court of public opinion.

Ultimately, longer-term policy legacies forged around the existing food security policy architecture exerted a strong influence on the NFSA. The legislation essentially worked through, and built upon, the existing policy architecture, but left other options such as cash transfers on the table for the future. From a different perspective, many members of the significant, diverse civil society campaign network that coalesced around the 'right to food' saw major missed opportunities in the bill—the failure to cement a truly universal 'right to food', to support local procurement and storage of food to help small and marginal farmers, and an overwhelming focus on cereals rather than pulses and edible oils that are also important sources of nutrients. This meant that by the time the bill reached Parliament, it had few full-throated advocates.

In this chapter, we first set out the historical background to India's approach to food security. We then analyse the process of policy formulation of what became the National Food Security Act as it passed from the PMO to the NAC to begin its slow passage through Parliament. We conclude by reflecting on the wider implications of the NFSA for understanding the politics of poverty reduction under the UPA government. The chapter draws on interviews with politicians, civil society activists, NAC members, officials and academics involved in the debates and process of policy formulation.

ORIGINS OF POLICIES TOWARDS FOOD SECURITY

India's approach to food security over time has stood on two pillars. The first pillar, since the 1960s, has involved a focus on achieving national self-sufficiency in food production to reduce dependence on food imports and food 'aid'. This has been achieved through public policies designed to boost domestic agricultural production including technological investments in the Green Revolution (and beyond), input subsidies for farmers, and the fixing of 'minimum support prices' at which the State will procure rice or wheat from farmers. These procurement policies, particularly input subsidies and pricing mechanisms, have crystallised into a fairly stable formation over time, reflecting an agrarian political settlement based on the increasing economic and political power of owner-cultivator farmers, often from middle castes, from the mid-1960s onwards (Rudolph and Rudolph 1987; Corbridge and Harriss 2000).

The second pillar has focused on the distribution of subsidised food (procured by the State) through the PDS. The origins of the PDS lay in wartime food rationing introduced in the 1940s, but it was maintained after Independence with the aim of keeping food prices stable. In this period, it was particularly focused on meeting the needs of urban and food 'deficit' areas to support an emerging working class (Suryanarayana and Geetha 1993). The PDS was gradually expanded as a corollary of the reforms to the public procurement of food in the Green Revolution era until by the 1980s—in theory—it covered the entire country, and was reoriented towards supporting food consumption in rural areas. In the post-reforms era, however, the PDS became subject to scrutiny again as the Central government sought to reduce its budgetary deficit. Food subsidies alone were equivalent to about 39 per cent of the total budgetary deficit in 1992–93 (ibid.: 2207). In 1997, the PDS was therefore converted into a targeted programme aimed at the 'Below Poverty Line' (BPL) population. This reform pushed responsibility for maintaining any more generous provisions under the PDS to the states. Some states responded by developing or maintaining their own food security regimes, but across India the move towards a targeted system increased inefficiencies in the PDS (see Khera 2011; Sen and Himanshu 2011). Under the targeted PDS, leakages increased (due to corruption, spoilage or transportation) as did exclusion errors since many of the poorest did not possess the requisite BPL card to access their entitlements.

By the late 1990s and early 2000s, several surveys drew attention to what became known as India's 'hunger paradox'. Despite rising incomes, and despite the achievement of national self-sufficiency in food production, India's population remained food insecure. Indeed, in the first phase of India's economic growth take-off (from the early 1980s to early 2000s), as Deaton and Drèze showed, calorie consumption declined despite rising incomes and overall consumption (Deaton and Drèze 2009).

The publication of the National Family Health Surveys (NFHS) in 1999 and 2006 galvanised and drew attention to the fact that India fared poorly in international comparison. Furthermore, the situation persisted despite rising incomes. The proportion of underweight children had remained virtually unchanged, for instance, at 46 per cent between 1998–99 and 2005–06 (ibid.: 50).

Against the backdrop of drought-induced hunger despite the enormous food stocks that India had built up, a civil society movement began to galvanise around the 'right to food'. In May 2001, the People's Union of Civil Liberties (PUCL, Rajasthan) submitted a writ petition to the Supreme Court seeking enforcement of the right to food under Article 21 of India's Constitution which enshrines the right to life. A series of Supreme Court orders from July 2001 onwards directed all states to ensure that all PDS shops, if closed, were reopened and functioning; that states must complete the identification of BPL families, issuing cards and distributing 25 kg of food grains per household; that every child be provided with a cooked midday meal at school under the Midday Meals scheme; and that other schemes such as National Old Age Pensions, and ICDS be implemented in full.[6]

Building on the Supreme Court interventions, as well as increasing domestic and international scrutiny of India's problems with hunger and undernutrition, legislation on a 'right to food' was included in the Congress Party's manifesto ahead of the 2009 elections. When the UPA were returned to power with an increased majority, it was included as part of the '100-day agenda' of the new government.

Formulation of the National Food Security Bill

The formulation of the NFSB was characterised by a lengthy process of debate and consultation, during which a diverse set of interests were mobilised. Congress president Sonia Gandhi's leadership was critical in ensuring that the bill saw the light of day. But what was ultimately enshrined in legislation was far from radical. Numerous drafting and revising committees struck different balances between commitments to a 'right to food' as already laid down by the Supreme Court, the perceived availability of food grains and the implied fiscal burden. The compromises enacted between different interest groups ensured that the eventual legislation did little to divert from the existing policy architecture for food security, permitting only a moderate expansion in legal entitlements under the PDS and falling short of a universal system which the Right to Food Campaign, among others, saw as integral to a truly rights-based approach.

Soon after the 2009 elections, on 13 July 2009, the prime minister tasked an 'Empowered Group of Ministers' with framing legislation on the issue. Thus, unlike some of the earlier social legislation of the first term of the UPA, this bill began its journey in the PMO. This reflected the fact that it took some time for the NAC to be reconstituted after the UPA's re-election in 2009: it was not reappointed until 2010. The Empowered Group consisted of Finance Minister Pranab Mukherjee, Agriculture Minister Sharad Pawar, Defence Minister A. K. Antony, Home Minister P. Chidambaram, Railway Minister Mamata Banerjee, Textiles Minister Dayanidhi Maran, Commerce Minister Anand Sharma, and Rural Development Minister C. P. Joshi, with the Deputy Chairman of Planning Commission being a Special Invitee. The initial draft was heavily criticised by the Right to Food Campaign and others for an apparently overriding concern 'not to ensure food security, but to contain the government's expenditure under the proposed NFS Act' (EPW editorial 2010). It focused on the continued operation of a Public Distribution System targeted to BPL households, and a reduction of the quantity of food grains they were already entitled to under Supreme Court orders.

This initial draft was rejected by Sonia Gandhi, and the task of drafting a bill was passed to the newly reinstated NAC. The NAC working group that drafted the bill was led by Harsh Mander, one of the Supreme Court Commissioners on the right to food cases who monitor implementation of court orders. As Mander explained, the bill required careful drafting. Unlike the MGNREGA which stipulated simply that every household would be entitled to 100 days' work, food insecurity needed to be approached from multiple dimensions. The NAC worked to build consensus among different groups such as those working on child malnutrition, destitute feeding, or with the homeless. Mander emphasised that the significance of legislating on these matters was to create legal duties for the State to provide food to those who are food insecure. This could be done through a variety of means including subsidised food, cooked meals, unconditional cash transfers such as maternity benefits, and old age pensions.[7] There was a long process of negotiation within the NAC, but also some indirect influence from the PMO. As Khera (2013) notes, the functioning of the NAC changed during the second term of the UPA. Rather than setting the agenda for legislation, as had been the case under UPA-I, the NAC was now just one of many players involved in negotiating the NFSA. Under UPA-II, the NAC's Secretariat was explicitly asked to facilitate wider consultations with outside experts and government ministries (Khera 2013). The draft bill which was eventually crafted, therefore, contained numerous compromises reflecting the large number of stakeholders involved.

Foremost among the compromises at this early stage was with the principle of universalism. Early NAC discussions favoured the idea of a universal PDS in the poorest districts,[8] but this was not retained in their draft bill. Instead, aware of the limited resources the government was willing to commit, the NAC tried to forge a middle ground by introducing two categories of eligible households: 'priority' households entitled to 35 kg of food grains per month and 'general' households entitled to 20 kg per household, covering a total of 90 per cent of the rural population, and 50 per cent of the urban population—or 75 per cent of India's population. Decisions on total population coverage were driven by calculations of total food production and availability. But this formula drew much criticism. Critics pointed out that identifying who belonged to these categories would be administratively complex and that previous BPL surveys had not been very reliable. They also argued that the new categories would introduce new exclusions: under the current system all APL (above poverty line) card holders could access the PDS, albeit at higher prices than BPL households. Under the new measures, many people would find themselves excluded altogether. At a more normative level, it was questioned whether a targeted provision could be considered a 'right to food'. As member of the (by then erstwhile) NAC Jean Drèze argued, a targeted system risked perpetuating inequality of access and undermining the social solidarity and sense of public ownership that universal schemes help to produce:

> Targeting is ... divisive: it prevents the emergence of a cohesive public demand for a functional PDS. And vocal demand is very important for the success of the PDS. This is one reason why the PDS works much better in Tamil Nadu than elsewhere: everyone has a stake in it. Chhattisgarh's recent success builds on the same principle—about 80 per cent of the rural population is covered. (Drèze 2010b)

Left parties, the Right to Food Campaign, and some academics therefore argued strongly in favour of universalisation. The RTF Campaign saw targeting as 'the thin end of the wedge, to lay the ground for gradual but eventual State withdrawal from the supply of public services' (Mander 2012: 272). Himanshu and Abhijit Sen (member, Planning Commission) argued that experiments with targeting in the PDS—introduced in 1997—had failed, creating new forms of exclusion among the most vulnerable and a significant increase in 'leakages'. They also argued that concerns about the food grain requirements of a universal PDS ignored the likelihood that a universal PDS may see lower leakages in the long run, and thus were arguably based on over-estimations of the total quantity of food grains required (Sen and Himanshu 2011).

However, opposition to full universalisation was raised on fiscal grounds and on grounds of the availability of food grains. It also reflected the continuity of a longer-term shift to targeting government programmes introduced in the 1990s. This was despite the fact that even some of the strongest early votaries of targeting, such as Kirit Parikh (former member, Planning Commission) had begun to recognise some of the problems with targeting and were starting to propose instead a move towards models of targeting based on exclusion criteria rather than on the identification of the poor.

Following the release of the NAC draft (including the compromise formula on coverage) in October 2010, the prime minister referred it to an 'expert committee' chaired by his Economic Advisor, C. Rangarajan. Along with the bill, the committee was referred a proposal by the Ministry of Rural Development to replace the existing BPL survey with a socio-economic and caste census to be conducted by the Registrar General and Census Commissioner of India. This Expert Committee reported in January 2011. It raised concerns about whether there would be adequate food grains available to meet what it described as the 'near universal' coverage proposed in the draft bill, as also about the impact of such high levels of public food grain procurement on open market prices. They also argued that the costs of the bill had been underestimated. To address these concerns, they recommended that the population entitled to Rs 2/kg wheat and Rs 3/kg rice should be defined as the percentage of the population below the official poverty line plus 10 per cent. Based on the Tendulkar poverty line, this would be equivalent to 46 per cent of the rural and 28 per cent of the urban population—roughly those designated as 'priority' households under the NAC draft. The rest of the population would be covered through an executive order and able to access food grains priced at the same as the 'minimum support price' (the rate paid by the government to procure food grains from farmers) on the basis of food grains available in any given year.

In the version of the bill that was eventually tabled in Parliament in December 2011, after redrafting by the Ministry of Food, the NAC's dual categories of priority and general households were retained. Yet the tabled bill included a new 'force majeure' provision under which the government would not be liable for any claim 'out of failure of supply of food grains or meals when such failure of supply is due, either directly or indirectly, to force majeure conditions such as war, flood, drought, fire, cyclone, earthquake or any act of God'. The Right to Food Campaign described this draft bill as a 'denial of the right to food,' saying that the bill had been written with the 'object of minimising the obligations of the government, restricting people's entitlement, and avoiding any accountability'.[9]

Role of the Parliamentary Standing Committee

Having been introduced to Parliament, the bill then sat under the consideration of the Parliamentary Standing Committee on Food, Consumer Affairs and Public Distribution for over a year until January 2013. The most decisive intervention by the committee was their recommendation to replace the dual priority/general categories with one category of entitlement. The revised provisions suggested by the Standing Committee and incorporated into the final bill covered the same total pool of beneficiaries—75 per cent of the population—but with only 5 kg of food grains per person per month (lower than the NAC proposals for 'priority' households of 7 kg, and higher than the general category). This new formulation followed a proposal for simplification made by a group of development economists in an open letter to the prime minister in 2012, and in deposition to the Standing Committee by Jean Drèze and Reetika Khera on 28th October 2012.

In an open letter to Prime Minister Manmohan Singh, some of the world's leading development economists from India, the United States and the United Kingdom came together to call for a simplification of the identification of beneficiaries to be covered by the PDS under the new legislation. While they held differing views over the means of delivering subsidies (many preferred cash or food coupons to the existing system of in-kind subsidies), they agreed that the 'complicated three-way division of the population between "priority", "general", and excluded households' was problematic on several grounds:

> First, there is no clarity as to how these different groups are to be identified .... Second, ... [it had] many of the weaknesses of "BPL targeting," which has proved so unreliable and

> divisive in the past. Third, this rigid framework ... would undermine the positive trend towards a more inclusive PDS .... Last ... [it] is confusing – simplicity and transparency are essential for the success of this legislation.[10]

Many NAC members approved of the Standing Committee's subsequent simplification of the categorisation of entitlements under the bill, although there was concern that the compromise had involved reducing the quantity of food grains from 35 kg/household per month to 25 kg (except for the poorest households covered by the Antyodaya Anna Yojana (AAY)).

The reduced level of entitlements reflected the other debate that raged beyond Parliament: that of whether the State could afford the increased expenditure. Fiscal hawks had become more vocal in the context of the slowdown in India's growth rates in 2011–12, which had a knock-on effect on the fiscal deficit (which rose from 4.9 per cent of GDP in 2010–11 to 5.7 per cent in 2011–12[11]). Numerous commentators in the media, sometimes drawing on vastly inflated figures to make their case,[12] argued that the NFSB represented a significant increase in State expenditure on 'entitlements' at a time when—they argued—the State could ill afford it.

The Right to Food Campaign, and others, hit back at the suggestion of a genuine fiscal squeeze by pointing out the amounts of revenue lost to the exchequer because of corporate tax breaks. Kavita Srivastava, convenor of the Right to Food Campaign asked: 'Why do the critics of the NFSB remain silent on the huge subsidies to the tune of more than Rs 4 lakh crore to corporate and service sectors through low taxation rates, tax waivers etc., that are depleting the exchequer, but are quick to suggest ways in which the government can cut costs in dealing with hunger' (Srivastava 2012). While opposition on fiscal grounds did not ultimately scupper the bill altogether, it helped to place limits on the generosity of the PDS entitlements it guaranteed.

In other respects, the Standing Committee attempted to dilute the bill's provisions. One major question concerned the extent to which legal entitlements would extend to the ICDS.

The Ministry of Women and Child Development (MWCD) had submitted to the committee that the ICDS was not yet ready to be held accountable under the bill. They stated:

> ICDS scheme is currently in transition and the on-going efforts are to improve delivery through implementation of revised feeding and nutritional norms with quality as well as reach out to the population through AWCs in all the 14 lakh habitation. The scheme is confronted with programmatic and operational gaps which would need to be addressed first. After then only the ICDS scheme would evolve to an acceptable level of performance in terms of delivery of services and outcomes. Therefore, the time is not ripe yet for making the entitlements legal through an Act of Parliament.[13]

Based on the MWCD evidence of programmatic and operational gaps in ICDS, the Standing Committee recommended that extra food grains should be provided to pregnant women rather than making a free meal at anganwadi centres a legal entitlement.[14] It also found that ICDS is not yet 'ripe' to implement provisions for children under two years, so again it recommended additional food grains instead of a cooked meal (p. 100). However, these amendments did not find their way to the bill, and ICDS did come under its purview.

The original draft bill as agreed by the NAC and published by the government in 2011 had also contained provisions in two chapters specifically geared towards the destitute, starving and homeless. The Standing Committee recommended that these be removed on the grounds that these groups will be difficult to identify, and that such a provision may increase their vulnerability by damaging the social fabric and reducing household support for the vulnerable.[15] These sections were removed from the new draft of the bill. Harsh Mander, the first architect of the NAC draft bill, argued that with the removal of such measures, the bill had been reduced to solely focus on the PDS, which was not the original intention of the NAC.[16]

After the Standing Committee had reported, the bill was approved by the cabinet in March 2013, and then reintroduced to the House by the Food and Civil Supplies Minister, K. V. Thomas, on 6 May 2013. Due to disruptions to Parliament, the bill was not debated. Instead, after tortuous negotiations within the government, the bill was initially introduced as an ordinance in July 2013, and received retrospective parliamentary approval in December 2013.

NATIONAL FOOD SECURITY ACT, 2013: MAIN FEATURES

- 5 kg of food grains per month under the PDS for every person in 'priority' households.[17] Households already covered by the AAY (introduced in 2000) will remain entitled to 35 kg per month.
- Total coverage of PDS entitlements extended to 75 per cent of the rural population, and 50 per cent of urban population, with state-wise coverage based on data from the National Sample Survey. The state governments will be responsible for identifying the AAY households.
- Cap of Rs 3/kg for rice, Rs 2/kg for wheat or Rs 1/kg for coarse grains for a period of three years under the PDS (and thereafter will follow a rate set by the Central government, and less than the Minimum Support Price).
- Every pregnant woman and breastfeeding mother will be entitled to a cooked meal through her local anganwadi centre, and a maternity benefit of at least Rs 6,000 over six months.
- Every child up to 14 years will be entitled either to a meal cooked to appropriate nutritional standards,[18] through an anganwadi centre (six months–six years) or through the midday meal at school (6–14). [This gives statutory underpinning to existing provisions through the ICDS and Midday Meal schemes.]
- Suggested reforms to the Targeted Public Distribution System (TPDS) including doorstep delivery of food grains, end-to-end computerisation; leveraging 'aadhaar' for identification; preference to be given to public institutions/bodies to run fair price shops; diversification of commodities included under PDS; support to local public distribution models and grain banks; and lastly, 'introducing schemes such as cash transfer, food coupons or other schemes to the targeted beneficiaries in lieu of their food grain entitlements...in such area and manner as may be prescribed by the Central Government'.[19]

WHY WAS THE NFSA SO CONTENTIOUS?

The NFSA was enacted in December 2013, shortly before the defeat of the UPA government in May 2014. It introduced universal rights to Midday Meals for school children, maternity benefits and ICDS, and delinked access to the PDS from 'Below Poverty Line' estimates. The bill did not dismantle or radically alter the existing architecture of food security policy. The success or failure of the implementation of its provisions would continue to rely on the role played by state governments, which have starkly differing records on effective administration of the PDS to ensure that food reaches the neediest (Drèze and Khera 2015). Nevertheless, the debates over the legislation opened far-reaching debates about the role of the State in poverty alleviation, and the framing of the bill deliberately left the door open to changes to delivery mechanisms including technology-enabled cash transfers in the future.

The biggest source of contention around the bill was whether subsidies in-kind and services delivered by the public sector are the most effective means of reaching the poor. The NFSA expanded in-kind subsidies by increasing direct food subsidies, but also indirectly by enabling the continuation of input subsidies and price support via public procurement from farmers. Supporters of the expanded provision pointed to states which have successfully reformed their PDS models—such as Chhattisgarh and Tamil Nadu—as examples that reform to public service delivery is possible even in apparently unlikely circumstances. But the notion that the PDS is inherently unreformable, or further that subsidies represent a distortionary intervention in agricultural markets that were ripe for reform, were powerful counter views.

The compromise that the eventual legislation rested on was to leave the existing PDS architecture in place, but to allow for future consideration for other schemes including cash transfers or food coupons in lieu of food grain entitlements. Many on the Left, and in the Right to Food Campaign, were concerned that the bill explicitly thereby left open the back door for cash transfers to replace the PDS. Opponents of cash transfers as a substitute for provision of food in-kind argued that there are factors specific to the Indian context that sharply qualify the likely effects of providing cash rather than food. These include poorly developed markets and social inequalities (caste and gender) that mean that in-kind subsidies provide stronger protection than cash. Furthermore, the poor are likely to bear heavy transaction and transition costs in the process of switching to a new system of cash transfers (Khera 2014). Others emphasised that there is no guarantee that cash transfers will tackle undernutrition—even in the context of poverty reduction in recent decades, calorie consumption has been falling—therefore increasing the amount of cash in the hands of the poor may not be a route to improving nutrition. Lastly, some feared that a shift to cash transfers is a prelude to dismantling the PDS altogether—both the distribution of subsidised food, as well as public procurement/ role of the State in setting minimum support prices for farmers. A more general issue—raised even by those more sympathetic to cash transfers—was the inadequacy of the existing banking infrastructure.

However, despite the concerns raised about cash transfers as a potential route to dismantling the PDS, there seemed to be little appetite anywhere in government or on the political spectrum for a shift towards a complete cash subsidy as a replacement for existing schemes—with a widespread recognition that it would be politically difficult for any government to abandon public procurement of food grains from farmers.

The bill also supported the use of the Unique ID Scheme—or Aadhaar—for identification of beneficiaries. At the time of the NFSB's passage, the Unique Identification Authority of India (UIDAI) saw Aadhar being used for 'last mile authentication'—that is, the identification of beneficiaries in fair price shops. East Godavari district in Andhra Pradesh was the first district in the country to pilot the use of Aadhar identification in PDS.[20] Biraj Patnaik, principal advisor to the Supreme Court Commissioners on the Right to Food case, argued that the use of Aadhar could 'revolutionise' the PDS by effectively making entitlements 'portable'. By allowing for online identification and monitoring of stock-flows, entitlement holders could access their rations from any shop, improving their choice and responding better to seasonal labour migration within families by allowing for a household's allocation to be accessed from multiple locations (Patnaik 2010). However, Aadhaar has since become a larger issue, closely connected with wider debates on the right to privacy, which go beyond the scope of this chapter.

Another source of opposition to the bill related to its potential impact on agriculture and farmers. Here the debate focused on whether sufficient food grains were available to meet increased demand under the expanded TPDS. This influenced the decision on the proportion of the population to be covered. The resulting coverage of PDS in the bill accords approximately to the existing rate of public grain procurement—it does not envisage a major increase in State procurement. The bill itself had relatively little to say about agricultural production apart from a brief reference in Clause 39 to a commitment to work towards objectives set out in 'Schedule 3' to improve 'food security', including agrarian reforms to help small/marginal farmers, and to encourage decentralised procurement. Some have described this as a missed opportunity. As Planning Commission member Abhijit Sen pointed out, this remains in essence a bill that is focused on the PDS, unlike Brazilian anti-hunger programmes, for instance, which included a focus on local procurement from small-holder farmers (this could have been insisted on for the Midday Meals scheme for instance).[21]

But an important secondary debate focused on the bill's impact on agricultural markets and on maintaining the State's role in procurement. Among others, Ashok Gulati—the head of the Commission on Agricultural Costs and Prices (CACP), the body responsible for setting the Minimum Support Price (MSP) offered to farmers—was a consistently loud critic of the NFSB because it gave a further lease of life to the infrastructure for procurement. He argued that the bill would have an adverse impact on open market prices and the diversification of agricultural production by encouraging a State monopsony in the grain trade and crowding out private players. The increase in, or perpetuation of, agricultural subsidies implied by the bill, he suggested, crowded out other longer term forms of investment which are needed in roads/rural infrastructure, research and development, education and public investment in irrigation etc. (Gulati et al. 2012). This view—shared by many economists—was one of the largest sources of intellectual opposition to the bill. These views often became reasons to oppose the bill altogether rather than seeing it as an opportunity to rethink the role of the State in agricultural procurement.

CONCLUSION

Food has a long history as a subject of electoral politics in India. This chapter has shown how the 'right to food' was put on the agenda by a civil society campaign that worked through the Supreme Court. It was subsequently included in the manifesto of the Congress Party in 2009, and intended to be a centrepiece of social legislation in the UPA's second term of office. However, negotiations over the legislation became the occasion for a vigorous debate about the role of the State in addressing poverty in India at a time when the UPA's wider political legitimacy was waning. While the bill did enact new legal entitlements for school children, pregnant and lactating mothers, as well as 75 per cent of the rural population and 50 per cent of the urban population, it disappointed many campaigners who had fought for a fully universal system of food security. It also disappointed many opponents of food subsidies who had fought for a more radical reform of the subsidy system altogether. The bill found few vigorous champions because it entailed so many compromises.

The very achievements of the first term of the UPA had also begun to establish new lines of political debate that affected the progress of social legislation under its second term. By the eve of the 2014 general elections, there was a more polarised debate in the media about the public provision of entitlements versus growth and jobs-led 'development'. These, far too often stylised views, crystallised most sharply in terms of their implications for welfare policy in the competing visions laid out by Bhagwati and Panagariya (2014), and Drèze and Sen (2013). The NFSB was caught in the crosshairs of this new ideological contestation. What is perhaps striking is that the NFSB—widely seen as being driven by electoral concerns and arising from a 2009 manifesto commitment—barely featured at all in the Congress' campaigns for the 2014 elections. This reflected an incumbent party on the back foot, which was not united across its rank and file by a strong ideological commitment to social democracy. The Congress Party itself served as a weak defender of the rights-based legislation it had introduced. But it also reflected the reality that the legislation took so long to negotiate that it had barely made itself felt on the ground by the time of the 2014 elections so that it could not serve as a prominent electoral appeal to its main potential stakeholders: the rural poor.

NOTES AND REFERENCES

1. Figures for 2010–12 given in the Food and Agriculture Organisation (FAO)'s *State of Food Insecurity* report, 2012 (cited in Pritchard et al. 2014: 19).

2. This implies a focus on the entire life-cycle from adequate nutrition for women during pregnancy, to the first 1,000 days of childhood, through to adulthood and old age.

3. See discussion of ICDS in Chapter 5.

4. See Swaminathan 2012.

5. Discussion on 13 June 2013 (all interviews for this chapter were conducted by Louise Tillin). Trinamool Congress MP Dinesh Trivedi made similar remarks in a discussion on 10 June 2013. Trivedi was the only MP to table a full speech in response to the re-introduction of the NFSB in May 2013.

6. See http://www.righttofoodcampaign.in/legal-action/supreme-court-orders (accessed 9 August 2019).

7. Discussion with Harsh Mander, 13 June 2013.

8. Minutes of the NAC meeting on 14 July 2010, originally available on the NAC website at http://www.nac.nic.in/press_releases/14_july_2010.pdf (accessed 30 April 2014; site discontinued).

9. 'Government Draft of National Food Security Bill: A Denial of the Right to Food', *Right to Food Campaign*, 26 July 2011.

10. 'A simple proposal on food security', open letter to Prime Minister Manmohan Singh in *The Hindu*, 12 March 2012. Available at http://www.thehindu.com/todays-paper/tp-opinion/a-simple-proposal-on-food-security/article2986061.ece (accessed 7 September 2017).

11. Union Budgets, various years. Available at https://www.indiabudget.gov.in/previous_union_budget.php (accessed 4 August 2019).

12. One set of inflated figures that were widely quoted come from a discussion paper published by the Commission on Agricultural Costs and Prices which estimates the total implied costs of the NFSB to be Rs 682,163 crore (c. £810 million) over three years (Ashok Gulati et al. 2012). However what was often misreported was that this was an estimate of total expenditure, not additional expenditure. By contrast, the Parliamentary Standing Committee estimated the total implied *additional* annual expenditure of the bill to be more like Rs 34,007 crore (c. £40.4 million—at the June 2013 exchange rate).

13. Report of the Standing Committee on Food, Consumer Affairs and Public Distribution (2012–13) on the NFSB, 2011, 94.

14. Ibid.: 97–98.

15. Ibid.: 104.

16. Discussion with Harsh Mander, 3 June and 13 June 2013, Delhi.

17. This was commonly described as 25 kg per household on assumption of a five-member household, but the bill itself provides an individual commitment—unlike the AAY scheme which operates at household level. This quantity of 25 kg is lower than the 35 kg per month at subsidised prices which the Supreme Court ruled in 2008 should be the entitlement for BPL families. (Interim order, 10 Jan 2008 in *PUCL v Union of India and Ors.* Supreme Court Writ Petition [Civil] No. 196 of 2001—see PRS Legislative Briefing, 26 September 2012.)

18. See reference to the 'biscuit lobby' in Chapter 5 and the concern that this clause, supported by the MWCD, favours private contractors able to meet the specified standards rather than local producers.

19. These suggested reforms built primarily on the reform model adopted successfully in the state of Chhattisgarh. For more detail on the Chhattisgarh reforms to the PDS, see Drèze and Khera 2017b; Puri 2012; and Tillin, Saxena and Sisodia 2015.

20. This was also reiterated in a conversation with Nandan Nilekani, chairman of UIDAI, 5 June 2013.

21. Discussion between Louise Tillin and Abhijit Sen in Delhi, 14 June 2013.

four

The Forest Rights Act, 2006

By the time the UPA led by the Congress took power after the general election of 2004, many in the new government and in the policy community more generally (including people in government and civil society) had concluded that things had gone badly wrong in the forestry sector. This was not a small matter. Upwards of one-quarter of the country's land mass is officially listed as forested,[1] and while no census of the forest population exists, estimates range from 275 million to 400 million.[2] Many of them are extremely poor. One authoritative analysis in 2000 estimated that of the 300 million people living below the official poverty line, 200 million were partially or wholly dependent for their livelihoods on forest resources.[3] The key questions that emerged as the new government took power in 2004 were whether poor forest dwellers should (i) have security of tenure over plots of forested land that they had long occupied; (ii) be able to use and market minor forest products; and (iii) play a role in the management of forests.

Earlier government initiatives to address these problems had proved ineffective. A Joint Forest Management programme which began in 1990 had drawn forest dwellers onto forest management committees in which they were supposed to influence decisions—along with the officers of the Forest Service who had long dominated forest areas, and who tended to regard forest dwellers as encroachers. But by 2004, these committees had largely become instruments controlled from above by Forest

Service officials.[4] That and other government initiatives to benefit and empower forest dwellers had gone the way of most legal provisions to benefit 'tribals' (Adivasis)—severely disadvantaged groups who numbered 84.3 million in 2011, 8.2 per cent of the Indian population, who loom large among forest dwellers. Those provisions have been widely unimplemented, in violation not just of law but also of the Constitution, both of which matter in India.

Other issues compounded the problem and, by mid-2004, had made it politically salient. The issue of security of tenure over forest lands was often discussed in terms of its implications for government revenues, rather than as a forestry matter—which, for complex reasons, implied that all the primary stakeholders (not least, poor forest dwellers) were left out. Most existing laws—from the Indian Forest Act of 1927 through the Forest Conservation Act of 1980, many state government acts, etc.—contained provisions to encourage proactive efforts by forest dwellers in defence of their interests. But little of this had actually occurred because of Forest Service resistance, and because forest dwellers suffered from a severe lack of political capacity (political awareness, confidence, skills and connections) which was an important dimension of their 'poverty'.

To make matters worse, India's Supreme Court had recently been persuaded by an extreme group of environmentalists who were impatient with human inhabitants of forests to ban the award of rights of occupation to poor forest dwellers, many of whom had long resided there. Many evictions ensued. Supreme Court rulings in India are 'law declared'—that is, they carry the same force as legislation, until the Parliament enacts measures to override them. Key figures close to the new government concluded that an 'historic injustice' had been done to forest dwellers,[5] who had responded to the Court's ruling with heated protests. Their anger also facilitated efforts by armed insurgents, so-called 'Maoists' or 'Naxalites', to recruit forest dwellers to their cause. These things left politicians from many parties badly rattled.[6]

The newly elected government in 2004 was also being pressed, from without and within, to act to address such problems. Civil society organisations reinforced 'tribal' protests.[7] One important example was a high-profile exercise called the 'Campaign for Survival and Dignity' led by Pradip Prabhu, general secretary of an association called the Kashtakari Sanghatana. In an indication of the links that many senior civil society activists had with India's 'establishment', Prabhu had previously been the dean of the School of Rural Development at the Tata Institute of Social Sciences—an elite research institution.

Such campaigns from outside the government were matched by efforts of several progressive insiders. They included certain advisors to Sonia Gandhi and at least two important officials within the PMO. The first was Pulok Chatterji who had earlier served as an executive director at the World Bank where he had absorbed ideas from some of the enlightened subcultures that exist there. The second and key force for change on the prime minister's staff was R. Gopalakrishnan, an immensely dynamic and socially committed civil servant. He had spent the previous ten years devising and overseeing successful poverty initiatives in Madhya Pradesh[8]—a state with substantial forested areas.

The CMP agreed upon by the parties in the new, Congress-led ruling alliance—including the two Communist parties that supported the government—made several sympathetic references to the plight of forest dwellers and promised several actions.[9] Thanks to pressure from without and to the efforts of such insiders,[10] it was soon decided that a new Forest Rights Act[11] should be introduced to address the problems noted above.

FORMULATION

What followed was a formulation process marked by (i) the quite open interplay of diverse interests; (ii) a certain amount of bargaining to accommodate some of those interests; (iii) a key intervention from Sonia Gandhi to prevent the bargaining from weakening the draft of the law; (iv) politically calculated haste;

and (v) a serious omission amid the haste which has severely limited the impact of the new Act. This episode exhibits the openness of India's policy-making process, at least in this case; the breadth of forces (within and outside the corridors of power) that were arrayed both for and against the new law; the loci of power within the government; and the dangers that haste poses to the wording of crucial elements of legislation.

On 19 January 2005, a small group of people with expertise on forestry issues—drawn from civil society, government and the legal profession—were summoned to the PMO and tasked with drafting such a law. The new committee was broad-based, including people with diverse views—some who advocated the rights of forest dwellers, and others who were sceptical out of a concern for wildlife—but with the former in the majority.[12] This was in accordance with Sonia Gandhi's wishes, since she and her key advisors hoped to reduce opposition to the new initiative by drawing some sceptics into the formulation process. She pressed for the inclusion of national parks and wildlife sanctuaries within the ambit of the new law, despite the opposition of the wildlife lobby.[13] She also sought speedy action, to deny opponents of the legislation time to muster pressure against it.[14]

The committee could not have been formed without clearance from Prime Minister Manmohan Singh himself. People who worked closely with him indicate that when he considered the rights-based initiatives being proposed by Sonia Gandhi and the NAC which she chaired—on the right to information, MGNREGA, and forest rights—he was neither an enthusiast nor an opponent. One key advisor recalls him saying 'next to nothing' on the subject. But he had good reason in early 2005 to permit such ideas to go forward. He was then newly anointed by Sonia Gandhi as the head of the government, and he needed to cement the support (from outside his government) of two Communist parties which held 61 out of 543 seats and were pressing for new legislation on, among other things, forest rights.

One of his former advisors also believes that by early 2005, Manmohan Singh had begun to make progress towards a goal which, if it came to fruition, would be 'his own signal achievement': an agreement on civil nuclear power with the United States. Since it was possible that Sonia Gandhi would be sceptical about this, and since it would be extremely difficult to sell it to the Communist parties, the prime minister almost certainly calculated that it made sense to cultivate both by enabling rights-based legislation to proceed.[15] He therefore approved the appointment of the committee to draft the new law on forest rights.

The committee's members were aware of two immense impediments that the eventual Forest Rights Act (FRA) would face during the implementation phase, and they sought to address them. First, they knew that many, probably most, members of the Forest Service would oppose the Act. It sought to confer property rights on individuals and communities among forest dwellers. That contradicted the view among members of the Service that they and not forest residents exercised something approaching 'ownership' of the forests. They saw themselves as conservators and (as we have noted) they tended to regard forest dwellers—even those who had resided there for generations—as illegal occupants, or as one journalist put it, 'encroachers...living at the whims of the forest department'.

Second, the architects of the Act knew that moneyed mining and logging interests had long made significant profits from forest products, which residents of forested areas would, under the new law, now control (and be able to use or sell). Those moneyed interests often shared their profits, through illicit payments, with politicians and some bureaucrats. To compound the problem, some state governments derived substantial revenues from the sale of forest products and/or from taxation on such sales. The new Act was a classic case of a particularly difficult type of devolution—when an attempt is made to transfer powers to individuals or elected councils at the grassroots in a sector (a) from which substantial profits are reaped by private individuals and/or government actors; and (b) from which governments derive significant revenues.

The framers of the Act responded to these problems as best they could, in the certain knowledge that it would encounter resistance from these sources. To tackle the Forest Service, they assigned the task of implementation not just to one but two Central government ministries: the Ministry of Environment and Forests (under which the Forest Service operates) and the Ministry of Tribal Affairs (since most forest dwellers come from disadvantaged 'tribal' groups). More to the point, in an attempt to counter reluctance in the Forest Service, the latter ministry was given the lead role in implementing the Act. To address anticipated resistance from state governments that would lose revenues, and from private interests and government actors who would lose profits, they inserted explicit provisions that were intended to ensure that poor forest dwellers would gain rights to land that they occupied and to forest products.

These two impediments persuaded some advocates of the new Act that it would largely be an 'aspirational' law—unlikely to prevail over interests that were certain to oppose it. Those advocates had become disheartened after years of thwarted efforts to assist severely disadvantaged 'tribals' both within and outside forests. They likened the new Act to a 1996 law that required the empowerment of elected local councils in 'tribal' areas[16] but which had gone almost entirely unimplemented. They regarded the failure to enforce both that law and indeed, even constitutional guarantees to 'tribals', as an indication of a scandalously weak commitment to the well-being of one of India's most vulnerable groups.

The formulation process did not end with the completion of the committee's draft bill. It was first sent to Sonia Gandhi's NAC which had devised other important rights-based initiatives. None of that Council's members had served on the drafting committee. The NAC submitted comments on the draft which contained a few far from radical suggestions, and passed the matter back to the executive branch.

Then, in the words of a lawyer on the initial drafting committee, 'politics took over'—diverse actors became involved in various stages of the post-drafting process. The lawyer's presence on the committee had ensured that the concepts set out in the text had clear, precise meanings. But as the draft passed through executive departments of government, then a Joint Parliamentary Committee, and then a 'Group of Ministers', several key words were changed and—quite possibly with no destructive intent—made more ambiguous.[17] Loose wording would create problems once implementation began, but there was nothing that the initial drafters could do to put this right.[18]

At that stage in the formulation of the MGNREGA, government ministries had greatly weakened the draft before forwarding it to a committee of Parliament for consideration. This did not occur in the case of forest rights. Some of the drafters of the forest bill testified before the Parliamentary Committee to counter arguments from two quite different sets of opponents of the bill: people who shared the Forest Service's proprietary views of forests, and extreme wildlife enthusiasts (the 'tiger lobby') who prefer forests to be free of human inhabitants even though vast numbers of them have long resided there.

To the surprise of people on all sides of this debate, the Parliamentary Committee greatly strengthened the content of the bill. It was chaired by a long-serving member of the Congress Party, V. K. C. Deo, a strong advocate for the rights of 'tribals' and other forest dwellers. The Committee went beyond the provisions in the draft bill which gave individuals security of tenure and added a similar—and radical—guarantee to communities residing in forests. It also extended the purview of the bill, the draft of which had referred only to 'tribal' residents of forests, to 'other traditional forest dwellers', of whom there were a great many. These changes delighted progressives, although the lawyers among them were dismayed by the insertion of certain vague, ambiguous words because they feared that these would be used in courts to defeat the purposes of the new law. The Law Ministry sometimes tightens up such wording, but that did not occur in this case, probably because of the haste with which advocates of the bill wished to proceed.[19]

Even though the bill had been strengthened by the Parliamentary Committee as it made its way towards enactment, certain concessions had been made to those who wished to dilute the draft—in order to minimise opposition. This alarmed members of the NAC who urged Sonia Gandhi to intervene. She asked the sole member of that Council with expertise in forestry issues[20] to draft a letter to the prime minister for her signature. The NAC insisted that several key provisions to benefit forest dwellers had to be included in the new law. Manmohan Singh ensured that these points appeared in the final text.

Despite this, two regressive provisions in the draft bill[21] remained in the Act which was eventually passed. The first was made after the Parliamentary Committee had concluded its work. It had given local-level mass meetings of forest dwellers (*gram sabhas*) the authority to make certain key decisions, with the proviso that appeals against them could go to the senior-most bureaucrat in the district (known as the Collector or Deputy Commissioner). The Ministry of Environment and Forests altered that provision to give the Collector full authority in such instances. The Tribal Affairs Ministry—which was also involved, and was made the lead implementing ministry because it was more sympathetic to forest dwellers—was at that time poorly led, so that it did not oppose this change. Sonia Gandhi, who might have intervened on advice from progressives in the NAC, preferred swift action (as noted above) and she was at that moment distracted by other matters, so she did not intervene.

The second provision—an oversight—was to prove much more damaging. The final text of the Forest Rights Act contained a single sentence (Section 13) which carries grave implications. It stated that: '...the provisions of this Act shall be *in addition to and not in derogation of* the provisions of any other law for the time being in force' (emphasis added). In other words, the new Act did not override earlier legislation on forests which the Forest Service had long used to deny forest dwellers the very rights which the new Act sought to promote. As we shall see, despite efforts since 2006 to give the new Forest Rights Act precedence, those old laws have served as potent obstacles.[22]

IMPLEMENTATION

In the implementation phase, the Forest Rights Act has faced far greater impediments than any of the Indian government's other recent rights-based initiatives, including the MGNREGA. The latter contained more formidable and thoroughgoing mechanisms to ensure proper implementation than the Forest Rights Act, but that does not take us very far in understanding the different histories of these two initiatives. Forest Rights has faced far more daunting opposition and obstacles.

Among the worst of these has been the indifference—and more often, the hostility—of Forest Service officers. They tend to regard poor, illiterate or semi-educated forest dwellers—many of whom were supposedly 'primitive' tribals—as unworthy intruders. In an uncanny echo of our work on the rural employment guarantee scheme, one especially knowledgeable informant stated that when dealing with these people, forest officers display an unusually acute form of an 'allergy' to transparency and downward accountability that afflicts most state actors in India.[23] But that comment understates the problem. An authoritative analysis by the main government committee to evaluate implementation found that the Forest Service was 'functioning as a "veto" in denying rights to the people'.[24]

The views of forest officers were well known at the formulation stage, which is why the Ministry of Tribal Affairs was given the lead role in implementation. But it was of course impossible to exclude the Ministry of Environment and Forests, and the Forest Service which works out of it, from the implementation of a Forest Rights Act. The problem that this entails is compounded by the fact that the Ministry of Tribal Affairs has no employees working below the (high-intermediate) district level—none at the grassroots where crucial actions occur under the Act. That ministry must rely on the Forest Service and on the Revenue Department (which also has other priorities) because they have officials working at district, sub-district and local levels.

If evidence were needed of the threat that this posed, the Minister of Environment and Forests sought to undermine the Act as the draft was being considered. He sent the Cabinet an official rebuttal of the draft which set out 18 points to demonstrate that there was no need for the new law.[25] Strangely, his arguments were not entirely spurious. He was correct in arguing that several previous initiatives had already provided forest dwellers with many of the rights that eventually figured in the new Act—on paper.[26] He failed to mention, however, that those initiatives had all been stymied by his very own Forest Service. It is hardly surprising then that, as one analyst puts it, since the passage of the Act, there has been 'a complete absence of buy in' by the Service.[27]

Further evidence of forest officers' opposition to the Act and to the conferral of rights on forest dwellers emerged from recent discussions by one of us with Forest Service officials in five Indian states. Their comments were universally negative. There is evidence that to discourage communities of forest dwellers from submitting claims to 'community' rights, forest officers told them (incorrectly) that by doing so they risked the loss of funds under the Joint Forest Management programme (Kothari 2011).[28] Their attitudes are patently demonstrated by the extraordinary decisions by forest officers' associations in two states, Odisha and Tamil Nadu, to file legal challenges to the validity of the Act. In the latter state, the High Court refused to invalidate the new law, but it ruled that no certificates giving security of tenure to forest lands could be issued. As a result, the Act is largely a dead letter in Tamil Nadu.

Resistance from the Forest Service—or what one campaigner described as the 'active sabotage' of the Act by the Service[29]—also had a destructive impact in several other states. One eminent commentator argued in early 2011 that eleven state governments 'are yet to implement the law'. Another analysis found that governments in Kerala, Rajasthan, Andhra Pradesh, Madhya Pradesh, Chhattisgarh and Jharkhand had made scarcely any attempts to acquaint forest dwellers with the contents of the Act or with their diverse rights under it. So, the implementation of the Act there mainly amounted to exercises in which politicians distributed certificates of land tenure as largesse.[30] Inaction in those six states is a deeply serious matter since the last four of them contain extensive forests which comprise a large proportion of India's forested areas. In recent times, two of those state governments—in Madhya Pradesh and Chhattisgarh—have become more active, because state elections were due in November 2013 and because forest dwellers have (and cast) votes.[31] But the overall implementation of the Act has been woeful.

For further evidence of this, consider an analysis by the Centre for Social Development (CSD) in 2010 which reached the following conclusions:

> All states have largely failed to respect the Act's historic provisions regarding role of the *gramsabhas* [which is to say that in no state were local-level mass meetings permitted to exercise powers to make decisions on forest issues or to oversee claims to rights];
>
> All non-land rights in the Act...have been largely ignored in implementation;
>
> District-level committees have been the site of numerous serious violations;
>
> The process in most states that have implemented the Act has been marked by haste and a total failure to provide information or engage in awareness-raising or trainings [to forest dwellers], including areas where the Rules specifically require authorities under the Act to perform these duties;[32]
>
> Eligible claimants have been denied rights, particularly in the case of other traditional forest dwellers [that is, non-'tribals'] whose claims have been overwhelmingly rejected in all states...; and
>
> The [C]entral government, and in particular the Environment Ministry, has continued policies that are in direct violation of the spirit and letter of the Forest Rights Act.[33]

The wretched implementation of the Act also emerges vividly when we examine the list of 13 rights which it affirms. The first of these is the 'right to hold and live in the forest land under the individual or common occupation for habitation or for self-cultivation for livelihood by a member or members of a forest dwelling Scheduled Tribe or other traditional forest dwellers'. That right has often (but not consistently) been upheld. The reference just above to politicians distributing certificates providing security of tenure is an indication of that. By July 2016, 3.845 million poor forest dwellers had received such certificates.[34] This is 'one of the largest land reforms in India's history' (Kumar, Singh and Rao 2017: 40–43), but it has still reached only a modest fraction of the total number of such people. In May 2012, the Tribal Affairs Minister stated that there were 'very few cases' in which their rights were being recognised. It was also the main positive outcome of the Act in the initial years. Little or nothing was done to deliver the other 12 rights set out in the new law. They include:

> [the] right of ownership, access to collect, use, and dispose of minor forest produce which has been traditionally collected within or outside villages boundaries;
> rights including community tenures of habitat and habitation for primitive tribal groups and pre-agricultural communities;
> rights over disputed lands under any nomenclature in any State where claims are disputed;
> rights for conversion of...leases or grants issued by any local authority or any State government on forest lands to titles;
> rights...which are accepted as rights of tribals under any traditional or customary law of concerned tribes of any State;
> any other customary right enjoyed by the forest dwelling Scheduled Tribes or other forest dwellers...which are not mentioned in [all previous clauses of the Act]...but excluding the right of hunting or trapping or extracting a part of the body of any species of wild animal; and
> [the] right to *insitu* rehabilitation including alternative land in cases where the Scheduled Tribes and other forest dwellers have been illegally evicted or displaced of forest land of any description without receiving their legal

entitlement or rehabilitation prior to the 13th of December 2005.[35]

So, when we consider 12 of the 13 rights that have been 'granted', the Forest Rights Act has largely been a failure.

The most severe of these disappointments has been the poor delivery on the second item in this list, the certification of forest rights to communities. That provision could potentially cover 85.6 million acres and 200 million forest dwellers in 170,000 villages. Community rights have been acknowledged for only 2.7 million acres, 3 per cent of the potential total.[36]

After mid-2011, things became somewhat more complicated. Key supporters of poor forest dwellers—some of them in very high places—have made strenuous efforts to implement the full array of progressive provisions in the Act. They have lacked the power to bring major changes to the bleak picture set out above, and they were eventually forced to accept a vastly damaging intervention from the very apex of the power structure. But their efforts are worth noting.

It is evident from another of our case studies—of the Jawaharlal Nehru National Urban Renewal Mission (JNNURM) (see Chapter 6)—that powerful actors in key government agencies can have a huge impact on the implementation of a programme, for good or for ill. In that case, negative reviews and, less significantly, the intervention by members of the NAC produced constructive changes, albeit limited.

The Forest Rights Act witnessed something similar, at ministerial level. During the first five years of implementation, those in charge at the Ministry of Tribal Affairs (the lead agency in implementing the law) felt little ownership of it and thus took only limited interest in it. They issued clarifications of certain import rules for implementation in 2008—to begin addressing problems caused by vague language in the law—but these were inadequate and had little impact.[37] Lax leadership by ministers at Tribal Affairs was a serious problem which triggered protests from advocates for forest dwellers. (Something similar happened with the anti-poverty aspect of the JNNURM.) The main analyst who called attention to this in early 2011 in a report of an official committee doubts whether the report was read within the ministry or forwarded to state governments for consideration.[38]

But then in June 2011, things changed dramatically. A new Minister of Tribal Affairs was appointed—V. K. C. Deo, the man who had chaired the Parliamentary Committee which strengthened the draft of the bill. He brought commitment and political sophistication to the role. He had been hamstrung by the fact that his ministry's personnel do not penetrate below the district (high-intermediate) level. But his energetic efforts to ensure that poor forest dwellers benefit from the Act—especially in obtaining certificates of land tenure—produced some results. He also saw to it that a further and much more complete set of clarifications of implementation rules was issued in 2012.[39]

Deo overlapped far too briefly (for just one month in mid-2011) with a sympathetic, dynamic and adroit Minister of Environment and Forests, Jairam Ramesh. The latter was very proactive: paying numerous visits to forested areas, pressing state governments to implement the Act more genuinely and energetically, and arranging certain key adjustments in practice to the terms of the Act. All of these efforts benefited forest dwellers.[40] But then prime minister Manmohan Singh—who was growing increasingly unhappy with the Act and with the minister's strenuous efforts—moved Ramesh to a different ministry and replaced him with a more malleable successor who did far less to promote implementation.[41] As we shall see, Ramesh's main 'sin' was to resist attempts from the very apex of government to permit—and indeed, to promote—major violations of the Act and of environmental regulations.

This brings us to a further major element in the explanation for the substantial failure of the Forest Rights Act. The hostility of the Forest Service had already done immense damage,[42] and then after mid-2011, the prime minister himself turned destructive.

During 2010 and 2011, major corporations in India felt and voiced acute frustration with the slow pace of economic liberalisation and initiatives to develop infrastructure, and with delays and refusals that emerged when they sought official approvals for new ventures. The prime minister was especially pained by these loud complaints because they were directed at him—even though he had (as finance minister) been the initiator of liberalisation in the early 1990s. The PMO felt besieged by hostility from the corporate sector and its friends in the media.[43]

To ease the tension, and to address slowing economic growth (which was partly the result of the international financial crisis), the prime minister began to respond to the discontents of what is called 'India Inc.'. Urged by Finance Minister P. Chidambaram, he established a team in the Cabinet Office to expedite clearances that had become ensnared in complex relations between the Central and state governments. Efforts were made to persuade Indian corporations to invest at home instead of abroad where delays and red tape caused less frustration. Much of the pressure from the corporate sector focused on impediments to proposed projects for the extraction of raw materials—the prices of which had soared—from forested areas. Some of those impediments emerged from the Forest Rights Act which sought to empower elected local councils and local-level mass meetings to grant or withhold permission for such projects.

In mid-2011, the prime minister began taking action to respond to corporate discontents. He moved Jairam Ramesh out of the Ministry of Environment and Forests mainly because the latter had made effective use of environmental rules and the provisions of the FRA to thwart proposed projects from extractive industries. Then in October 2012, the prime minister compelled reluctant ministers at Tribal Affairs and at Environment and Forests to relax the provisions of the Forest Rights Act. He first ordered that proposals for 'linear' development projects (roads, power and telecommunications lines, pipelines, etc.) which would pass through forested areas should proceed without the agreement of elected local councils and local-level mass meetings. Then he went much further and forced those ministers to deal similarly with non-linear projects like mines and factories, which would occupy large tracts.[44] Such things had already been happening in some states, but this was a blatant violation of the law from the very apex of the political system.

This was music to the ears of many chief ministers who head state governments in this federal system. A major (though largely unnoticed) trend in India over the last 20 years has been the radical centralisation of power within many (though not all) state governments in the hands of chief ministers. At the end of 2013 roughly 60 per cent of Indians in lived in states where governments were characterised by one-person dominance or near dominance. The main change which has enabled many chief ministers to centralise has been the flow of massive, covert, illicit financial 'contributions'—directly to them—by industrialists who seek official approvals for large undertakings. These funds are then used by chief ministers to intimidate and buy off subordinates and others—partly to compensate them for the loss of power that they experience as chief ministers centralise control of state-level systems. Many of the industrialists who provide such 'contributions' seek permission to engage in mining in forested areas (Manor 2015). State governments have offered no resistance to the prime minister's extraordinary violation of the Forest Rights Act.

The pliable new Minister of Environment and Forests did not protest the prime minister's intervention, but V. K. C. Deo at Tribal Affairs—who was committed to the Act and to poor forest dwellers—made his discontent apparent.[45] Perceptive observers who have dealt with him since this change have stated that Deo appeared to feel 'helpless'.[46] He had tried to overcome the problems caused by the statement in the Act that it was 'not in derogation' of other laws, which forest officers have used to obstruct implementation. Deo had formally stated that since the Forest Rights Act post-dated other laws, it took precedence over them. But this changed nothing since in law, he was wrong. Such failures, plus resistance from the Forest Service and the prime minister's disregard for the Act inspired his sense of helplessness—which accurately reflected his and the Act's plight.

IMPACT AND IMPLICATIONS

Most of the key points on the impact and implications of the Forest Rights Act are already apparent from the discussion of its implementation. Hence, when assessing its impact, we are compelled to focus mainly on its limitations, on things that did *not* happen. Its only significant outcome has been the award of certificates for security of land tenure to 1,406,971 poor forest dwellers (by 30 September 2012). This is not trivial, but even this sole achievement pales when we weigh that number against at least 275 million people who reside in forested areas.

It is also dwarfed by the large number of intended impacts which have not occurred. Here is a partial list of things which the law not only aspired to, but required. Elected local councils and local-level mass meetings were hardly ever permitted to make decisions on the management of forests on claims to rights. So, the intention of the Act to draw communities into important roles—which had also been a stated aim of the Joint Forest Management initiative in 1990—went unfulfilled once again. Thus, the Central and state governments—and more specifically the Forest Service—continued to violate both the spirit and letter of the Act.

In most states, next to no information about the content of the Act was disseminated, and scarcely any efforts were made to raise the awareness of forest dwellers. Here we encounter the same acute 'allergy' among most political actors in India to transparency and downward accountability that was apparent from the implementation of the MGNREGA. But the Forest Rights Act lacked the potent transparency mechanisms built into that latter programme, so that misdeeds in the forest sector were not visible to poor people to the degree that they were in the latter initiative.

Many eligible claimants were denied rights set down in the Act, and claims to rights by non-tribal forest dwellers were overwhelmingly rejected in all states. In several states, rejections occurred even when claimants submitted full supporting evidence.

All non-land rights in the Act have been largely ignored. Perceptive analysts of the Act emphasise the supreme importance of one of these: the provision that is intended to unlock access to forest products. They argue that the sole achievement on the Act—the award of land certificates—provides forest dwellers with a 'safety net'. Access to forest products would, by contrast, provide them with a 'springboard', a means of enhancing their livelihoods and escaping severe poverty. The Act has delivered the 'safety net', at least to a small fraction of forest dwellers, but they have largely been denied the 'springboard'.[47]

There were certain exceptions to this bleak verdict since implementation, and thus outcomes, varied—not just between states or regions of India,[48] but between localities within individual regions.[49] But when we consider the overall picture, it is impossible to disagree with Ashish Kothari's view that in terms of impact, the Act is an 'abysmal failure', or with his arguments that 'the government itself is proving to be the biggest obstacle in its implementation', and that in the forest sector, India 'has hardly begun the journey towards changing governance' (Kothari 2011).

NOTES AND REFERENCES

1. The United Nations Food and Agricultural Organisation gives a figure of 19.5%.

2. The low figure is a World Bank estimate. India's Ministry of Environment and Forests estimates the number at between 350 and 400 million; see Nayak, Kohli and Sharma (n.d.: 5).

3. Khare et al. 2000, initially cited in Bose 2010.

4. This is a common trend with such 'user committees' in India and across the developing world. For more detail, see Manor 2005b. For more detail on Joint Forest Management, see Saxena 1997; and Ravindranath and Sudha 2004.

5. These words eventually appeared in the Preamble to the FRA.

6. The comments above emerge in part from interviews in New Delhi with Sanjay Upadhyay, 22 November 2013, and N. C. Saxena,

21 November and 3 December 2013. (All interviews cited in this chapter were conducted by James Manor).

7. For useful details on campaigns by civil society organisations, and on the formulation process, see Bose 2010: 13–14, 18–24.

8. He was, for example, the co-author with another civil servant—Amita Sharma, who herself took on the day-to-day management of the MGNREGA—of the Madhya Pradesh Education Guarantee Scheme. It brought basic primary schooling to roughly half of the villages in that state. Gopalakrishnan served as the right-hand man of the progressive chief minister there, Digvijay Singh. For a detailed analysis of that state government (1993–2003) and of the Education Guarantee Scheme, see Melo, Ng'ethe and Manor 2010, chapter three. Gopalakrishnan could not be interviewed for this study because he passed away in 2011.

9. The Congress Party's manifesto made no clear reference to forested areas or forest dwellers. The UPA CMP stated that the new government would urge state governments in the federal system to make laws conferring ownership rights on forest dwellers in respect of forest produce. It also affirmed that evictions of forest dwellers would be ended, and that the government in New Delhi would safeguard the rights of 'tribal' communities over mineral resources, water resources, etc., as laid down in existing legislation.

10. Individual civil servants within relevant government departments, such as Rajeev Kumar in the Ministry of Tribal Affairs, also contributed to these efforts.

11. Its full formal title is: 'The Scheduled Tribes and Other Traditional Forest Dwellers (Recognition of Forest Rights) Act, 2006'.

12. The committee included civil servants, a Supreme Court advocate with expertise in the forestry sector and other knowledgeable persons—not including any members of Sonia Gandhi's NAC.

13. For an analysis of the political tensions between environmental concerns and social justice in pursuit of forest rights in India in a comparative perspective, see Kashwan 2017.

14. Interview with environmental lawyer Videh Upadhyay, New Delhi, 6 December 2013. The committee appointed to draft the bill was initially told to finish their task within two weeks, but they pleaded successfully for a little more time since they needed to study various existing laws, court rulings, etc. Interview with Sanjay Upadhyay, another environmental lawyer, New Delhi, 22 November 2013.

15. Interviews in New Delhi with two former senior advisors to the prime minister, on 14 June and 24 November 2013; and with a member of the technical support group that worked with the Ministry of Tribal Affairs after the draft of a new Forest Rights Bill had been completed, New Delhi, 26 November 2013.

16. This law was the 'Panchayats (Extension to Scheduled Areas) Act, 1996', commonly called 'PESA'. It sought to give substance to provisions for elected local councils in 'tribal' areas set out in Part IX of India's Constitution.

17. Terms now included, like 'habitat rights' and 'other forest dwellers' (which seemed to refer to non-'tribals') were examples that would prove hard to define—so that they would assist those resisting implementation once the Act came into force. The Act states that communities within forested areas will be 'empowered' (a fashionable but somewhat vague word), but does not use more legally precise words like 'authority' and 'responsibility'. The powers and duties of '*gram sabhas*' (local-level mass meetings) were also vaguely set out—which later gave opponents openings to claim they had exceeded their powers and failed to perform their duties. Interviews in New Delhi with N. C. Saxena, 3 December 2013, and Videh Upadhyay, 6 December 2013.

18. Interview with Sanjay Upadhyay (the advocate in question), New Delhi, 22 November 2013.

19. Interview with two members of the drafting committee, New Delhi, 22 November and 3 December 2013.

20. This was N. C. Saxena, who (full disclosure) advised us in our studies of the five programmes.

21. To this might be added an omission: the failure of the Act to address the need to clear forest dwellers of criminal offences for seizing forest land and collecting forest products before 2005. The Act legalises these things. See Bandi 2013.

22. Interview with Videh Upadhyay, New Delhi, 6 December 2013.

23. The informant was N. C. Saxena, New Delhi, 3 December 2013. Our research on India's rural employment guarantee (Chapter 2) found this 'allergy' to be a crucial feature of the Indian State—a theme developed at length in Jenkins and Manor 2017.

24. These words are from a reference to that report by Bandi, 'Implementation of the Forest Rights Act...', p. 21. He was referring to the *MANTHAN: Report (of) National Committee on Forest Rights Act*, December 2010, available at www.indiaenvironmentportal.org.in/files/

file/Final%20Report_MoEF_FRA%20Committee%20report_Dec%20 2010.pdf (accessed 9 September 2019). This was a high-powered committee appointed jointly by the Ministry of Environment and Forests and the Ministry of Tribal Affairs. For a useful account of how the committee conducted its investigation, see Kothari 2011. See also, Vasundhara and Kalpavriksh, 'A National Report on Community Forest Rights under the Forest Rights Act: Status and Issues' at www.fra.org.in.

25. Interview with Videh Upadhyay, New Delhi, 6 December 2013.

26. Interview with N. C. Saxena, New Delhi, 21 November 2013.

27. Interview with Videh Upadhyay, New Delhi, 6 December 2013. He adds that forest officers know that bureaucrats in India are seldom hauled up on charges of dereliction of duty.

28. This point was made independently by a former Planning Commission member in an interview, New Delhi, 28 November 2013.

29. At a meeting of senior officials and analysts from eight states in Ranchi, the Forest Department was accused of encroaching on 'tribals'' livelihoods.

30. Note, however, that in Madhya Pradesh, the state government pressed forest officers to make processes on the ground genuinely participatory; see Bandi 2013: 23, citing a study by S. K. Sampath. Bandi adds that in many states, apart from Madhya Pradesh, state governments have been misrepresenting the Act (ibid.: 23).

31. Rajasthan also went to the polls at that time, but it is far less forested than the other two, so political pressure to act was less intense. It is worth noting, however, that state governments in Madhya Pradesh and Chhattisgarh were re-elected while the one in Rajasthan was not.

32. For evidence of this failure see, 'Tracking the Forest Rights Act', *Kalpavriksh*, 1–11, 29 July 2008 (first cited in Bandi 2013, 'Implementation of the Forest Rights Act', 22).

33. Centre for Social Development, New Delhi, 'State of Implementation of the Forest Rights Act – Summary Report', 2010.

34. This figure was provided by sources in the Ministry of Tribal Affairs.

35. For the full list, see Chapter Two of the Act.

36. See Kumar, Singh and Rao 2017: 41. For a useful context, see Shankar Gopalakrishnan 2017. For details on impediments and resistance to implementation of the full potential of the Act, see Sahu, Dash and Dubey 2017: 45–47.

37. For the full text of those clarifications, see *Gazette of India, Extraordinary,* Part II, Sections 3, Sub-section (i), 1 January 2008.

38. Interview with that author, N. C. Saxena, New Delhi, 21 November 2013.

39. The clarifications made it clear, for example, that people whose dwellings were just outside forested lands but who entered those lands to collect forest produce—on which they were mainly dependent for their livelihoods (an important provision in the Act)—should be granted the formal right to do so. Unfortunately, a new chief bureaucrat in the ministry who arrived in 2012 declined to issue further clarifications of this kind, which is a setback. Interview with N. C. Saxena, New Delhi, 3 December 2013. For the full text of the clarifications, see *Gazette of India, Extraordinary*, Part II, Section 3, Sub-section (i), 6 September 2012.

40. For example, when Ramesh visited a forested area of the western state of Maharashtra, he discovered that forest dwellers depended upon the harvesting of bamboo, but that the state government refused to recognise bamboo as a 'forest product'. Ramesh pressed them (successfully) to change that.

41. Jairam Ramesh was Minister of State (that is, a junior minister, but with independent charge) for Environment and Forests between May 2009 and July 2011. Thereafter, he was a full Minister for Rural Development.

42. An analysis by the CSD in New Delhi was scathing. It spoke of 'large-scale interference by the Forest Department in the rights recognition process' and referred elsewhere to 'sabotage'. See their 'State of Implementation of the Forest Rights Act – Summary Report', 2010.

43. Interview with a senior advisor to the prime minister (name withheld), New Delhi, 24 November 2013.

44. An NGO estimated that the potential areas for mining in forested areas extended over 1.1 million hectares. The PM's actions marked a change from earlier in 2012. In April, for example, the Ministry of Environment and Forests had pressed the Himachal Pradesh state government to conform to the Forest Rights Act when considering large projects in forested areas.

45. See for example V. K. C. Deo's interview with *The Indian Express*, 9 June 2013.

46. Interviews with two civil servants (names withheld) who have worked with V. K. C. Deo, New Delhi, 30 November and 5 December 2013.

47. Interview with Videh Upadhyay, New Delhi, 6 December 2013.

48. In some states, governments were especially unsympathetic. The Gujarat High Court had to order the state government there to adhere to the FRA after it had seen evidence that the Forest Department was not accepting the evidence of 'tribals' in applications for security of land tenure. Up to the end of June 2011, it had rejected 113,700 of these.

49. See for example, Kumar 2013.

five

The (Re)Making of India's Integrated Child Development Services

INTRODUCTION—THE INDIAN ENIGMA

When, in January 2007, the TV network NDTV (New Delhi Television Limited) aired a series of reports called 'The Republic of Hunger', many middle-class Indians were shocked to hear that almost half of the children in the country were malnourished. Equally shocking was the news that child malnutrition was being reduced at an excruciatingly slow pace and that, in the previous seven years, it had increased in eight states and remained stagnant in seven others (Dasgupta et al. 2012). How was it possible that such shocking levels of malnutrition persisted despite three uninterrupted decades of spectacular economic growth?

To put it bluntly, India's performance at ensuring the welfare of its children has been woeful. Table 5.1 shows malnutrition trends in India since the early 1990s.

Despite recent improvements, malnutrition rates remain alarmingly high: almost 40 per cent of India's children under the age of five are stunted, over a third are underweight, and over a fifth are wasted.[1] There is quite a striking variation in malnutrition rates across Indian states (Table 5.2): while 'only' around a fifth of the children are stunted in Goa and Kerala, the figure is close to 50 per cent in states like Uttar Pradesh, Bihar and Jharkhand. Generally speaking, states with high

TABLE 5.1: Stunting and underweight trends in India, 1992–2015

	% of stunted children under 5	*% of underweight children under 5*	*% wasted children under 5*
NFHS 1 (1992/93)	52*	53.4*	17.5*
NFHS 2 (1998/99)	45.5**	47**	15.5**
NFHS 3 (2005/06)	48	42.5	19.8
NFHS 4 (2015/16)	38.4	35.7	21

*Refers to children under 4.
**Refers to children under 3.
Source: National Family Health Survey (NFHS), rounds 1–4.

malnutrition rates are also states with high fertility rates. This means that the absolute number of malnourished children is not declining much. Moreover in some of the richest states like Gujarat or Maharashtra, well over a third of the children are stunted, underscoring the far from perfect correlation between GDP growth and population well-being.

TABLE 5.2: Stunting rates across Indian states, 2005–2016 (low to high)

State	*NFHS-4 (2015–16)*	*NFHS-3 (2005/06)*	*Percentage reduction 2005–2016*
Kerala	19.7	24.5	−24.37%
Goa	20.1	25.6	−27.36%
Tripura	24.3	35.7	−46.91%
Punjab	25.7	36.7	−42.80%
Himachal Pradesh	26.3	38.6	−46.77%
Tamil Nadu	27.1	30.9	−14.02%
Jammu & Kashmir	27.4	35	−27.74%
Mizoram	28	39.8	−42.14%
Telangana	28.1	47.4	−68.68%
Nagaland	28.6	38.8	−35.66%
Manipur	28.9	35.6	−23.18%
Arunachal Pradesh	29.4	43.3	−47.28%
Sikkim	29.6	38.3	−29.39%
Andhra Pradesh	31.4	47.4	−50.96%

(contd)

Table 5.2 (contd)

State	NFHS-4 (2015–16)	NFHS-3 (2005/06)	Percentage reduction 2005–2016
New Delhi	32.3	42.2	−30.65%
West Bengal	32.5	44.6	−37.23%
Uttarakhand	33.5	44.4	−32.54%
Haryana	34	45.7	−34.41%
Odisha	34.1	45	−31.96%
Maharashtra	34.4	46.3	−34.59%
Karnataka	36.2	43.7	−20.72%
Assam	36.4	46.5	−27.75%
Chhattisgarh	37.6	52.9	−40.69%
ALL INDIA	**38.4**	**48**	**−25.00%**
Gujarat	38.5	51.7	−34.29%
Rajasthan	39.1	43.7	−11.76%
Madhya Pradesh	42	50	−19.05%
Meghalaya	43.8	55.1	−25.80%
Jharkhand	45.3	49.8	−9.93%
Uttar Pradesh	46.3	56.8	−22.68%
Bihar	48.3	55.6	−15.11%

Source: NFHS-4 and NFHS-3. Figures for Andhra Pradesh and Telangana in column 2 (NFHS-3) refer to the undivided state of Andhra Pradesh and are therefore not strictly comparable.

India's indicators are worse or comparable to those of neighbouring (and much less prosperous) countries such as Bangladesh, Myanmar and Sri Lanka (Table 5.3). Even Nepal, whose per capita GDP is less than half of India's, has lower child mortality rates (UNICEF 2013) and has made important progress in maternal care.[2] Conflict-ridden South Sudan has comparable levels of wasting among children. The comparison of change over time (Table 5.3) with other emerging economies such as China, Brazil and South Africa shows the important progress made in terms of children's well-being in these countries (including India), but the pace of progress in India has been dramatically slower than in the others. In fact, at the current rate, India will achieve the stunting rates of China by 2055 (IFPRI 2016b).

If we extended the comparison to other human development indicators, the results would be very similar (Maiorano and Manor 2017).

TABLE 5.3: Stunting, infant mortality rates (IMR) and child mortality rates (CMR) in selected countries

Country	*% Stunted children*	*IMR (1990–2016)*		*CMR (1990–2016)*	
		1990	*2015*	*1990*	*2015*
Bangladesh	42	99.7	30.7	143.7	37.6
Brazil	7.1	50.9	14.6	60.8	16.4
China	9.4	42.1	9.2	53.8	10.7
India	38.4	88.3	37.9	125.8	47.7
Myanmar	35.1	78.3	39.5	109.9	50
Nepal	40.5	97.7	29.4	140.7	35.8
South Africa	23.9	47.4	33.6	59.9	40.5
Sri Lanka	14.7	18.1	8.4	21.2	9.8

Source: World Development Indicators (latest available data). Data for India are from the NFHS–4.

A fairer comparison can be made with low or middle-lower income Sub-Saharan countries. India's child malnutrition rates are higher than those in most of them. Indeed, 'few countries have such disastrous indicators of child well-being' (Drèze 2006: 3710).

This chapter will examine the political and policy processes that led the UPA government to reform the Integrated Child Development Services (ICDS), India's main policy to promote child development and well-being. The ICDS was introduced in 1975 in 33 blocks (sub-districts) throughout the country. It is the flagship programme of the Ministry of Women and Child Development (MWCD).[3] It provides a package of six services to children below six years of age, to pregnant and lactating mothers, and to women between 15 and 45 years of age. Table 5.4 summarises the services provided. The scheme is not targeted on the basis of census,[4] caste or other criteria. Everyone can access the programme.

TABLE 5.4: ICDS services and target population

Services	*Target group*
Supplementary nutrition	Children below 6; pregnant and lactating mothers
Immunisation	Children below 6; pregnant and lactating mothers
Health check-up	Children below 6; pregnant and lactating mothers
Referral service	Children below 6; pregnant and lactating mothers
Pre-school education	Children 3–6
Nutrition and health education	Women (15–45 years)

Source: Ministry of Women and Child Development, https://icds-wcd.nic.in/icds.aspx (accessed 4 August 2019).

Services are provided at ICDS centres called anganwadis (AWC), in both rural and urban areas, and are open every day except weekends. An anganwadi worker (AWW) runs the centre. The AWW, a woman from the community, is the key functionary at the grassroots and oversees the provision of all services and is assisted by an anganwadi helper.[5] Health-related services are provided in convergence with personnel from the Health Department at block-level Primary Health Centres (PHC).[6]

While the basic policy infrastructure of the ICDS has not changed much since the introduction of the programme in the 1970s, the UPA did introduce some significant changes, which will be analysed in detail below. First, and very importantly, the UPA granted significant additional resources, which made it possible to move towards the universalisation of the programme. Second, responding to a wealth of evidence that became available since the 1990s, the restructured ICDS focuses greater attention on children below three years of age, after which period much of the damage suffered due to malnutrition is irreparable. Third, the reform aimed at strengthening coordination across different government departments in order to tackle malnutrition using a multi-sectoral approach—again responding to research showing that malnutrition is not only and perhaps not principally due to lack of food, but is due to a combination of causes. Fourth, the UPA government started running the ICDS in 'Mission Mode', in an attempt to streamline implementation and to evaluate its effectiveness against measurable outcomes.

PUTTING ICDS ON THE POLICY AGENDA

The need to restructure the ICDS arose from two sets of concerns. First, in the two decades before the 2004 elections, a growing body of research had shown that the consequences of child malnutrition had important repercussions on all dimensions of human development and had severe implications for economic growth. Malnutrition during the first two years of a person's life has irremediable consequences in terms of cognitive and physical development (Gragnolati et al. 2005), which have a major impact on school performance and on labour productivity.

Given India's extremely high malnutrition rates, this is perhaps the greatest waste of human capital in history. A recent World Bank report (Galasso and Wagstaff 2018) estimates that about two-thirds of the workforce in India earns on average 13 per cent less than what they would have if they had not been stunted during childhood. A recent study by Save The Children estimated that India will lose as much as US$ 46 billion by 2040 due to malnutrition (POCUS 2014: 8), while other studies show that reducing child malnutrition can have immense economic benefits at very little cost (Alderman, Behrman and Puet 2017). These ideas penetrated the policy community in New Delhi and contributed to a broader understanding of the nature of the problem and the importance of tackling it.

However, the ICDS had been affected by severe implementation shortcomings and by important policy-design issues, which limited its impact. First, until 2005–06, the scheme was seriously underfunded. This was evident from stagnant financial allocations[7] despite the parallel expansion of the programme. Underfunding caused several problems. Many AWCs lacked the most basic infrastructure or did not have their own building so that children gathered in schools, temples, cattle sheds or under a tree (CAG 2013b). The *Comptroller and*

Auditor General Report showed that 52 per cent of the AWCs lacked toilets and 32 per cent did not have drinking water supply (CAG 2013b: 37; Venugopal 2012: 74). This is an important aspect as the quality of the AWC can encourage (or discourage) parents to send their children to the centre, not to speak of the inherent contradiction of running a child development centre in unhygienic and potentially harmful conditions.

Lack of funds affected the programme coverage, too. Despite the objective of universalising the scheme, progress has been slow, until recently.[8] In 2005 there were about 600,000 operational AWCs, compared to an estimated need of 1.4 million.[9]

A second major implementation problem related to the staff running the programme. On the one hand, it suffered from a severe staff shortage. On the other, village level functionaries, the AWWs, are not regular employees of the state. Rather, they are considered 'volunteers' who receive an 'honorarium', which, at Rs 4,500 (US$ 65) per month in 2012[10], is not only below the minimum wage, but is also often paid irregularly.[11] Furthermore, the workload assigned to the AWWs is unrealistic.[12] They are asked to take care of *all* aspects of the programme at the local level.[13] Paperwork alone accounts for about 40 per cent of their time[14] (Planning Commission 2011a: Table 6.11). AWWs are expected to keep eight different registers, feed children, impart pre-school education, provide health counselling, organise immunisation sessions, conduct regular home visits, provide take-home rations for pregnant women and children under three years of age, coordinate actions with staff from the Health Department, attend meetings with supervisors and child development project officers (CDPOs), and monitor children's growth—to name just their principal tasks. Moreover, the local administration tends to assign all sorts of additional tasks to the AWWs, including management of other schemes, plus census and electoral duties.[15] Given their vulnerable position—they have no job security—the AWWs often give preference to these non-ICDS duties and keep the AWC closed. This unreasonable workload undermines the programme's main stated aim of assisting children between three and six years of age, to prevent irreparable damage. A report of the Planning Commission (2012: 40) shows how the AWWs simply have no time to take care of younger children (who cannot travel to the AWC) as their working hours barely suffice to open the centres, feed older children, and complete monitoring tasks and paperwork. The motivation of the AWWs and their training are two other important issues that have affected their overall performance.

Another problem concerning the ICDS staff was the quality of civil servants in charge of implementing the programme. The MWCD is considered to be a very low-profile ministry,[16] and this affects both political[17] and bureaucratic appointments. Most officials spend most of their time trying to find ways to leave the ministry;[18] and there is no 'excitement' about or interest in the scheme. In 2013, the Health Ministry proposed to stop the NFHS, which is the *only* comprehensive source of data on child malnutrition. A member of the NAC recalls that not even one official from the MWCD tried to defend the survey.[19] The very fact that the fourth round of the NFHS was then delayed for years—thus creating a huge data gap—is revealing about the commitment of the MWCD officials. The fact that most officials, especially at lower levels, are men does not help.

The third major implementation problem, closely related to the points noted above, is that the ICDS, while conceived as a comprehensive scheme for promoting child development, has in fact been implemented as a feeding programme (Drèze 2006). The problem here is the confusion—widespread in the MWCD at all levels—between hunger and malnutrition. The two problems are connected but they do not entirely coincide. Research shows that India's exceptionally high levels of child malnutrition can be explained by a combination of widespread poverty, the low status of women in society, and poor sanitation (Jayachandran and Pande 2017; Coffey and Spears 2017). Thus, malnutrition is a multidimensional problem and simply giving more food to children will not solve it. However, this is what the scheme has been focusing on since its inception.

This was due to at least two things. First, linking malnutrition to the lack of food sounds logical and most officials in the MWCD, lacking technical expertise on nutritional issues, followed that logic. Second, food is the domain where the highest amount of illicit money can be made at all levels. The reports submitted by the special commissioners to the Supreme Court on the status of supply of take-home rations for the ICDS leave little doubt about the extent of corruption that surrounds the procurement of food for the scheme.[20] Similarly, an evaluation of the ICDS in Gorakhpur district of Uttar Pradesh by the National Human Rights Commission (2011) showed, on the one hand, that despite repeated Supreme Court orders to provide hot cooked meals, *all* centres supplied ready-made food containing only 100 calories as against the prescribed 500 calories; and on the other hand, that as much as 63 per cent of the funds were misappropriated.

The influence of contractors is huge at all levels. At the top, they provide political parties with substantial kickbacks. We will see below how the Union minister for Women and Child Development insisted upon procuring food Centrally, and how allegations about her corruption were widespread in policy-making circles. At the state level, one observer recalled that at a Planning Commission meeting in 2011, one member suggested that Uttar Pradesh's (centralised) system of food procurement not be discussed because elections in the state were due soon, and the 'biscuit lobby' was an important source of (illicit) money for the ruling party (which was supporting the Central government from the outside).[21] At the bottom of the system, contractors often collude with local self-help groups (SHGs) or Panchayati Raj institutions representatives to provide substandard food to the children, who sometimes refuse to take it, or fall ill after eating it (Venugopal 2012). In some cases, AWWs sold the food meant for children as cattle feed (Sinha D. 2006). In short, food procurement is where the money is to be made—about 40 per cent of the funds for supplementary nutrition are siphoned off (Planning Commission 2011a)—which constitutes an incentive for the administrators and politicians to focus their attention on this aspect. The results were major disruptions in the food supply, and the problem was compounded by a high degree of administrative incapacity at all levels (Biswas and Verma 2009).

In some AWCs, food was unavailable for up to 200 days a year (out of 300 envisaged by the scheme) (Venugopal 2012: 78).

The focus on supplementary nutrition has meant that other very important components have been neglected. In particular, counselling and nutrition education for mothers have not received the attention they deserve. Child malnutrition can be effectively tackled by explaining to mothers the importance of colostrum for the new-born, exclusive breastfeeding for the first six months, and simple hygienic actions like washing hands before eating or preparing food. There is ample evidence that child-rearing practices are 'highly unscientific' (Saxena 2012: 11), and that promoting maternal behavioural change could lead to important results.

A fourth problem has been the extremely centralised design of the programme, in line with the political environment at the time when the scheme was introduced (the mid-1970s). Consider a few examples. The norms for renting a building for an AWC were decided Centrally. Renting a building in Delhi or in rural Bihar was assumed to cost the same. Similarly, population norms for the establishment of an AWC were decided in New Delhi, not taking into consideration the extremely varied demographic environments (especially in the north-eastern states) in a huge country like India.

Fifth, the ICDS suffers from a severe lack of monitoring and accountability mechanisms. According to the Comptroller and Auditor General, the monitoring system has underperformed 'on all fronts' (CAG 2013b: 127). Recent attempts to introduce a new monitoring unit (in 2006–07) did not result in much better results, and administrators did not appoint a single consultant out of the six that were supposed to run the unit (ibid.: 128).

In fact, the ministry's monitoring (in)capacity is such that the MWCD proved unable even to estimate the cost of its own staff. Out of a total staff expenditure of Rs 2,853 crore (c. $416 million) in 2008–11, the MWCD budgeted (and released) only Rs 1,753 crore (c. $255 million) (CAG 2013b: 115). Moreover, the quality of available data available is abysmal. Basic figures such as per child expenditure are not available with the ministry.[22]

State governments deliberately report incorrect figures.[23] The data tables on the MWCD's website, for instance, show that most states report figures for severe malnutrition as being below 2 per cent, despite ample evidence coming from independent surveys (like the NFHS or the *Hungama Report* 2012) showing much higher figures. In as many as 18 states, the figure for grade II (mild) malnutrition was reported as being 0.00 per cent![24] A district collector told Special Commissioner to the Supreme Court, N. C. Saxena, that reporting correct figures was a 'high-risk and low-reward activity!' (Saxena 2012).

Finally, and perhaps more importantly, the ICDS has suffered from a serious failure of inter-ministerial coordination. For the ICDS to work on the ground there must be coordinated action between three ministries, namely MWCD, Health and Family Welfare (MHFW) and the Sanitation Department (part of the Rural Development Ministry). Coordination scarcely occurs at the grassroots and is virtually absent at the top of the system.[25] According to a member of the NAC, MWCD officials 'never' attend meetings at MHFW.[26] Rivalry between different ministries also plays a role (Reich and Balarajan 2012: 44).[27] At lower levels, there are some efforts at coordinating action between different departments through joint committees, but meetings are infrequent or do not happen at all (CAG 2013b: 23). Furthermore, coordination failures regularly occur (Sinha, D. 2006). At the grassroots, some coordination between the accredited social health activist (ASHA), the auxiliary midwife nurse (AMN)[28] and the AWW exists. However, the AWW and the ASHA/AMN report to different departments, with little or no sharing of information.[29] In short, the ICDS 'works in isolation from other departments and is also poorly integrated with the community' (Sinha, D. 2006: 3691).

The combination of these factors resulted in the limited impact of the ICDS. However, two remarks are in order. First, in those areas of India where it has worked reasonably well, the impact on malnutrition and infant mortality rates has been positive. This is largely true in Tamil Nadu (Rajivan 2006), and in pockets in other states (FOCUS 2006). Also, in remote areas the AWC is the only 'health' centre available and it represents an important reference point for the population. Furthermore, as we will see in the concluding part of this chapter, there have been some significant improvements in implementation in recent years.

Second, ICDS alone could not (and could not be expected to) solve the problem of child malnutrition. This is because malnutrition is a multidimensional problem that needs to be tackled from different angles at the same time. The persistence of poverty and the fact that, according to the Global Hunger Index (IFPRI 2016a), 15.2 per cent of the Indian population is food insecure is a major contributing factor to high levels of child malnutrition. This is reflected in the alarmingly high number of children—300,000 per year, according to a recent UNICEF report—who die annually for lack of adequate nutrition[30] and in the persistence of starvation deaths across the country, including in the national capital.[31]

Moreover, a large proportion of those who can afford to buy enough food—also thanks to the Public Distribution System—cannot afford to have a diversified and balanced diet. According to the NFHS-4, less than 15 per cent of children below two years of age receive an adequate diet. The shortage of food—and its poor quality and lack of variety—impacts especially on the nutritional status of women who, in many cases, eat whatever is left, *if* something is left. Several studies in recent years have recognised that gender inequality and women's disempowerment are directly linked with children's well-being and malnutrition levels (Vir 2016). Diane Coffey and Payal Hathi (2016) showed that 42 per cent of pregnant women in India are underweight and that, by the *end* of the pregnancy, they weigh less than their Sub-Saharan African counterparts do at the *beginning* of their gestation. This is an important way in which malnutrition is transmitted across generations as underweight mothers tend to give birth to underweight children (Coffey, Khera and Spears 2013). Moreover, families tend to invest more resources—including resources that result in better nutrition indicators—on the first son, systematically neglecting the other children, especially girls (Jayachandran and Pande 2017).

A third important determinant of malnutrition is sanitation. Particularly important is the percentage of people who defecate in the open. There is a robust literature that shows how exposure to faecal germs at an early age results in semi-chronic illness that in turn results in an inability to absorb nutrients and leads to a diversion of nutritional energy from growth to defence (i.e. the production of antibodies) (Chambers and von Medeazza 2013). According to the *Census of India* (2011), 53 per cent of Indian households defecate in the open. No country in the world has a higher rate of open defecation than Bihar, while Uttar Pradesh alone accounts for 12 per cent of all people worldwide that practice open defecation (Spears 2013b). The corresponding figure for Sub-Saharan Africa is about 25 per cent. This difference alone provides much of the explanation for India's exceptionally high rates of stunted children (Spears 2013a).

The ICDS, in short, could not be expected to tackle child malnutrition on its own. Recent research indicates that it is effective to a certain extent (Mittal and Meenakshi 2015), particularly for girls (Jain 2015), but as one MWCD official put it, 'a nutritional lens should be applied to every scheme' for malnutrition to be effectively tackled.[32]

ICDS Restructuring under UPA-I

The drive to restructure the ICDS did not originate within government circles. Pressure came from two other sources, namely the Supreme Court and civil society. In April 2001, the People's Union for Civil Liberties (PUCL) filed a petition in the Supreme Court.[33] As discussed in Chapter 3, this petition argued that the State had failed to protect the right to life (Article 21 of the Constitution) because it had failed to ensure the right to food to a majority of the population.

The Right to Food case has recently been closed after almost 16 years.[34] During this quite prolonged period of time, the Supreme Court issued a number of interim orders that applied for the duration of the case. Crucially, these orders direct the Central and the state governments to implement specific policy measures in order to ensure the right to food. In other words, the Supreme Court recognised that State institutions were responsible for the prevention of hunger and starvation.[35]

To monitor the implementation of its orders, the Supreme Court appointed two special commissioners, and gave them extensive powers to enquire into any violation of its orders and to demand appropriate action.[36] Moreover, the Court made the chief secretaries of the state governments responsible for the prevention of starvation and malnutrition-related deaths in their states. (This created incentives for the state governments to underestimate the extent of malnutrition and to instruct officials to deny the occurrence of starvation deaths.[37])

The Supreme Court issued orders covering a wide range of food-related government programmes. Some of them concern the ICDS. The first one was issued on 28 November 2001. This order transformed the provisions of eight government schemes[38] (including the ICDS) into legal entitlements. The Court also mandated the universalisation of the ICDS and established minimum caloric requirements of the meals served under the scheme. The order was largely ignored by the National Democratic Alliance (NDA)'s government in New Delhi (which governed until May 2004) and by most state governments. However, this order constituted a turning point for India's social policies as it galvanised many activists, academics and progressive civil society members to push for the respect of the order and to keep the government accountable.

In April 2004, shortly before the general election and at a time when the Congress was 'looking for ideas that would resonate with the "common man"' (Khera 2013: 8), a series of hearings on the ICDS were held. This served as a 'wake-up call' for the Congress, which decided to insert the universalisation of the ICDS into its electoral manifesto.[39] When the Congress-led UPA unexpectedly won the election, the universalisation of the ICDS found its place in its CMP, which formed the programmatic base for the legislature and the political foundation for the support that the Left parties decided to offer the UPA government from the outside.

Despite the electoral promise, the government was slow to act. On 7 October 2004, the Supreme Court issued another order, directing the government to do four things. One, it ordered an increase in the number of AWCs from the existing 600,000 to 1.4 million, so that every habitation[40] in the country would be covered. The Court also asked the government to provide a time frame for the universalisation of the ICDS. Two, the Court ordered a doubling of the per capita expenditure on supplementary nutrition (from 1 rupee to 2 rupees per child per day). Three, the Court excluded BPL criteria for the identification of beneficiaries, thus reinforcing the idea that the services provided under the ICDS had to be considered as rights, and were therefore not subject to (questionable) exclusion criteria. Four, the order banned contractors from supplying food to the AWCs.

The order was largely ignored. Fifteen years after the order, the number of operational AWCs had not reached the prescribed 1.4 million, although, according to official figures, 1.34 million AWWs are operational, covering most villages and urban areas in India. The government never issued a time frame for the universalisation of the ICDS as requested. The doubling of the expenditure norms was cleared by the Cabinet only in 2008–09. Finally, many state governments have continued to provide food through private contractors. Maharashtra even moved in the opposite direction, deciding to provide packaged food procured centrally, rather than freshly prepared food procured locally.[41] Madhya Pradesh, as late as April 2018, awarded to one public sector company and its three privately-owned joint ventures a contract to supply take-home rations to the ICDS in violation not only of the Supreme Court order but also of a high court order prohibiting the companies to participate in the tender because of their involvement in money laundering.[42] However, the 2004 orders had the effect of mobilising the policy community for reforming the ICDS. As we shall see below, the NAC, the Planning Commission, and civil society groups started proposing ideas for reforming the scheme.

The next turning point was the order dated 13 December 2006.[43] It not only reiterated that 1.4 million AWCs had to be operational, but it gave the government two years to reach the target.[44] Moreover, the order was issued shortly before the release of the FOCUS report (2006) that, as we shall see, revealed the extent of child malnutrition and caught the media attention. Although the target was not reached by December 2008, the order put enough pressure on the government to make it start working for the universalisation of the ICDS. The number of AWCs increased significantly in the following years, and so did the allocation of funds, from Rs 2,931 crore in 2004–05 (US$ 428 million) to Rs 16,058 crore (US$ 2.3 billion) in 2013–14, i.e. an increase of almost 450 per cent in nine years[45] (Figure 5.1). However, the increased budget was barely enough to cover the expansion of the programme and the increased spending norms per children in supplementary nutrition (revised again through a Supreme Court order in 2009).[46]

FIGURE 5.1: Expansion of the ICDS and budgetary allocations 1975–2015

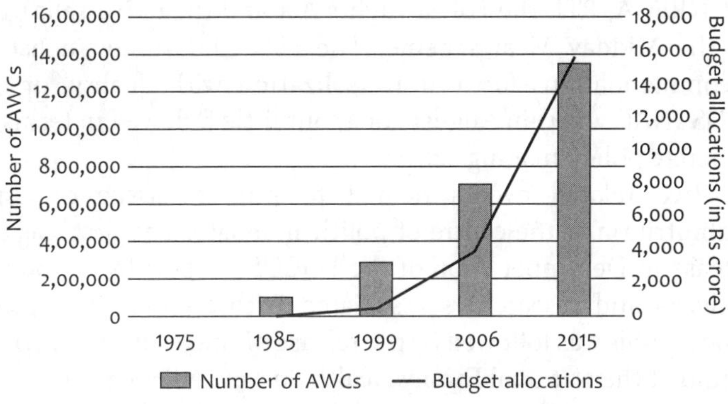

Source: MWCD data tables and personal communication by Dr. Shreeranjan (MWCD). Budget documents 1975–2015 (all revised estimates).

Amid the rush to universalise the programme, various actors within the policy community had started to prepare concrete policy plans for reforming the ICDS. The key actors were the RTF Campaign (a group of activists, academics, and concerned citizens who have been struggling to ensure the right to food), the NAC, and the Planning Commission. It is important to note at this point that the boundaries between these sets of actors are rather fuzzy. Many people associated with the RTF Campaign played multiple roles. Some of them were, or had been, members of the NAC; others were advisors to the Planning Commission or the MWCD or other ministries; still others were assistants/advisors to the two special commissioners to the Supreme Court. One of the two special commissioners (Harsh Mander) had a long association with the RTF Campaign and served on the NAC, while the second (N. C. Saxena) was also a member of the NAC. In other words, the ideas generated within the RTF Campaign penetrated to a significant extent into policy circles, and the exchange of views among these actors occurred on a continuous basis.

However, the reform of the ICDS was not a policy priority for any of these actors, let alone for the government.[47] Most of the political and advocacy energy expended during the UPA-I government was focused on other pro-poor policy initiatives, like MGNREGA, RTI, the Forest Rights Act and the universalisation of the Midday Meal scheme. The NAC did submit a list of recommendations for a 'universalization with quality' of the ICDS (NAC 2004) in August 2004, but little followed in terms of concrete policy-making action.

Two related events helped to put the issue of child malnutrition at the centre of political debate. The first was the release in December 2006 of the FOCUS[48] report by a group of activists and researchers associated with the RTF Campaign (2006). This was followed by the release of the results of the third round of the National Family Health Survey (NFHS-3 2007). The two reports got the attention of the national and international media.[49] Several newspapers started reporting malnutrition-related issues[50]. NDTV aired a series of reports in January 2007 called 'The Republic of Hunger'. The extent of child malnutrition revealed by the reports shocked the country, especially the urban middle class. A senior journalist working as political editor in a major newspaper at that time admitted she was completely taken by surprise when she heard that half of the children in the country were malnourished. Indeed, she was even more surprised that after decades of work as a political journalist, she had not even heard once about the existence of this problem.[51]

The Supreme Court order of December 2006 and the two reports stimulated various groups to mobilise. First, the Planning Commission, which was preparing the Twelfth Plan at that time, allocated significantly more resources for the ICDS (from Rs 10,000 crore during the Tenth Plan, to Rs 42,000). It also advocated a restructuring of the ICDS (Planning Commission 2008b: 210) along the lines of the NAC and the RTF Campaign's recommendations.[52]

Second, Professor M. S. Swaminathan—a highly respected figure—organised the National Nutrition Conclave (NNC) in August 2007, advocating placing the issue of child malnutrition at the centre of the policy agenda (NNC 2007). This conclave, which later evolved into the Coalition for Sustainable Nutrition Security in India, involved a large number of very high-profile policy-makers (including ministers and MPs), nutrition experts (including advisors to the government and Planning Commission), donors' representatives and international NGOs. The Conclave was perhaps the first to present a list of a few essential things that needed to be done to tackle child malnutrition to high-level policy-makers and political leaders. However, the role of the Coalition subsequently vanished as other actors acquired a more prominent role.

Third, the release of data on child malnutrition—and the media attention they received—made the prime minister refer to the issue in his Independence Day speech in 2007; child malnutrition was a 'national shame'. From then on, Manmohan Singh regularly addressed the problem in his Independence Day speeches (in 2008, 2009 and 2011). He also started being moderately interested in the ICDS. Shortly after the release of the two reports, he wrote a letter to the chief ministers calling for 'urgent action' to be taken to 'tone up' the ICDS.[53] The prime minister's interest helped to keep the media's attention on the topic, which in turn stimulated further action in government circles. For example, the prime minister decided to include child malnutrition in the agenda of the National Development Council (NDC).

Fourth, a group of young MPs[54] (from across party lines) formed an informal advocacy group called Citizens' Alliance against Malnutrition. The group associated with some NGOs (like the Naandi Foundation), donors (UNICEF) and journalists (like Neerja Chowdhury) with the objective of giving visibility to the issue of child malnutrition. Their strategy was fourfold. First, the MPs started visiting AWCs throughout the country[55] in order to expose the poor implementation of the ICDS and to get the attention of the media. Second, they held a series of high-level meetings with the prime minister, the speaker of the Lok Sabha, the leader of the Opposition, various chief ministers, Sonia Gandhi, Deputy Chairman of the Planning Commission, Montek Singh Ahluwalia, and several editors of newspapers.[56] Third, they sought the involvement of celebrities (most notably actor Aamir Khan) to give even more visibility to the issue. Subsequently, the MWCD launched a nation-wide information campaign, mainly through a series of TV advertisements starring Aamir Khan himself. Fourth, the Alliance supported the Naandi Foundation's *HUNGaMA Survey Report* (2011), which showed the extent of malnutrition in the poorest 100 districts of the country. Thanks to the intercession of these MPs, the prime minister himself released the report.[57]

In short, the Supreme Court order of December 2006 and the release of the FOCUS and NFHS-3 reports (followed in 2008 by the Lancet Reports, which added an international perspective to the debate)—and the media coverage that followed—set the policy-making machine in motion. After 2007, a constant process of consultation under the aegis of the Planning Commission occurred. However, progress was slow. The only significant initiative taken by the UPA-I government was the establishment in November 2008 of the PM's National Council on India's Nutrition Challenges, a high-level body entrusted with the task of proposing policy solutions to the problem of widespread child malnutrition. However, the Council was not convened until November 2010.

During the last part of the UPA-I government, a single policy issue was discussed, namely the procurement of food for the supplementary nutrition component of the scheme. Two options were discussed. The first one, championed by the Minister for Women and Child Development, Renuka Chowdury, was centralised procurement of ready-to-eat food. The minister's argument was that providing fortified food through Central procurement would be more hygienic and easy to monitor. Also, she pointed out—in consonance with ready-to-eat food manufacturers—that the role of micronutrients can play a key role in determining a child's health status. However, the minister was quite isolated. The rest of the policy community largely preferred locally-produced, culturally-appropriate and freshly-cooked meals for children. Opponents of centralised procurement included the PM, several Cabinet ministers, the Planning Commission, the NAC, the Supreme Court, the RTF Campaign[58] and most nutrition experts (Baru et al. 2008). They argued that centralised procurement would facilitate corruption,[59] that the quality of pre-packaged food was often extremely poor and most importantly, that a full meal is more nutritious than any fortified pre-packed biscuit, which can also be difficult for malnourished children to digest.[60] Further, freshly cooked meals could foster social equality[61] and provide employment for women (Prasad and Sinha 2008). Finally, the Supreme Court order of 2004 had banned contractors. In other words, Renuka Chowdury was largely isolated, despite strong support from the so-called 'biscuit lobby' and partial support from donor agencies. Two years were lost discussing what was largely a non-issue.

ICDS Restructuring under UPA-II

The story of the restructuring of the ICDS was marked by slowness. We have seen that the first proposals for reform came in August 2004 from the NAC, which had advocated 'universalization with quality', and from the RTF Campaign and the Planning Commission in 2007. But the political irrelevance of child malnutrition until the release of the FOCUS and NHFS-3 reports resulted in these proposals being largely ignored by the government.

Things accelerated after 2007, but the ICDS remained low on the policy agenda during the UPA-II government (2009–14). The principal reason for this low prioritisation was the limited political appeal of tackling child malnutrition. MPs and MLAs by and large do not see any significant political advantage in addressing the problem. Elected representatives respond to their constituencies, which ask for employment, a new road or a new hospital, but not for addressing child malnutrition. Part of the problem is that childcare in India is considered a responsibility of women, and given their low social status in India their demands commonly tend to be ignored. But even women, for whom the issue of child malnutrition is very important from a personal point of view, are not likely to demand that their elected representatives tackle the problem as a political priority.[62] Malnourished mothers often do not recognise their children's malnutrition (unlike hunger) or they accept it as a normal fact.[63] The problem is that 'all but the most extreme manifestation of undernutrition has no visible symptoms' (Gillespie et al. 2013: 3); and if a problem is invisible, it is unlikely that politicians will do anything to solve it.

In fact, in 2012—the year when a restructured ICDS was finally approved—only 3.5 per cent of the questions asked in Parliament were related to children (POCUS 2014: 7). Showing 'too much' support for policies aimed at tackling child malnutrition could even be politically harmful as a section of the urban middle class does not readily accept that their taxes should be used to feed the children of families that, in their view, cannot afford to have them.[64] Significantly, not a single political party has ever mobilised support for restructuring the ICDS, not even the parties of the Left and not even their women's cells. The limited political significance of child issues can also be inferred from the rarity of discussions held in Parliament on the topic (Biswas and Verma 2009; Sinha, S. 2006). In fact, the words 'nutrition' or 'malnutrition' appear in the Lok Sabha debates only 393 times between 2004 and 2017—as against, for instance, 'education', which appears 1,624 times.[65]

A second reason for the slow pace of the policy-making process to restructure the ICDS is that the nodal ministry lacked the administrative capacity to approach a redesign. In 2007, many bureaucrats in the MWCD did not know the difference between hunger and malnutrition or between an underweight and a stunted child. In 2007, many officials heard for the first time that the focus of policy action should be on children under two years of age, or about the role of micronutrients. Therefore, it took time for the bureaucracy to get a basic understanding of malnutrition and to figure out how they should proceed in tackling it.[66]

Perhaps the clearest indication of the low priority accorded to the reform of the ICDS was the process that followed the establishment, in response to strong pressures from civil society groups, of the PM's National Council on India's Nutrition Challenges in November 2008. On the one hand, this seemed to be a signal that the political leadership seriously intended to take rapid action against malnutrition. On the other, the first and only (two-hour long) meeting of the Council took place two years later, in November 2010. It took a lot of energy to get the Council convened. Civil society groups extensively lobbied MPs and the PMO to convene a meeting, to no avail. According to Arun Gupta (a Council member), the PM finally summoned the Council after Gupta convinced a Congress MP to write a letter (which was signed by other MPs) to Sonia Gandhi, who in turn spoke to the PM.[67] According to another source who was involved in the process, the PM was aware of the differences between Renuka Chowdhury and some members of the Planning Commission regarding the issue of Central procurement of food, and he did not want this controversy to come out in the open, so he delayed the meeting until the former was replaced after the 2009 elections.[68]

When the Council eventually met, it took four decisions: the ICDS would be strengthened and restructured; a multi-sectoral programme to address maternal and child malnutrition would be prepared and implemented in 200 selected high-burden districts;[69] a nation-wide information campaign would be launched; and the Council would invite the ministries dealing with Health, Education, Sanitation and Agriculture to adopt a nutrition focus in their programmes.

Since then, supporters of the ICDS have been asking to convene a meeting of the Council every six months to monitor the implementation of these four decisions (a task included in its terms of reference), to no avail. Similarly, the demand for the establishment of a national authority with full-time staff reporting to the Council has not been accepted. It took two more years for the 'restructuring and strengthening of the ICDS' to be approved, despite repeated promises to launch the reformed scheme on 1 April 2008 (Planning Commission 2008b: 143) or by the beginning of 2012 (Manmohan Singh 2011).

Most of the time after the release of the FOCUS and the NHFS-3 reports was spent in an extensive process of consultation under the aegis of the Planning Commission. The RTF Campaign and the NAC were asked to submit updated recommendations (RTF 2012; NAC 2011). The MWCD and the MHFW were invited to prepare a joint paper on the restructuring of the ICDS (Planning Commission 2011b).

The Planning Commission organised a 'multi-stakeholder retreat' in August 2010 (Planning Commission 2010). The remarkable fact about the policy papers produced during this consultation process is that they all look very similar. All stress the need to focus on children under two–three years of age; all point out the necessity to hire a second AWW, at least in selected districts; all call for a more decentralised design and community involvement; all underline the need to strengthen convergence with other programmes and departments; all advocate for the introduction of AWC-cum-crèches in at least 5–10 per cent of the AWCs; all ask for substantially more resources to be invested in the construction/maintenance of buildings for AWCs; all suggest the provision of (locally produced) take-home rations for children under three and pregnant mothers, and freshly cooked meals for children above three; and finally, all ask for a strengthened system of monitoring and accountability. Most of these proposals (the exception being the NAC's) also proposed to run the scheme in 'mission mode', learning from the experiences of the Sarva Shiksha Abhiyan and the National Rural Health Mission. Differences did exist, but they entailed minor details. It is in fact not surprising that a broad consensus emerged. All of these recommendations were prepared by (or based on the input of) a relatively small group of people that, as we saw above, play multiple roles in different policy-making agencies.[70]

There were two interconnected issues that blocked the approval of the restructuring of the ICDS for so long. The first was that politicians and bureaucrats asked for easily implementable solutions, whereas the nutrition community could not (and did not want to) come up with a list of ten bullet points easily understandable by non-experts.[71] However, as knowledge about the complexity of malnutrition increased among the bureaucracy, the idea that what was needed was a holistic approach became by and large accepted.

The second problem was more difficult to overcome. The proposed plans shared another important feature. They all required significant resources to be invested. We have seen that budgetary allocations for the ICDS increased by almost 400 per cent[72] between 2004–05 and 2012–13. However, these additional resources were barely enough to cover the expansion of the programme and the increased expenditure on supplementary nutrition.[73] All the proposed plans envisaged a much higher expenditure. An important part of the policy community—most notably the PM, the Finance Ministry and the Deputy Chairman of the Planning Commission—simply did not want to allocate these additional resources.

This was not just a problem of fiscal conservatism. India's spectacular economic growth during the UPA-I government, coupled with the even more spectacular increase in revenues since 2003, left significant space for expansionary policies.

However, policy-makers were skeptical about investing significant resources in a programme which had worked rather poorly, whose impact on malnutrition rates had been limited, and which was unlikely to bring significant political dividends. The widespread feeling in policy circles that, at least during UPA-I, the MWCD was run by a minister more interested in making profits out of the ICDS[74]—a feeling reinforced by her insistence on centralised procurement of food—than in making the scheme work right, certainly did not help to speed up the process. Moreover, the administrative incapacity of the MWCD made even supporters of the programme skeptical about the very possibility of reforming the ICDS.

In fact, it was the MWCD itself that acknowledged its own incapacity to run the programme. As described in Chapter 3, in 2011, part of the ICDS (supplementary nutrition) was inserted into the National Food Security Bill. The MWCD strongly opposed the inclusion of the ICDS into the bill since that implied its transformation into legally enforceable entitlements (Aggarwal and Mander 2013). The MWCD argued that the ICDS was marked by several implementation gaps, which would take time to fix. Only then would the ministry agree to be held accountable for its implementation (Lok Sabha 2013: 94). The Standing Committee on Food, Consumer Affairs and Public Distribution accepted the ministry's viewpoint and excluded the ICDS from the NFSB. However, apparently at the insistence of Sonia Gandhi,[75] it was later put back in by the Cabinet and was eventually included in the approved version of the Act.

Sustained lobbying by both State and non-State actors proved decisive in winning approval for the restructuring of the ICDS. A great deal of this lobbying was done through personal contacts in key policy-making agencies. Members of the NAC pushed friends in the PMO to allocate more resources.[76] RTF Campaign activists, through their contact in the Planning Commission, made their ideas heard by its administrative head, Montek Singh Ahluwalia[77]—who was also lobbied by progressive members of the Commission such as Abhijit Sen, Syeda Hameed and Mihir Shah. RTF Campaign activists also talked with many MPs. The long process of consultation described above kept the attention of the media and the government focused on the issue, along with extensive research efforts by academics. Finally, malnutrition has increasingly emerged as a key issue in international fora, including at recent G20 summits, which is likely to have caused some embarrassment to India, which accounts for one-fifth of all malnourished children worldwide.

Further, a decisive argument was that, given the Supreme Court orders, the Indian government had to spend significant resources on the ICDS anyway. Thus, the options were either to cancel the scheme altogether—an idea that was discussed during the UPA-I government—and substitute it with something new, or to try to make the ICDS work better. The latter option was probably considered easier and more cost-effective.

RESTRUCTURED ICDS—MAIN FEATURES

The government finally approved the restructuring of the ICDS in December 2012 (MWCD 2012). The prime minister's Council had asked the Planning Commission to coordinate an inter-ministerial group for the restructuring, which submitted its report in September 2011. The total budgetary allocation suggested by the inter-ministerial group was Rs 183,778 crore (US$ 27 billion) over the five-year Twelfth Plan period (2012–17). Then the proposed plan went through the Expenditure and Finance Committee of the Cabinet, which cut the financial allocation by about 30 per cent to Rs 123,580 crore (US$ 18 billion). However, up to the financial year 2016–17 (the last of the Plan period), the government had allocated only about 65 per cent of the funds (Kapur, Joshi and Srinivas 2016).

The restructured ICDS envisages a set of programmatic, management and institutional reforms. Programmatic reforms include most of the recommendations made by civil society groups (notably the RTF Campaign), the NAC, and the Planning Commission. The most important issue that was left out of the restructuring was the regularisation of the AWWs—they remain 'volunteers' who receive meagre honoraria.

Important reforms cover three main areas. First, the focus of the scheme was shifted to children under three years of age. A second AWW would be hired in 200 high-burden districts for improved family contact and home visits. A separate service for care and nutrition for children under three was introduced and special counselling sessions on infant and young child feeding were envisaged. All other services (which were slightly reorganised) include specific interventions for younger children (MWCD 2013: 14).

Second, funds were allocated for the construction of about 700,000 AWCs (in convergence with the MGNREGA) and for their maintenance and up-gradation. The opening hours of the AWCs have been extended to six hours, and 5 per cent of the AWCs will run as AWC-cum-crèches.

Third, there was an effort to strengthen human resources at all levels. The most significant innovation was the creation of a separate cadre for the recruitment of ICDS personnel. This provision was intended to enable the employment of ICDS-dedicated staff and put a limit on frequent transfers from other departments. Another potentially important provision was the creation of monitoring offices at the sub-block level, for supervisors to establish offices. This was intended to bring more consistency to the role of supervisors, which until that point had been limited to (rare) *ad hoc* visits to AWCs. Finally, a system of incentives for AWWs was established, especially by giving them the possibility of becoming supervisors.

The main aim of reforming the management structure of the ICDS was to decentralise its design. States were given more flexibility and encouraged to run the programme according to local needs. The main instruments to ensure decentralisation were the Annual Programme Implementation Plans. These would be done at the state and district levels and were supposed to include suggestions from below. A new five-tier (Central, state, district, block, village) system of monitoring was introduced. However, elected local bodies were substantially excluded. At the district level these were represented only by their executive wing (the CEO, a bureaucrat). At the block level, elected representatives were excluded altogether, whereas at the AWC level one ward member would chair the monitoring committee, along with representatives from community-based organisations of various kinds (MWCD 2013: annexure XX).

The principal potentially significant step to encourage the involvement of communities in the management of child malnutrition was the inclusion of malnutrition in the ambit of the village health and sanitation committee. These are committees created under the NRHM with the task of creating awareness about health services and monitoring implementation of the NRHM at the village level. With the inclusion of nutrition within its ambit, the implementation of the ICDS will be included among its tasks. States were also 'encouraged' to grant official 'notification' to the committee as a sub-committee of the *gram panchayat* (the lowest level elected village council). Many state governments have long declined to take such steps.

Institutionally, the ICDS was to be run in 'mission mode' between 2012 and 2017. This meant that over the duration of the mission (2012–17), the ICDS had a set of quantifiable outcomes (for details, see MWCD 2013: annexure ID). Most targets were based on the data collected in 2005–06 for the NFHS-3 Report. So, for example, the ICDS Mission had the objective of reducing underweight children by 10 percentage points by 2017. However, this was a rather unambitious target as the simple continuation of the (very disappointing) trend would have ensured a reduction in child malnutrition of 5.62 percentage points over the 2005 data. In fact, the actual reduction as recorded by the *Rapid Survey on Children* (MWCD 2015) (based on data collected in 2014) shows that this unambitious target had in fact already been met even before the ICDS started being fully implemented in mission mode! As we have seen, the NFHS-4 data show that the decline of malnutrition rates has indeed accelerated, although still slowly: 38.4 per cent of the children are still stunted. Even though the acceleration seen in recent years should be celebrated, one should keep in mind that Thailand, for example, managed to reduce the percentage of underweight children by 25 percentage points between 1980 and 1986 (Tontisirin, Kachondham and

Winichagoon 1992), while Bangladesh recorded a 26 percentage point reduction in child stunting between 1997 and 2007 (Headey et al. 2015).

The institutional arrangements for the implementation of the ICDS were supposed to change and a number of new committees had to be set up at the Central, state and district levels. Probably the most significant change was the creation of state and district child development societies—i.e., separated from line ministries and more flexible entities—which were to be in charge of the implementation of the scheme. The rationale behind creating these structures was to leave more flexibility (and discretion) to government officials in the management of funds and the recruitment of contract employees. These societies would administer the funds supposedly in a more efficient and rapid way than line departments. It should be noted that the flow of funds was still quite centralised, and elected councils were not involved in any meaningful way.

In short, although the restructured ICDS included many of the suggestions coming from the nutrition community and from supporters of the ICDS, the degree of restructuring appears quite limited, especially if we look at what has happened on the ground five years after the formal approval of the restructuring of the programme. Indeed, the MWCD has recently called for the need of another restructuring of the programme.[78] In particular, there is at best a half-hearted effort to involve the community in the management of child malnutrition. The gram panchayat, the only local institution that is somewhat accountable to the people, is involved only marginally. Of course, it is far from certain that panchayats can play a progressive role, especially in some parts of the country. But more than 40 years of experience with a centralised programme should have taught that child malnutrition cannot be eradicated from the top.

CONCLUSION

As we have seen in the first part of this chapter, the ICDS has suffered from serious implementation faults since its introduction in the mid-1970s. However, there has been significant improvement in recent years. This was due to two parallel and intertwined processes that took place in Delhi and at the state level. On the one hand, the UPA government reformed the ICDS in two overlapping ways. First, it introduced a number of changes—such as increased budgetary resources, modification of minimal nutritional norms, adjustment to field staff salaries etc.—that were then implemented by the state governments as they were introduced. This has resulted in the sharp increase in coverage: in 2006, about 600,000 AWCs were operational. Today, there are 1.34 million AWCs covering virtually all villages in India.[79] Furthermore, there have been significant qualitative improvements, which is remarkable in a context of rapid quantitative expansion of the programme (Drèze and Khera 2017a). For instance, in the six states surveyed for the FOCUS (2006) and POCUS (2014) reports, 53 per cent of the AWCs now have their own building (up from 33 per cent in 2004) and 59 per cent have a toilet (up from 20 per cent). Between 2005 and 2014 the percentage of children attending an AWC has increased from 23 to 38 per cent and those who receive supplementary nutrition through the programme has doubled from 24 to 49 per cent (POCUS 2016: 15). In Bihar, where Nandini Nayak and N. C. Saxena (2006) had reported that in 2006, 85 per cent of the posts of supervisors and 21 per cent of the CDPO posts were vacant, the shortage of staff has been effectively addressed and by 2015, no CDPO post is vacant in the state, although 22 per cent of the supervisors were still not in place then (MWCD data tables). Furthermore, the state governments introduced their own specific reforms, which resulted in significant improvements in implementation (Kapur, Joshi and Srinivas 2016). For instance, many states have introduced eggs as part of the supplementary nutrition component of the scheme, which is an important qualitative improvement as eggs are an excellent source of most fundamental nutrients. Also, implementation in some states like Chhattisgarh, Odisha (Sharma et al. 2009) and Maharashtra,[80] (IFPRI 2014) where the state government set up a dedicated nutrition mission to run the scheme, has improved remarkably.

Second, and at the same time, the Central government worked with different stakeholders to restructure the design of the ICDS, which, as we have seen, took a final shape in late 2012. Despite the limited restructuring that has occurred, the new design of the programme is less centralised and has provisions to facilitate inter-department coordination, which has helped in ensuring better implementation.

Perhaps more important than the (limited) restructuring of the ICDS itself, is the fact that more attention is now paid to child malnutrition in government circles. The then finance minister Pranab Mukherjee in his Budget Speech for 2012/13 included malnutrition among the five key issues that had to be tackled as a priority (Budget Speech 2012/13 par. 6[81]). New schemes have been introduced like the Integrated Child Protection Scheme and a multi-sectoral programme to which we referred above. Six states (Uttar Pradesh, Maharashtra, Odisha, Karnataka, Gujarat and Madhya Pradesh) have set up dedicated nutrition missions. Part of the ICDS (the supplementary nutrition component) was inserted in the National Food Security Act (2013), thus becoming a legal entitlement.[82] The NFSA, moreover, universalised a cash-transfer programme piloted in selected districts in recent years to provide maternity benefits (Rs 6,000 in installments) to all lactating mothers for the promotion of exclusive breastfeeding during the first six months. However, at the time of writing—more than four years after the enactment of the Act—this provision is yet to be implemented.

Child malnutrition is also getting the attention of the government from another perspective. Its *Economic Survey 2012/13* dedicated a chapter to the 'demographic dividend'. India will provide the single largest contribution to the global workforce in the decades to come (Aiyar and Mody 2011), as a result of a late demographic transition. This could well be India's best hope to experience an 'economic miracle' comparable to that of East Asia (Kelkar 2004). However, the quality of this workforce will be extremely low if urgent action is not taken. We have seen how malnutrition during childhood affects an individual's lifelong ability to be intellectually and economically productive.

Having a huge but low performing workforce will not do much to promote India's economic miracle. In fact, the demographic dividend could turn into a demographic nightmare. States with higher malnutrition rates also have higher fertility rates, implying that the number of malnourished children may not decrease much in the years to come. Overall, the cost of not tackling child malnutrition as a top policy priority could be huge losses in terms of the accumulation of human capital, the creation of human capabilities and hence future economic growth.[83]

The BJP-led government elected in 2014 has sent contrasting signals. On the one hand, it seems that it is indeed building on the work done by the UPA governments and is putting nutrition relatively high on the agenda. In the *Economic Survey 2015/16*, an entire chapter is dedicated to malnutrition, its impact on future economic growth, and the cost-effectiveness of investing more resources on tackling it (MOF 2015). On 5 November 2015, the Niti Aayog (the newly established body that replaced the Planning Commission in January 2015) held a meeting with the MWCD and the MHFW to develop a national nutrition strategy, which was launched in September 2017. It promises to put nutrition at the centre of the country's development agenda. It remains to be seen what impact it will have at the grassroots.

On the other hand, however, the recent restructuring of Centre–state fiscal relations in the wake of the recommendations of the Fourteenth Finance Commission resulted in a declining financial commitment by the Central government on the ICDS. Although the 50 per cent drop in financial allocation for the ICDS in 2015–16 was partially reversed, the ICDS budget was cut by over 15 per cent between 2014–15 and 2016–17. In real terms, this constitutes a rather dramatic drop. The Central government's argument is that, given that it decided to transfer additional resources to the states, it is now up to them to decide what Centrally Sponsored Schemes they want to prioritise by allocating additional resources. Given the very low political appeal of the ICDS, these changes mean that the future of the programme is a question mark. Overall, the share of the budget (2016–17) dedicated to children was as low as 3.32 per cent of the total (POCUS 2014: 7). Moreover, the government has so far not implemented yet the provision of maternity entitlement as prescribed by the NFSA. This indicates that even though that nutrition has found a higher place in the agenda at the rhetorical level, it hardly results in concrete policy intervention.

A positive element of the new approach is that it recognises that nutrition must be tackled by different angles and that it is not (only) about the lack of food. The launch by the BJP-led government of the Swachh Bharat (Clean India) mission in 2014 and the inclusion of the construction of toilets among permissible works under the MGNREGA are welcome steps and could partly ameliorate the terrible state of sanitation infrastructure, especially in rural areas. However, much more effort must be made to raise awareness about correct sanitation and health care practices. Toilets are useless if they are used as cattle sheds. Recent evidence collected by the r.i.c.e. Institute shows that 40 per cent of those who own a working latrine in their house have at least one family member that still defecates in the open (Coffey et al. 2014). Furthermore, as shown by Coffey and Spears (2017), a key reason why open defecation remains widespread is caste norms that associate the management of human waste with 'impure' castes. This constitutes a potent and difficult-to-eradicate barrier to the use of toilets in rural areas, where they cannot be connected to sewage systems and therefore need to be emptied manually.

The reformed ICDS that we described in this chapter is thus just part of the solution to child malnutrition, although an important one. The AWC is often the only 'health' centre available in remote areas and can constitute a crucial point of reference for the population. However, it is crucial that effective monitoring is exercised at all levels and a greater effort is made to give a sense of ownership of the ICDS to local communities. Only if and when child malnutrition is recognised as a social problem will it capture the imagination of politicians and bureaucrats, and will it be effectively tackled. The interests of the political authorities (and the perceived political advantage resulting from effective implementation of the ICDS) will be crucial elements in determining the programme's impact and in ensuring convergence among different ministries and departments.

NOTES AND REFERENCES

1. Stunted children are too short for their age; underweight children weigh too little for their age; wasted children weigh less than they should for their height.

2. 'Growth or Safety Net?', *The Economist*, 21 September 2013.

3. This ministry was created in 2006. Earlier it was a department within the Ministry of Human Resource Development (MHRD).

4. This was clearly stated by the Supreme Court (order issued on 28 November 2001) which mandated the government to abandon the targeting criterion based on the official poverty line.

5. Some states (e.g. Tamil Nadu) pay a higher honorarium to AWWs and helpers from their own budgets.

6. For a list of the responsibilities of the AWW, see Planning Commission 2011a: 22.

7. The ICDS is a centrally sponsored scheme. Until 2005–06 the Central government funded 100 per cent of inputs except supplementary nutrition (SN), which was funded by the state governments. In 2005–06 the Central government started providing 50 per cent of SN costs. In 2009–10 the Centre increased its share of SN costs to 90 per cent for states in the north-east of the country and decreased its assistance for general costs to 90 per cent. This restructuring of the financial norms was paralleled by a significant increase in the overall allocation for the ICDS (more details below).

8. We will see below that the recent rush to universalise the scheme was mainly due to the intervention of the Supreme Court that ordered the government to open an AWC in every habitation of the country.

9. MWCD Data Tables (available at https://www.icds-wcd.nic.in/icdsdatatables.aspx).

10. 'Overworked ICDS workers on measly pay', *The Times of India*, 27 November 2012.

11. Interview with Hemalata, All India Federation of Anganwadi Workers and Helpers (AIFAWH), New Delhi, 15 March 2013. Interviews in this chapter were conducted by Diego Maiorano.

12. For a list of the responsibilities of the AWW, see Planning Commission 2011a: 22.

13. On the role played by the AWWs (often beyond their duties), see Ghosh 2005.

14. 'An Organizational Problem'. *LiveMint*, 25 January 2012.

15. Interview with Hemalata (AIFAWH), New Delhi, 15 March 2013.

16. This came out of virtually every interview conducted in New Delhi and in some states capitals in March–July 2013.

17. Two perhaps extreme examples of the quality of political appointments in the MWCD at the state level come from Gujarat and Karnataka. In the latter, the MWCD minister was caught watching a porn movie in the Assembly. In Gujarat, the minister was recently sentenced to 28 years in jail for her role in the Naroda Patiya massacre that occurred during the 2002 pogroms.

18. Interview with N. C. Saxena, NAC and Special Commissioner to the Supreme Court, New Delhi, 9 August 2013.

19. Interview with A. K. Shiv Kumar, NAC, New Delhi, 26 March 2013.

20. Both reports were written by Biraj Patnaik, Principal Adviser to the Special Commissioners to the Supreme Court. They are available at: http://www.sccommissioners.org/Reports/stateadvisers.html (accessed 29 August 2013; site discontinued). See also the CAG Report 2013b: 93 and ff.

21. Interview, New Delhi, March 2013 (names withheld).

22. Interview, A. K. Shiv Kumar, NAC, New Delhi, 26 March 2013.

23. I thank N. C. Saxena for pointing this out to me.

24. MWCD data tables, available at https://icds-wcd.nic.in/icdsdatatables.aspx (accessed 4 August 2019).

25. Interviews with Mridula Bajaj, Mobile Crèches, New Delhi, 30 July 2013, and Gayatri Singh, UNICEF India, New Delhi, 25 March 2013.

26. This is probably an overstatement, but the same was expressed by many other observers.

27. Here the problem seems to be that officials in the MWCD resent the fact that in government circles malnutrition is seen as their failure only (interview with Dr. Shreeranjan, Joint Secretary, MWCD, New Delhi, 20 March 2013).

28. Both work under the MHFW.

29. Interview with Gayatri Singh, UNICEF India, New Delhi, 25 March 2013.

30. See Patel 2018.

31. 'Death of 3 Delhi sisters: Stomach was absolutely empty, they died of starvation, says doctor', *Hindustan Times*, 26 July 2018.

32. Interview with Dr. Shreeranjan, MWCD, New Delhi, 20 March 2013.

33. This Public Interest Litigation (PIL) is known as '*PUCL vs. Union of India and Others*', Writ Petition (Civil) 196/2001.

34. A useful summary of the Right to Food case was written by Yamini Jaishankar and Jean Drèze and is available here: http://www.corteidh.or.cr/tablas/27433.pdf (accessed 4 August 2019).

35. The order dated 8th May 2002 made state governments responsible.

36. Supreme Court Order 8th May 2002.

37. See Raman 2013.

38. Beside the ICDS, these are the PDS, the Antyodaya Anna Yojana, the Mid-day Meal scheme, the Annapurna, the National Old Age Pension Scheme, the National Maternity Benefit Scheme and the National Family Benefit Scheme.

39. According to many sources, it was Jairam Ramesh who drafted most of the Congress manifesto. See also Hasan 2013, chapter 5.

40. The Supreme Court also requested the government to start with SC/ST habitations.

41. 'Replacing hot cooked meals with packaged food mixes will affect children's health, say nutritionists', *scroll.in*, 1 September 2017.

42. 'How three tainted companies retained their grip over Madhya Pradesh's nutrition scheme for children', *scroll.in*, 30 May 2018.

43. Many interviewees (including Jean Drèze, Santosh Mehrotra, Biraj Patnaik and Dipa Sinha) agreed that it was the 2006 order that set the policy-making machine on track.

44. Another important provision of the order was the introduction of the 'anganwadi-on-demand'.

45. At current prices.

46. Interview with Dr. Shreeranjan, Joint Secretary, MWCD, New Delhi, 20 March 2013.

47. Interview, Jean Drèze, New Delhi, 22 March 2013; and Mridula Bajaj, Mobile Crèches, New Delhi, 30 July 2013.

48. Acronym for Focus On Children Under Six. The report (along with many others reports cited in this chapter) is available on the Right to Food Campaign website, which is a phenomenal source of information. http://www.righttofoodcampaign.in/pre-school-nutrition/campaign-material (accessed 23 October 2015).

49. 'Even amid its wealth, India finds, half its small children are malnourished', *The New York Times*, 10 February 2007.

50. For example, 'Investing in our children', *The Hindu*, 30 December 2006.

51. Interview with Neerja Chowdhury, New Delhi, 9 August 2013.

52. Both had been invited to submit recommendations (NAC 2004 and 2005; RTF 2007).

53. 'Urgent action needed to tone up ICDS', *The Hindu*, 17 January 2007.

54. The most active members were Jay Panda, Sachin Pilot and Supriya Sule. An interesting interview with Sachin Pilot was published by *The Economic Times* on 11 February 2008.

55. Their first visit was to Madhya Pradesh, a BJP-ruled state. They then decided to go to a Congress-ruled state, Maharashtra, and then to a regional party-ruled state, Uttar Pradesh. According to the young MPs involved, this strategy was part of a larger effort to keep the issue apolitical and to avoid blaming each others' parties for poor implementation of the ICDS (interview, Neerja Chowdhury, New Delhi, 9 August 2013).

56. Interview, Jay Panda, MP, New Delhi, 1 August 2013.

57. Interview, Rohini Mukherjee, Naandi Foundation, Hyderabad, 5 August 2013.

58. 'Biscuit Lunch', *Outlook*, 31 March 2008.

59. See N. C. Saxena's letter to the prime minister dated 7 September 2007, available at: http://www.righttofoodindia.org/data/copy_of_letter_to_pm_regarding_corruption_icds2007.pdf (accessed 23 October 2015). See also 'Contractors? That Means Pilferage', an interview of Montek Singh Ahluwalia in *Outlook*, 31 March 2008.

60. 'Hard to Swallow', *Outlook*, 10 December 2007.

61. One of the most evident signs of caste discrimination is the refusal of upper castes to dine with lower status people. Making children eat together irrespective of caste boundaries could make a great difference over the long term.

62. Interviews with MPs and MLAs conducted in New Delhi, Hyderabad, Jaipur, Visakhapatnam and Lucknow.

63. Interviews with civil society activists conducted in New Delhi, Jaipur and Hyderabad in 2012–13.

64. Interview with Mobile Crèches staff, New Delhi, 30 July 2013.

65. Calculation by Diego Maiorano.

66. Interview with Dipa Sinha, New Delhi, 16 March 2013.

67. Interview with Arun Gupta, Breastfeeding Promotion Network of India, New Delhi, 14 March 2013.

68. Interview, March 2013 (name of source withheld).

69. According to some experts, this programme could be the game changer as it will be designed with a multi-dimensional perspective, which alone can ensure effective action against malnutrition.

70. Interview with Vandana Prasad, New Delhi, 21 March 2013.

71. Interview with Dipa Sinha, New Delhi, 16 March 2013.

72. At current prices.

73. Not only were the norms for expenditure per child for supplementary nutrition doubled twice (in 2008 and in 2009), but the Central government's share of costs for this service changed in 2005–06. Before that date, the supplementary nutrition component was paid entirely by the state governments; after, 50 per cent of the costs were covered by the Centre.

74. This is something that came out of virtually every interview conducted for this project.

75. Interview with Jean Drèze, New Delhi, 22 March 2013.

76. Interview with A. K. Shiv Kumar, NAC, New Delhi, 26 March 2013.

77. According to some observers, the presentation of the 'Strategies for Children Under Six' by groups associated with the RTF Campaign in 2011 was decisive in convincing Ahluwalia. Apparently he began the meeting by saying, 'Convince me that what you propose will work'.

78. 'We need a Nutrition Mission', *The Hindu*, 23 July 2016.

79. As of 31 December 2015 (MWCD data tables, https://www.icds-wcd.nic.in/icdsdatatables.aspx).

80. Maharashtra has been celebrated has an exemplary success story. *The Global Nutrition Report 2014* (IFPRI 2014), for example, claimed that the state had reduced stunting from 36.5 to 24 per cent between 2005/06 to 2012. However, the recently released NFHS-4 data show that the decline in stunting in children under five was from 46.3 to 34.4 between 2005/06 and 2015. This is still a good performance.

81. Available here: http://indiabudget.nic.in/budget2012-2013/bspeecha.asp (accessed 19 September 2013).

82. See Chapter 3 on the Food Security Act.

83. Many studies have attempted to estimate the loss in terms of economic growth and productivity due to child malnutrition. For a useful summary see Gragnolati et al. 2005: 7–8. See also Kelland 2013.

six

The Jawaharlal Nehru National Urban Renewal Mission and Urban Poverty

The MGNREGA, seen as the flagship anti-poverty programme of the UPA-I government, was followed within three months by the launch of the JNNURM on 3 December 2005. While not primarily an anti-poverty programme, its objectives included tackling the daunting mass poverty that is an inescapable feature of the urban Indian landscape. Along with the development of urban infrastructure and the reform of urban governance, the provision of basic services to the urban poor was identified as an important component. This chapter seeks to understand the politics of why despite this recognition of the importance of tackling urban poverty, the anti-poverty aspect of the JNNURM came to be treated as very much a secondary element within a wider programme of urban renewal.

ORIGINS AND FORMULATION

The 2004 Congress general election manifesto included a commitment to a 'comprehensive programme of urban renewal based on public–private partnerships', also mentioning the provision of social housing for the poor to deal with the proliferation of slums. This subsequently found its way into the UPA's CMP. Yet, unlike MGNREGA there was no significant civil society campaign pushing for it. Much of the impetus behind the launch of JNNURM seems to have come from senior bureaucrats, especially in the Ministry of Urban Development, as well as a few influential voices on urban affairs outside government such as Ramesh Ramanathan, a former Citibank executive-turned-social entrepreneur who in 2001 co-founded Janaagraha, an urban policy think-tank[1] based in the southern city of Bangalore, India's chief information technology (IT) hub.

An important rationale for a national programme of urban regeneration was that the locus of economic activity in the country had shifted decisively towards the urban sector in the wake of economic liberalisation in the early 1990s with the urban share of GDP rising from 46 per cent in 1990 to 58 per cent by 2008 (McKinsey Global Institute 2010: 17). An example of what might be done had been set in Bangalore in the early 2000s where the Bangalore Agenda Task Force (BATF), constituted by the Congress state government of Karnataka led by S. M. Krishna but privately funded, acted as an advisory and oversight body tasked with reforming and improving urban institutions and services (Raman 2006: 78–83; Manor 2007: 428–433). Chaired by Nandan Nilekani, co-founder of the Indian IT software giant Infosys, it also included Ramesh Ramanathan. Although BATF was dissolved after Krishna left office in 2004 following the Congress' loss of its majority in state assembly elections (Raman 2006: 160), Nilekani and other erstwhile BATF members, notably Janaagraha's Ramanathan, subsequently sought to persuade politicians and bureaucrats in Delhi of the need for a national mission for urban change (Nilekani 2008: 228; Raman 2006: 229)—Ramanathan credits Nilekani with opening doors in government and the UPA.[2]

A key figure in bringing the JNNURM to fruition was Anil Baijal, one of India's most senior civil servants. Following the 2004 election he had been removed from the powerful post of home secretary only a few months after having been appointed by the BJP Home Minister L. K. Advani. In July he was appointed secretary of the Ministry of Urban Development at the instance of Ghulam Nabi Azad, the Congress minister with whom he had a good relationship, having twice worked with him in the past.[3] Baijal came to the post with something of a reputation as a versatile troubleshooter. For instance, immediately prior to his appointment as home secretary he had received positive press coverage when serving briefly as vice-chairman of the Delhi Development Authority (DDA) after his predecessor had been arrested in connection with a land scam.[4]

Initially a bit upset at what could be seen as a demotion, Baijal was open to ideas about doing something significant in the urban sector when the opportunity presented itself at a 'retreat' discussion on the subject in Goa in autumn 2004. Apart from Baijal the discussion also included Professor O. P. Mathur of the National Institute of Public Finance and Policy (NIPFP) (a former director of the National Institute of Urban Affairs or NIUA), K. C. Sivaramakrishanan of the leading Delhi think tank, the Centre for Policy Research, who had served as secretary for urban development from 1988 to 1992, and Junaid Ahmad. Ahmad, a dynamic Bangladeshi who was the World Bank's urban lead specialist, had arrived in India having worked on the Bank's urban programme in post-apartheid South Africa.[5] Baijal put the ideas emerging out of the Goa discussions to Azad, who welcomed them. The initiative was also supported by other key figures, notably Prime Minister Manmohan Singh, Finance Minister P. Chidambaram and Montek Ahluwalia, the new deputy chairman of the Planning Commission.[6]

Historically, the political and economic discourse on poverty in India has focused on the rural sector: Prime Minister Singh even began his speech launching the JNNURM by saying, 'There is no doubt that India by and large still lives in our villages'.[7] In the last decade this rural bias in addressing the issue of poverty has been reinforced by concern about the spread of Maoist insurgency in many districts across rural central and eastern India with a concentration of marginalised tribal people, a threat that Singh, from 2006 on, repeatedly described as 'the single biggest internal security challenge ever faced' by India.[8]

Against this backdrop, there was no step change in how JNNURM sought to confront the problem of the urban poor. Both the main components in this aspect of the programme—Basic

Services for the Urban Poor (BSUP) in the 63[9] 'mission cities' (including seven with a population of over 4 million, 28 with between 1–4 million and 28 under a million) and the Integrated Housing and Slum Development Programme (IHSDP) in other towns and cities—had numerous precursors including the Minimum Needs Programme (1974), Environmental Improvement of Urban Slums (1974), Urban Basic Services for the Poor (1990), the Prime Minister's Integrated Urban Poverty Eradication Programme (PMIUPEP, 1995), and the National Slum Development Programme (NSDP, 1996).

JNNURM envisaged a total investment of over Rs 123,700 crore including Rs 50,000 crore (revised to Rs 66,085 crore in 2009) of Central government funding allocated for the programme over seven years and Rs 45,070 crore actually budgeted in the period (Planning Commission 2013: 323; CAG 2013a: v). Although the greater share was devoted to urban infrastructure and governance (UIG) in the mission cities and the Urban Infrastructure Development Scheme for Small and Medium Towns (UIDSSMT), over a third was allocated to the two anti-poverty components—Rs 16,357 crore billion (24.75 per cent) to BSUP and Rs 6,828 crore (10.33 per cent) to IHSDP (Planning Commission 2013: 323). However, with a new scheme, Rajiv Awas Yojana (RAY) launched in 2011, by 2013–14 the BSUP allocation of JNNURM funds was down to 13 per cent and IHSDP to 8 per cent (Accountability Initiative 2013: 2).

While this was easily the biggest ever consolidated investment of public funds made in the urban sector in India, the JNNURM never received the kind of political and media attention that MGNREGA attracted. In large part this was because it was mainly borne out of a bureaucratic and technocratic impulse rather than a political initiative or one driven by civil society engagement. Unlike say MGNREGA and the Food Security Act passed in 2013, it was also not a programme that the NAC formed under Congress president Sonia Gandhi played any part in formulating or one that entailed parliamentary legislation. Critics of the JNNURM perceive the politics of the programme in the ideological orientation of its design with the aim, albeit substantially unrealised, of attracting large-scale private investment through public–private partnerships[10]. Others credit its primarily bureaucratic impetus for the programme being better designed than say the PDS or the ICDS (considered in Chapters 3 and 5).[11]

Yet there was a political as well as an economic dimension to the new focus on urban India that predated the UPA. The 'India Shining' image projected by the ruling BJP-led NDA coalition in the 2004 general election campaign was widely characterised in the media as focused on the glitz of urban India and the burgeoning middle class. Though the UPA came to office presenting more of a rural emphasis on '*aam aadmi*' (the common man), it was also not oblivious to the growing electoral significance of urban constituencies. As Congress New Delhi MP Ajay Maken, who served as Minister of State for Urban Development from 2006 to 2009 and Minister of Housing and Urban Poverty Alleviation from 2012 to 2013, noted, 'With about 147 cities with a population of 3 lakhs and above comprising 168 parliamentary constituencies, urban areas and urban issues have become extremely important, politically as well'.[12] The authoritative Lokniti National Election Study classifies 57 of the 545 Lok Sabha constituencies as urban and another 144 as semi-urban. In being returned to power in the 2009 election the UPA won 34 urban seats with 42 per cent of the vote, and in 81 semi-urban constituencies with 39.3 per cent of the vote, thereby eliminating the relative advantage that the NDA had enjoyed in urban areas even when it lost in 2004 (Palshikar and Yadav 2009: 39–40).

Ajay Maken, one of the younger and more dynamic leaders in the Congress (he was 41 when he was appointed Minister of State for Urban Development in 2006), was exceptional among the ministers and ministers of state in the two ministries of Urban Development and Housing and Urban Poverty Alleviation, responsible for delivering JNNURM in showing a lively interest in the programme including its anti-poverty aspect. The only one of the seven ministers who bore responsibility for JNNURM between 2005 and 2013 from a metropolitan constituency, his interest was seen by some as driven by concern with nursing his New Delhi seat. Of the others, Jaipal Reddy, Minister for Urban Development from 2005 to 2011, was described by a veteran urban activist as 'clueless' and content to leave the JNNURM to the bureaucrats in his department to shape.[13] His successor, Kamal Nath, was widely regarded as more involved but primarily interested in high-visibility large-scale urban infrastructure projects.

A significant constitutional constraint on the capacity of the Union government to act on social development and combating poverty in India's cities is the fact that responsibility for a lot of what needs to be done falls under the governments of the 29 states. As N. C. Saxena, a former secretary of the Planning Commission, puts it, this means that the Centre effectively acts as a donor agency when it comes to the implementation of social programmes such as BSUP and IHSDP.[14] An additional complexity was that responsibility for JNNURM was shared between the Ministry of Urban Development (MoUD) and that of Housing and Urban Poverty Alleviation (MoHUPA).

There are different views about the impact that this has had on the efficacy of the anti-poverty aspect of JNNURM. While the division could be mitigated by peculiar factors, like the personal rapport Anil Baijal, the MoUD Secretary, enjoyed with his counterpart in MoHUPA, Chitra Chopra, who also belonged to the 1969 batch of entrants to the Indian Administrative Service (IAS), Baijal's opinion was that it was unfortunate and resulted in an unavoidable compartmentalisation with different schemes aimed at tackling urban poverty housed in different ministries. The fact that the allocation of funds for JNNURM favoured city-wide infrastructure also meant that, as K. C. Sivaramakrishnan in his account of JNNURM puts it, 'the shadow fell on the declared policy of inclusive growth' (Sivaramakrishnan 2011: 21).

PROBLEMS OF IMPLEMENTATION

Prior to JNNURM urban poverty, like urban development more broadly, was a relatively neglected policy area. The Seventh Plan

(1985–92) was the first to explicitly recognise the problems of the urban poor (Kundu 2011: 45) and in 1997 the Swarna Jayanti Shahari Rozgar Yojana (SJSRY) was launched, subsuming the Nehru Rozgar Yojana, the PMIUPEP and BSUP, with the objective of addressing urban poverty through helping provide gainful employment and fostering self-managed community groups.[15] However, in an omission criticised by urban poverty specialists, the JNNURM did not extend to addressing urban livelihoods; its seven objectives only including two related to the urban poor:

> (e) Scale-up delivery of civic amenities and provision of utilities with emphasis on universal access to the urban poor; and
> (g) Provision of basic services to the urban poor including security of tenure at affordable prices, improved housing, water supply and sanitation, and ensuring delivery of other existing universal services of the government for education, health and social security. (JNNURM 2005: 5)

Infrastructure over Poverty Alleviation

Urban poverty was therefore not the main focus of the JNNURM. The programme was intended to make an impact on urban India through Central investment that linked asset investment to maintenance, aiming to improve financial health, credibility and reform of urban governance with reforms of antiquated urban land ceilings and rent controls opening up the urban land market. Based on a trilateral memorandum of understanding between the Government of India, the state government and urban local bodies (ULBs), the idea was to offer cities a big enough carrot to get them to accept reform so that success in even just a quarter of the 63 cities could showcase successful urban change. As Urban Secretary Baijal recalls telling the prime minister, 'If you get your urban story right, you get the India story right'.[16]

Although the mandatory reforms that ULBs were supposed to undertake under the scheme referred to the JNNURM's urban poor objectives (JNNURM 2005: 12), the programme's main storyline was urban infrastructure—the procurement of thousands of new low-floor buses bearing the JNNURM logo across Indian cities became its most publicly visible feature (Sivaramakrishnan 2015: 75). When a Technical Advisory Group (TAG) was constituted in February 2006, it was for the Sub-Mission on Urban Infrastructure and Governance and its terms of reference omitted any mention of the urban poor.[17] Chaired by Ramesh Ramanathan, it initially also included Professor O. P. Mathur and Sheela Patel, Director of the Mumbai-based Society for the Promotion of Area Resource Centres (SPARC), one of the country's first urban NGOs (established in 1984), subsequently adding K. C. Sivaramakrishnan, M. P. Vasimalai, Executive Director of DHAN (Development of Humane Action), an anti-poverty NGO based in the southern city of Madurai, and Professor R. V. Rama Rao, Director of the Institute of Development and Policy Studies (IDPS) in the southern port city of Visakhapatnam.

From the outset there was concern in TAG that the urban poverty dimension of JNNURM might get lost. At its first meeting in June 2006 Sheela Patel noted that of the two responsible ministries only MoUD was 'really active in operationalising the mission' giving rise to concern about how urban poverty issues would be adequately represented. Another problem she raised was the poor data available.[18] A study of Ahmedabad, Bangalore and Patna found that the three cities had no data on social indicators and Bangalore and Patna did not even have a list of slums, let alone data on the level of services (Mahadevia 2010: 271). Concerns were also expressed by Vasimalai, who found little for the poor in JNNURM, and Sivaramakrishnan, and at its fourth meeting in November 2006 Professor Mathur described the picture as regards urban poor as 'very dismal'.[19]

Design Faults

It soon became clear that there were serious drawbacks in the design of JNNURM that hampered its effective delivery on aspects relating to urban poverty. One was the weak structure. Neither the MoUD nor the MoHUPA were set up to handle such an ambitious programme, and dividing its direction between the two ministries was unhelpful.[20] The urban poor rarely appeared to figure much in the perspective taken by the MoUD.[21] Specifically, the funding arrangements and benchmarks for mandatory and optional reforms to be undertaken by urban local bodies and states proved far too ambitious.

Under the scheme the ULBs and parastatal agencies in the mission cities were supposed to implement six mandatory reforms. These included two focused on the urban poor—earmarking of budgets for basic services for them, and provision of basic services including security of tenure at affordable prices, improved housing, water supply and sanitation—as well as ensuring delivery of other existing universal services of the government for education, health and social security. Also listed was double entry accounting, introduction of e-governance, reform of property tax, and the phased levy of full cost service recovery charges on urban consumers. State level mandatory reforms included implementation of the decentralisation envisaged in the 74th Constitutional Amendment Act (1992), repeal of the Urban Land Ceiling and Regulation Act and reform of rent control laws, rationalisation of stamp duty, public disclosure of fiscal plans and performance information by ULBs and parastatal agencies, enactment of the Community Participation Law, and assigning and or associating ULBs with city planning. Additional to these were a further ten optional reforms from which states could pick two annually to implement; these included earmarking 20–25 per cent of developed land in all housing projects, public and private, for the economically weaker section and lower income group (JNNURM 2005: 12–13).

The realisation of the reforms relied on the capacity and will of states and ULBs. However, the reforms were not effectively built into the design, and were weakened by wishy-washy conditionality, meaning that states and ULBs saw the liberal funding released under JNNURM as 'soft money' that would be received irrespective of progress on reforms.[22] Much of the infrastructure funding was really irreversible—a flyover could not be left half built! Apart from slow reform, another consequence of this was that while the public sector investment was meant to leverage private money and generate the growth of public–private partnerships, Central government funding crowded out the private sector in an urban market that could really only effectively absorb a fraction of the projected investment.[23]

While the conditionality attached to JNNURM funding was not very effective in delivering reform, its cumbersome mechanism was also blamed for holdups. Attending a TAG meeting in May 2007 P. K. Mohanty, the Joint Secretary and JNNURM Mission Director in MoHUPA, said with planning done by the Central ministries, sanctioning by the Mission Directorates, the release of funds by the Finance Ministry, and project implementation by state governments, there was a lack of synchronisation.[24] Addressing a seminar in Bangalore five months later, another problem that Mohanty identified was the difficulty that many ULBs in the 1 to 4 million population Category B faced in coming up with the 30 per cent of project funding to match the 50 per cent from Central government and 20 per cent from state government.[25] The respective percentages for the seven metropolitan cities (Category A)—Mumbai, Delhi, Kolkata, Chennai, Bangalore, Hyderabad and Ahmedabad—were 50 project, 35 Central and 15 state; for mission cities with populations of under a million (Category C), 10, 80 and 10; and cities in the North East and Jammu and Kashmir, 0, 90 and 10.

City Development Plans and the Poor

The BSUP component of JNNURM suffered from the fact that both the municipalities and the urban planners were more interested in infrastructure development and in elite localities. Amitabh Kundu, one of the leading experts on India's urban economy, saw it as reasonably successful as an infrastructure programme but one that was rather about 'cleaning up' urban poverty than inclusion.[26] According to Kundu a significant problem with the approach taken by JNNURM came in the 'City Development Plans' (CDPs) or vision statements that the mission cities were required to furnish, along with 'Detailed Project

Reports' (DPRs), to get the approvals needed from the state nodal agency (urban development departments, development authorities or urban infrastructure and financing organisations) and a Central Sanctioning and Monitoring Committee (CSMC) chaired by the secretary of MoUD. These were often 'quick-fix' documents prepared by global or national research agencies that reflected a 'manufactured consensus' containing much rhetoric about equity and social justice but scant detail, and with slum dwellers allowed to play no more than a 'decorative role' as token stakeholders (Kundu 2011: 44). The result was that, for example, BSUP largely became a housing programme unaffordable for the really poor.[27]

The deficiency of CDPs is a recurring theme in assessments of JNNURM given by both those closely involved in the programme and reviewers. K. C. Sivaramakrishnan, in the first narrative account of the programme, noted how CDPs failed to address the need for the convergence of infrastructure development and housing for urban poor while officials in the two responsible ministries showed little enthusiasm for creative interaction (Sivaramakrishnan 2011: 59–60). Given the number of CPDs referred to advisory bodies such as the NIUA, NIPFP, the Centre for Environmental Planning and Technology (CEPT, Ahmedabad) or the Administrative Staff College (Hyderabad), 'the appraisals tended to be less than thorough' (ibid. 2010: 9). He also remarked on how, by diminishing public ownership of land, the philosophy of economic liberalisation also made it harder to earmark land for housing the poor (ibid. 2011: 187).

As early as June 2007, 19 months after the launch of JNNURM, the Hazards Centre, a Delhi-based NGO focused on the urban poor, based on a review of 15 CDPs, was outspoken in its criticism of the inherent bias of the programme:

> By aggressively promoting the idea that it is concerned with financing high-profile infrastructural initiatives above all else, the JNNURM is perhaps encouraging cities to indulge their own instinctive biases against the everyday lives and livelihoods of the lowest rungs of their workforces. Apart from questions of fair distribution, this orientation also

> makes the overall development goals of these cities virtually unachievable, given that the poor—and their places of work and residence—constitute the most visible as well as statistically significant components of every JNNURM city's fabric. (Hazards Centre 2007: 17)

Noting the patchiness of the focus on the poor in the CDPs, it related this to the programme's lack of clarity about their place in the development of the mission cities with no serious stakeholder consultations and relatively little funding allocated to the BSUP component (Hazards Centre 2007: 22, 28, 33). Subsequent reports by SPARC, the urban NGO headed by TAG member Sheela Patel, also criticised how organisations of the urban poor were typically ignored in city visions (SPARC 2011–12: 7), indicating that not much changed with reference to housing as the programme proceeded.

Social audits of BSUP projects undertaken under JNNURM indicate that an overall lack of community involvement in design and delivery of habitat has led to communities being dissatisfied with what they have, with many houses being built but families unwilling to live there and many projects either incomplete or not started (SPARC 2010–11: 28).

At a meeting attended by A. K. Mehta, Director JNNURM in MoUD, in October 2007 the two urban poverty specialists on TAG, Sheela Patel and M. P. Vasimalai, cautioned that urban poverty reduction should not be reduced to housing provision.[28] Urban activists such as Dunu Roy of the Hazards Centre have been vigorous in questioning MoHUPA's emphasis on housing as a way of lifting people out of poverty, advocating instead a broader focus on livelihood.[29] Nevertheless, in December 2008 a High-Level Task Force on Affordable Housing for All chaired by Deepak Parekh, Chairman of the Housing Development Finance Corporation (HDFC), the country's largest mortgage company, recommended the doubling of JNNURM funds for affordable housing with part of this devoted to *in situ* development assisted by NGOs and community based organisations (CBOs) (Parekh et al. 2008: 22). Yet the situation showed little improvement with a lot of the BSUP and IHSDP housing poorly serviced in terms of transport and utilities—as of 1 October 2013 over a third of the 731,391 units completed (of the 1,562,728 sanctioned) remained unoccupied.[30]

Poor Political and Civic Engagement

A significant factor in how JNNURM was implemented was the weak political engagement of ULBs with the programme. One important reason was the differentiated impact of the empowerment of ULBs under the 74th Amendment Act. Greater autonomy favoured the major metropolitan centres and larger cities with the capacity to do more with their greater municipal revenues and generally stronger finances (Kundu 2011: 37–38), and this also applied to JNNURM projects. Elsewhere there was widespread lack of awareness and apathy among community leaders and even municipal corporators—at a TAG meeting in May 2007 Professor Rama Rao asserted that ULBs and their elected representatives were still totally oblivious of JNNURM 18 months after its launch.[31] There was scant public and hardly any political debate on what was termed a 'Mission' but implemented as yet another government scheme. In many cities CDPs were not even discussed by the elected representatives (National Social Watch Coalition 2009: 173).

While part of the reason for this was the lack of attention paid to capacity building in urban governance, also pertinent was the relative powerlessness of elected representatives and city mayors as compared to municipal commissioners and IAS officers appointed by the state government as the executive heads of city corporations.[32] A 2010 report by the McKinsey Global Institute notes:

> India's cities do not have empowered leaders ... While many cities have mayors, their tenures are short and they rarely have the power to drive new investments, hire key personnel, fund projects, or reorganise departments ... In large cities, power is distributed between the municipal commissioner and the Municipal Corporation in a way that makes neither fully accountable for the city's decisions ... commissioners

> ... have no long-term stake in the city and invariably shy away from making the big decisions important for the city's long-term health. (McKinsey Global Institute 2011)

Within this context municipal corporations were reluctant to assume the responsibility for implementing reforms enjoined by JNNURM when the relevant agreements had been reached between the Central ministries, state governments and municipal commissioners.

When it came to the urban poverty aspect of JNNURM there were additional factors at play. In Mumbai, for instance, while mobilisation on particular issues such as legal recognition of the housing rights of slum dwellers by organisations like SPARC has had a political impact on elected municipal corporators, this political influence of the urban poor diminishes the higher the level of politics. After all, the majority of ministers in the state or national governments do not represent urban areas, still less possess any political ties to the urban poor.[33] In this, India is quite unlike, say, Brazil where far more of the decision makers on urban poverty issues are local and national politicians strongly connected to urban areas.

There was also only limited civic engagement with JNNURM. In 2009 a Citizen's Report on Governance and Development produced by the National Social Watch Coalition (NSWC), a network of civil society organisations, criticised the response of civil society to the programme:

> The section of civil society, which opposed this scheme even before its formal announcement, has shunned the entire scheme ... As a result, it has provided a free hand to the state to conceive and implement the scheme in the way it thinks fit. The section of civil society that welcomed the scheme and collaborated with the state has allowed the state to use them selectively without providing them real participation in design and implementation ... Finally, another section of civil society comprising mainly of stakeholders (beneficiaries) are engrossed in cornering maximum benefits from the scheme and are not concerned with [the] design or impact or equity aspects ... (NSWC 2009: 169)

The need for civil society engagement had been highlighted at the outset by TAG, but by May 2009 Sheela Patel was outspoken in her conviction that TAG had failed to fulfil its terms of reference which called for it to, among other things, involve citizens in service delivery and governance, enlist their involvement at the grass root level through ward committees, area sabhas and voluntary technical corps, and mobilise the support of civil society and elected representatives for reforms in urban governance.[34] In fact, one of the most urban NGOs campaigning on behalf of the urban poor, the Hazards Centre, found itself excluded from meetings organised by TAG (Roy 2009: 4) and the free market oriented Centre for Civil Society stopped working with the NIUA in 2008 when it became clear that the reform aspect of the JNNURM in which they were mainly interested was not being realised.[35]

Four years after the launch of JNNURM the conclusion that K. C. Sivaramakrishnan reached was that if anyone was 'in charge of the city' it was the consultants and developers, blaming this on the paradigm of 'a rising tide [that] will lift all boats ignoring the reality that many are mired in the mud and debris accumulated over the years and now held down by inequity' (Sivaramakrishnan 2010: 48). Even the semblance of consultation that did take place was dominated by the contribution of residents' welfare associations of the upper and middle class who, in the absence of effective representation of the poor, were able to capture urban community space.[36]

The reality of the urban context, especially of the urban poor in the bigger cities, is one of a more transient and diverse population, and consequently, of weaker community structures and social solidarity. In contrast to rural areas there are also relatively fewer NGOs active in cities.[37] As a result, beyond the role played (or often not played) by elected councillors or corporators, only consultation, not active wider community involvement, is really feasible.[38] Typically, the mandatory community participation laws were passed by states, but then left unimplemented.[39] Furthermore, MoHUPA, unlike ministries such as Education, Rural Development, Health and Panchayati Raj, lacked experience of working with NGOs and CBOs (SPARC 2010–11: 28).

TAG, MoHUPA and Programme Implementation

The effort to engage civil society organisations in regenerating cities and address urban poverty proved stillborn. In the initial presentation of the structure under JNNURM, the Technical Advisory Group chaired by founder of Janaagraha, Ramesh Ramanathan, appeared to have a key role in appraising proposals, alongside a National Steering Group (NSG), to be chaired by the Minister of Urban Development and co-chaired by the Minister for Housing and Urban Poverty Alleviation (and only met thrice between 2006 and 2009), and the CSMC chaired by the Secretary of MoUD. In the words of former Urban Development Secretary Anil Baijal, TAG's aim was to achieve a 'critical mass'.[40] In the event with barely a handful of support staff and administrative support from the NIUA, and mainly reliant on MoUD and MoHUPA, for information, the impact it had proved limited. Although it held 33 meetings between June 2006 and August 2010, only four of these were attended by the joint secretaries who acted as the JNNURM directors within MoUD and MoHUPA (each attended two), the last being in February 2008. Since the National Steering Group met only three times in three years (Sivaramakrishnan 2010: 45), much of the formal business oversight of JNNURM took place in the CSMC (which had met 127 times by October 2013[41]).

While never formally dissolved, TAG was effectively wound up through being undermined and neglected by the ministries (although the minutes of the CSMC meetings continued to state that they were to be circulated to the six TAG members). There were repeated complaints about CSMC minutes not being provided and the fact that JNNURM city monitoring reports by evaluating agencies such as the NIPFP did not follow a common template and were not routinely provided to TAG by the ministries.[42] In June 2009 the TAG members signed a letter raising their concerns jointly addressed to Jaipal Reddy, Minister of Urban Development, and Kumari Selja, Minister of Housing and Urban Poverty Alleviation. They received no response.[43]

With few city governments effectively controlling JNNURM activities, most had understandably little enthusiasm for involving civil society organisations in monitoring or implementation. When TAG came up with modified guidelines for City TAGs or City Volunteer Technical Corps that the Secretary of MoHUPA agreed with, MoUD nevertheless omitted the City TAG component from the version circulated to all the states, leaving TAG feeling, as Ramanathan told the MoUD Secretary, 'excluded and demotivated'.[44] In the event City TAGs or Corps, of variable efficacy, were established in only six of the 67 mission cities (Sivaramakrishnan 2010: 45).

The JNNURM Mission Directorate responsible for the anti-poverty parts of the programme (i.e. BSUP and IHSDP) was located in MoHUPA, and from September 2006 to January 2013 the Director was P. K. Mohanty, an Odisha-born 1979 Andhra cadre IAS officer who had previously worked in the Ministry of Urban Development and Poverty Alleviation for several years in the 1990s. He was therefore in a better position than most to influence the implementation of JNNURM, and his work received mixed reviews.[45] Some criticised him for concentrating too much on building houses rather than taking a holistic approach to improving services for the urban poor. However, others noted the constraints arising from the programme structure and gave Mohanty high marks for initiative, for example, crediting him with helping draft a Street Vendors Bill that for the first time recognised and gave rights to the hundreds of thousands of street vendors in Indian cities (although this was also criticised for limiting vendors to particular areas). Mohanty's successor, Sanjeev Kumar, was a younger man with less experience of urban affairs who defined his brief more narrowly: implementing policy in conjunction with state governments rather than concerned with evaluating or critiquing the programme ('a job for others').[46]

Implementation of JNNURM projects and reforms were the responsibility of state governments and municipal authorities and thus dependent on their size, revenue and other resources, as well as capacity and commitment. The already more developed states and cities possessed a superior capacity to implement reforms and to come up with projects. Thirty-seven per cent of Central assistance up to 2010 was claimed by just five of the 67 mission cities: Delhi, Hyderabad, Kolkata, Mumbai and Pune (Sivaramakrishnan 2010: 20). By the end of 2012, while over half the projects sanctioned in Tamil Nadu, Andhra Pradesh and Gujarat had been completed, none had in Bihar. Again, while Gujarat led in terms of at least the nominal implementation of reforms (87 per cent), Bihar lagged behind with a score of 35 per cent (Accountability Initiative 2013: 4–5).

When it came to the BSUP component, a study found that its implementation in Bangalore and Patna was poor (Mahadevia 2010: 270). A June 2013 CAG audit report found that only 4 per cent of the work on an ambitious project to make Bangalore 'slum free' had been done within the seven-year mission period.[47] It was often a similar story elsewhere—in Kochi, the Corporation had only managed to utilise 35 per cent of allocated JNNURM funding by mid-2013.[48] Apart from problems such as a lack of local funds to acquire the land needed for projects (which the Centre would not provide), as in Kochi, a common issue was the release of land by Central agencies such as the National Highway Authority, the Railway Board, the Airports Authority, the Ministry of Defence and major port trusts. Some of the largest owners of urban land, they were often not very cooperative in assisting projects to tackle urban poverty.[49] At the state level the exercise of political initiative occasionally helped, as in 2012 when Shanti Dhariwal, Minister of Housing and Urban Development in the northern state of Rajasthan, took the lead in getting the state government to approve a transfer of land by the Forest Department to build 12,000 houses for slum dwellers in Jaipur under RAY, the follow up to JNNURM, following an intervention by the NGO PRIA.[50]

EVALUATING JNNURM: ASSESSING IMPACT AND MAKING CHANGES

Assessing the social impact that JNNURM has had on the mission cities is not easy. A 2009 mid-term report by the Hazards Centre that focused on six cities ranging from Kolkata (Category A) to Bodhgaya (Category C) noted significant gaps in the socio-economic profiles of those affected by projects, and its benefits to them, as well as 'The general level of ignorance about the genesis of projects, the lack of public participation in the preparation of plans, [and] the inability to distinguish JNNURM projects from non-JNNURM ones' (Roy 2009: 45). While the report did not come up with an overall evaluation, the burden of its findings was, unsurprisingly, negative.

It was an assessment that found echoes to varying degrees in subsequent studies conducted from different perspectives. In 2011 the leading accountancy and business consultancy firm Grant Thornton India submitted its report as the appraisal agency for JNNURM. It confirmed many of the misgivings expressed earlier in TAG as well as by critics. It found that city development plans were not 'owned' by the elected wing of the urban local body and were typically one-off hurried exercises prepared by external consultants to avail of funding (Grant Thornton 2011: 37). Apart from a few cities where NGOs had been actively engaged in the past (e.g. Ahmedabad), the level of consultation with the urban poor or NGOs representing their interests was seen to be uniformly low (ibid.: 49). Field visits to a few sample cities showed that housing projects undertaken under BSUP/IHSDP (the responsibility of MoHUPA) did not converge with UIG/UIDSSMT projects (the responsibility of MoUD) (ibid.: 258).

Another report on Indian Urban Infrastructure and Services was submitted in 2011 by the High Powered Expert Committee (HPEC) set up by MoUD. Chaired by the economist Isher Judge Ahluwalia[51], among its other eight members were two members of TAG, Ramesh Ramanathan and Professor O. P. Mathur. This report also criticised the CDPs as 'hastily put together' with a lack of community involvement, notably of elected ULB representatives and slum dwellers (HPEC 2011: 25, 33). It further noted the sluggish implementation of reforms in governance and financing and the rather limited success in promoting public–private partnerships, as well as how JNNURM had served to expose the lack of capacity of local governments to prepare and implement urban infrastructure projects (ibid.: 33–34). The Committee recommended a new improved and expanded (two and a half times as large) JNNURM with a 20-year duration and a unified mission structure under a single Ministry of Urban Affairs and Housing (Brazil's Ministry of Cities was cited as an exemplar), more resources allocated to capacity building (the example of the South African Municipal Infrastructure Programme was cited), and action by Central and state governments to encourage and facilitate ULBs to engage in PPP in areas including low-income housing (HPEC 2011: xxix, 79, 94, 100–102, 116–117).

These two reports were followed in 2012 by that of a committee chaired by Arun Maira—a former management consultant and Planning Commission member—which had been constituted by the Planning Commission in response to a request from Kamal Nath, the Minister for Urban Development. The brief of the committee was to make recommendations for the design of a 'JNNURM-II'; the 25 other committee members included 20 Union and state government officers and Planning Commission officials, Isher Judge Ahluwalia, three TAG members (O. P. Mathur, Sheela Patel and Ramesh Ramanathan), Renana Jhabvala of SEWA, and Hari Shankaran, Managing Director of Infrastructure Leasing and Financial Services Ltd., a Mumbai-based infrastructure development and finance company. Reflecting on JNNURM-I, the Maira Committee report made the following recommendations to address inadequacies:

> (i) a robust mechanism to ensure city and regional level planning to address the absence of carefully drawn CDPs and the near absence of any long term city or regional plans and the exclusion of peri-urban areas;
> (ii) lack of monitoring of service level outcomes (including social and gender audits) and not just expenditure;

> (iii) a separate Mission Directorate, more efficient and streamlined governance structure and greater investment (10 per cent of total funding) in capacity building to deal with the lack of the capacity necessary for effective delivery;
> (iv) calibration of reforms and norms for varied cities rather than a "one size fits all" approach;
> (v) devolution of financial powers to ULBs to address the major failure to attract private investment and develop PPP;[52]
> (vi) higher priority to be given to the completion of reforms with 10 per cent of funds to be allocated to an Incentive Fund for states carrying out reforms;
> (vii) simplification of implementation processes to address the slow, process heavy JNNURM-I mechanisms. (Maira 2012: 6–9)

The first two of the six key objectives set out were the removal of urban poverty and the improvement in urban services, including basic services for the urban poor (Maira 2012: 10). The Maira Committee recommended that JNNURM-II be of a ten-year duration following a two-year interim period (beginning 2012–13). It also recommended the discontinuation of BSUP and IHSDP and that RAY become a sub-mission of JNNURM-II to achieve better convergence (ibid.: 14). However, in its response the MoUD opined that RAY should be separate, that MoHUPA decide on discontinuing BSUP and IHSDP, and that the allocations for RAY and slum rehabilitation for cities be under MoHUPA, with UIG and capacity building under MoUD. It also rejected the need for a National Steering Group co-chaired by the ministers for Urban Development and Housing and Urban Poverty Alleviation (Maira 2012: Annex 10, pp. 8–14).

Some of the recommendations of the Maira Committee and HPEC reports were presaged in a 2010 McKinsey Global Institute report which notably cited London, Johannesburg and Shanghai as urban exemplars for transforming urban India (McKinsey Global Institute 2010: 88–92). It had recommended tripling annual funding for JNNURM and RAY, more radical reform of urban governance including the introduction of empowered, directly elected mayors in the biggest cities with a new incentive fund for states prepared to embark on more ambitious reform, greater investment in capacity building, and increased support for smaller, poorer cities (ibid.: 99, 152, 156–157, 163–165). However, looking forward to an India where by 2030, 53 per cent of the population could potentially be middle class, urban poverty was not a major focus of the report—the only mention of the poor in McKinsey's recommended urban operating model was with reference to affordable housing as it noted that an estimated 35 per cent of urban households could not afford a house and a quarter lived in slums 'that deface the urban landscape' (ibid.: 22, 46, 120, 138).

Perhaps the most damning report on JNNURM was the performance audit carried out by the CAG. With reference to the anti-poverty aspects, the BSUP and IHSDP completion rates compared poorly to the UIG and UIDSSMT projects—by March 2011 only 1.6 and 1.37 per cent had been completed as against 19.73 and 16.44 per cent of the latter (CAG 2013a: 7). In 2012, of 82 BSUP and IHSDP projects audited, only one had been completed, seven had not started and one had been abandoned. Delay in acquiring land was the major reason for slow completion. Eleven instances of deficiencies in the identification of beneficiaries were also identified, including a case in Kochi where those in three colonies were Corporation employees with a regular income who were not eligible under BSUP (CAG 2013a: viii). In September 2013 the mission period for projects sanctioned under BSUP and IHSDP, already extended from 31 March 2012 by two years, was further extended by a year to 31 March 2015 with no new projects to be sanctioned in the meantime[53] (in May 2015 the BJP-led NDA government elected in 2014 extended this by another two years to 31 March 2017[54]).

Political Response and the Emergence of RAY

The political reaction to all these evaluations was muted since those participating in the debate around them were mainly government bureaucrats and a few interested NGOs and civil society organisations. While one view is that the latter benefited from being able to, for the first time, critique national urban policy through evaluating the JNNURM,[55] others are more skeptical. In a controversial commentary, N. C. Saxena described many NGO activists as populists who think with their hearts, not their brains, catering to a constituency of 'habitual seminar participants' (Saxena 2013a: 4)! To gain the active engagement of key politicians in early 2010, K. C. Sivaramakrishnan reported to TAG that he had met Rahul Gandhi and suggested that he talk to his party and get its stand on metropolitan planning.[56] He also wrote to Saugata Roy, the All India Trinamul Congress Minister of State for Urban Development, who agreed that the issue demanded immediate engagement; Digvijay Singh, Congress general secretary and former chief minister of Madhya Pradesh, did not respond. Although other TAG members were positive about Sivaramakrishnan's efforts to engage key politicians, nothing came of it.

President Pratibha Patil's speech to the new Parliament following the UPA's return to power in the 2009 election included an extravagant promise to create a slum-free India in five years through the Rajiv Awas Yojana for slum dwellers and the urban poor.[57] An influential voice close to the prime minister who was particularly concerned that JNNURM should address the plight of the urban poor was R. Gopalakrishnan, Joint Secretary and then Additional Secretary in the PMO from 2004, until shortly before his premature demise in 2012. Having advocated the extension of property rights to slum dwellers under the JNNURM recommendation for affordable security of tenure for the urban poor (Gopalakrishnan 2009), he was credited with contributing to the genesis of RAY.[58] Gopalakrishnan was convinced that assigning property rights to the quarter of the urban population living in slums allowed for *in situ* rehabilitation, while unlocking the potential for partnership with the private sector in investing in education and healthcare to create new social development zones' in India's cities: 'The hope is that the more articulate urban poor who understand that "crumbs of bread, are well, crumbs of bread, and not the whole loaf", may be able to wrest more, beginning with property rights under RAY' (Gopalakrishnan 2011).

Unlike with JNNURM, seen primarily as an infrastructure programme, the NAC chaired by Sonia Gandhi also sought to participate in formulating RAY. Sandeep Chachra, a social anthropologist and Executive Director of ActionAid India, drafted the recommendations of a working group on urban poverty on reforming RAY, which were communicated to the government in December 2011.[59] The recommendations aimed at ensuring that no slum dwellers were left out from the purview of the scheme, that the necessary major investment was made in providing them with basic services, that 25 to 40 per cent of land in city development plans should be dedicated to housing the urban poor to prevent future slums, and that there was effective community participation. In September 2013 MoHUPA Secretary A. K. Misra reported to the NAC that these recommendations had been factored into the implementation strategy for RAY and the new National Urban Livelihood Mission (NULM) approved by the Union Cabinet on 3 September 2013[60]. RAY, having completed its initial two-year preparatory phase, was to run together with the NULM, a restructuring of the Swarna Jayanti Shahari Rozgar Yojana, from 2013 to 2022.[61]

CONCLUSION

It is clear from the record that the economic and social impact of JNNURM on urban poverty is debatable. In the last decade although the annual rates of decline for both rural and urban poverty have increased, the latter has declined less while the increase in urban inequality has been greater, taking it to 0.4 per cent compared to 0.31 per cent in rural India (Saxena 2013b: 8, 11). It has not been transformative or inclusive, entrenching existing patterns and building some infrastructural capacity without necessarily improving services, certainly for the poor. Perhaps the most important impact that JNNURM has had is to make urban issues, and thus also urban poverty, part of the national policy agenda. Although this has not yet translated into the national political agenda, there is now a greater likelihood that it may and that a national urban programme is here to stay. This was evident with the advent of the BJP-led NDA government of Narendra Modi in 2014. In June 2015 Modi launched three huge flagship urban programmes, superseding JNNURM and RAY—the Atal Mission for Rejuvenation and Urban Transformation (AMRUT), the Smart Cities Mission, and Housing for All (Urban).[62] However, the new government's ambitious vision also did not have tackling urban poverty at its centre, and a recent study asked:

> If the predominant visual of the 'smart city' is one in which there is no space for the poor, who are these cities being created for, and can this be a sustainable and equitable model to be pursued at this stage of India's development? (HLRN 2017: 3)

The starting point for a politics that addresses urban poverty is a genuine recognition of the reasons for the presence and scale of the urban poor. This will only come about through the invigoration of urban politics which requires substantive reform of the institutions of urban governance, something that JNNURM could not accomplish and its successor programmes do not address.

NOTES AND REFERENCES

1. Janaagraha claims credit for having successfully lobbied for, and contributed to, the design of the JNNURM, originally available at http://www.janaagraha.org/content/artifact/jawaharlal-national-urban-renewal-mission (accessed 9 August 13; site discontinued).

2. Interview with Ramesh Ramanathan, by James Manor, New Delhi, 27 November 2013.

3. In December 2016, Baijal was appointed lieutenant-governor of Delhi by Narendra Modi's NDA government after his predecessor's resignation following disagreements with Delhi Chief Minister Arvind Kejriwal's Aam Aadmi Party administration. However, he soon also found himself engaged in a prolonged bitter confrontation with Kejriwal.

4. 'Anil Baijal new Home Secy', *The Times of India*, 29 January 2004. Available at http://articles.timesofindia.indiatimes.com/2004-01-29/delhi/28345440_1_anil-baijal-delhi-development-authority-subhash-sharma (accessed 16 October 13).

5. However, as it turned out, the World Bank's subsequent involvement in JNNURM was peripheral and it was not until 2011 that the Bank signed a credit agreement with the Government of India, committing US$ 60 million to a Capacity Building for Urban Development Project 'for building the capacity of select Urban Local Bodies (ULBs) to improve their skills for better urban management and thereby reduce urban poverty' (press release: http://www.worldbank.org/en/country/india/whats-new?qterm=JnNURM&lang_exact=English (accessed 27 September 13); and interview with Barjor Mehta, World Bank India urban specialist, New Delhi, 13 September 2013).

6. Interview with Anil Baijal, New Delhi, 13 August 2013.

7. 'Jawaharlal Nehru National Urban Renewal Mission launched'. Available at http://pib.nic.in/newsite/erelcontent.aspx?relid=13823 (accessed 30 September 17).

8. 'Naxalism is gravest internal threat: PM', *The Times of India*, 13 April 2006. Available at http://articles.timesofindia.indiatimes.com/2006-04-13/delhi/27823231_1_naxal-hit-states-internal-security-time-tested-strategy (accessed 16 October 13).

9. Subsequently increased to 67.

10. Interview with Dunu Roy, Director, Hazards Centre, New Delhi, 12 August 2013.

11. Interview with N. C. Saxena, member, NAC, New Delhi, 11 September 2013.

12. Speech to 24th Session of the Governing Council Meeting of UN-Habitat, Nairobi, April 2013. Available at (www.unhabitat.org/downloads/docs/12085_1_595016.pdf (accessed 11 October 13).

13. See also 'S. Jaipal Reddy, 57 Minister of Urban Development', *The Indian Express*, 21 May 2009. Available at http://www.indianexpress.com/news/s.-jaipal-reddy-57-minister-of-urban-development/463847/0 (accessed 31 July 2019).

14. Interview with N. C. Saxena, New Delhi, 11 September 2013.

15. http://mhupa.gov.in/pdf/guidelines-scheme/urbanemp-povallev/Swarna%20Jayanti/ReGuidelinesSJSRY.pdf (accessed 22 October 13).

16. Interview with Anil Baijal, New Delhi, 13 August 2013.

17. GoI Notification No. K-14012/101/2006-NURM, dated 27 February 2006. Available at http://mail.sarai.net/pipermail/urbanstudygroup_mail.sarai.net/2006-September/002497.html (accessed 14 October13).

18. Manoj Rai, Director of the 'Action Learning Initiatives' of another NGO working in urban India, Participatory Research in Asia (PRIA), says, 'Urban data collection is in a mess with uncertainty even about the number of slums in a city. This makes nonsense of urban planning'. (Interview with Manoj Rai, New Delhi, 7 August 2013).

19. Minutes of TAG meetings on 17 June, 18 October and 23 November 2006. Originally available at http://jnnurm.nic.in/minutes-of-tag-meeting-2.html (accessed 6 August 13; site discontinued).

20. Interview with Shubhagato Dasgupta, Senior Fellow, Centre for Policy Research, and formerly team leader of the Support to National Policies for Urban Poverty Reduction project, a Department for International Development, UK, and MoHUPA partnership project, New Delhi, 8 August 2013.

21. For instance, an article (see Krishna 2013) on JNNURM by Sudhir Krishna, Secretary, MoUD, from 2011, arguing the need for a public–private partnership omitted any mention of the poor except implicitly in referring to the expansion of slums.

22. Interview with Parth Shah, President, Centre for Civil Society, New Delhi, 9 August 2013.

23. Interview with Anil Baijal, New Delhi, 13 August 2013.

24. File No.: K-14012/156/06-NURM, Minutes of 7th Technical Advisory Group Meeting, 17 May 2007. Originally available at http://jnnurm.nic.in/minutes-of-tag-meeting-2.html (accessed 6 August 2013; site discontinued).

25. 'Local bodies not able to raise funds', *The Hindu*, 27 October 2007. Available at http://www.hindu.com/2007/10/27/stories/2007102752690500.htm (accessed 6 August 2013). This point was also stressed by K. J. Sohan, a former mayor of the port city of Kochi in Kerala and chairman of its Standing Committee for Town Planning, who said it was unrealistic to expect these cities to foot such a share of the cost (interview with Vagomon, Kerala, 30 March 2013); Funding Shares by City Categories, originally available at http://www.jnnurm.co.in/funding-shares-by-city-categories.htm (accessed 29 October 13; site discontinued).

26. Interview with Amitabh Kundu, New Delhi, 11 September 2013; see also Kundu 2011: 47–48.

27. Ibid.

28. Minutes of 9th National TAG Meeting, 10 October 2007. Originally available at http://jnnurm.nic.in/minutes-of-tag-meeting-2.html (accessed 6 August 2013; site discontinued).

29. Interview with Dunu Roy, New Delhi, 12 August 2013.

30. Over All Progress of JNNURM under BSUP and IHSDP – National Level As on 01/10/2013. Originally available at https://jnnurmmis.nic.in/jnnurm_hupa/jnnurm/Jnnurm_Ray_AHP_Progress_Report/Jnnurm_Glance_All_Progress.pdf (accessed 29 October 13; site discontinued).

31. File No.: K-14012/156/06-NURM, Minutes of 7th Technical Advisory Group Meeting, 17 May 2007. Originally available at http://jnnurm.nic.in/minutes-of-tag-meeting-2.html (accessed 6 August 2013; site discontinued).

32. Manoj Rai of PRIA cited the example of the frustration experienced by Vani Rao, the Mayor of Bilaspur in Chhattisgarh (interview with Manoj Rai, New Delhi, 7 August 2013).

33. Interview with Sundar Burra, advisor, SPARC, New Delhi, 12 September 2013.

34. Minutes of 1st and 22nd JNNURM TAG meetings, 17 March 2006, and 4 May 2009. Originally available at http://jnnurm.nic.in/minutes-of-tag-meeting-2.html (accessed 6 August 2013; site discontinued).

35. Interview with Parth Shah, New Delhi, 9 August 2013.

36. Interview with Amitabh Kundu, New Delhi, 11 September 2013. See also Kundu 2011: 39.

37. Interview with Manoj Rai, New Delhi, 7 August 2013. Available at http://www.pria.org/in-focus-strengthening-voices-of-civil-society-on-urban-poverty/voices-on-urban-poverty (accessed 6 August 2013).

38. Interview with Shubhagato Dasgupta, New Delhi, 8 August 2013.

39. Interview with Partha Mukhopadhyay, Senior Research Fellow, Centre for Policy Research, New Delhi, 8 August 2013.

40. Interview with Anil Baijal, New Delhi, 13 August 2013.

41. http://jnnurm.nic.in/minutesofthemeetingsofcsmc.html (accessed 30 October 13; site discontinued).

42. File No.: K/14012/156/06-NURM, 8th National Technical Advisory Group Meeting, 2 August 2007; Minutes of 22nd and 25th National Technical Advisory Group Meetings, 4 May 2009, and 15 October 2009. Originally available at http://jnnurm.nic.in/minutes-of-tag-meeting-2.html (accessed 6 August 2013; site discontinued).

43. Minutes of 23rd and 25th National Technical Advisory Group Meetings, 26 June 2009, and 15 October 2009. Originally available at

http://jnnurm.nic.in/minutes-of-tag-meeting-2.html (accessed 6 August 2013; site discontinued).

44. Minutes of 25th National Technical Advisory Group Meeting, 15 October 2009. Originally available at http://jnnurm.nic.in/minutes-of-tag-meeting-2.html (accessed 6 August 2013; site discontinued).

45. Interviews by James Manor and James Chiriyankandath with, amongst others, Shubhagato Dasgupta, Renana Jhabvala (Chairperson, Self-Employed Women's Association Bank, Ahmedabad), Partha Mukhopadhyay, Dunu Roy and Parth Shah, April to August 2013.

46. Interview, New Delhi, 14 August 2013. See also Complete Biodata, Executive Record Sheet Generator (IAS Officers), originally available at http://www.persmin.nic.in/ersheet/MultipleERS.asp?HiddenStr=01MH042000 (accessed 13 September 13; site discontinued).

47. 'JNNURM funds drained out', *The Times of India*, Bangalore, 7 June 2013. Available at http://timesofindia.indiatimes.com/city/bengaluru/JNNURM-funds-drained-out/articleshow/20468219.cms (accessed 30 August 13).

48. 'Kochi city scores low in JNNURM report card', *The Hindu*, 15 July 2013. Available at http://www.thehindu.com/todays-paper/tp-national/tp-kerala/kochi-city-scores-low-in-jnnurm-report-card/article4916433.ece (accessed 30 August 13).

49. Sundar Burra, interview, New Delhi, 12 September 2013. See also Sundar Burra's Presentation to the Planning Commission, 25 January 2007: 17 Urban Development, 'Shri Sundar Burra, SPARC', 25/01/07. Available at http://planningcommission.nic.in/data/ngo/index.php?data=b_ngobody.htm (accessed 4 August 2019).

50. Manoj Rai, interview, New Delhi, 7 August 2013. See also http://terraurban.wordpress.com/2012/05/17/rajasthan-govt-clears-biggest-rehabilitation-scheme-for-slum-dwellers/ (accessed 12 October 13).

51. She is married to Montek Singh Ahluwalia, Deputy Chairman of the Planning Commission.

52. In its response to the report the MoUD accepted that JNNURM-I had not attracted sufficient private investment yet remarked 'but we may not call it a failure' (Maira 2012: Annex 10, p. 4).

53. Office Memorandum No. N-11027/3/2012-BSUP/IHSDP/JNNURM/FTS-5089, MoHUPA, 18 September 2013. Originally available at http://mhupa.gov.in/W_new/OM_18_09_2013.pdf (accessed 26 September 13; link discontinued).

54. Office Memorandum No. N-11027/63/2014-PPG/FTS-12160, MoHUPA, 12 May 2015. Originally available at http://jnnurmmis.nic.in/jnnurm_hupa/jnnurm/JnNURM_Extention_16-17.pdf (accessed 1 September 17; site discontinued).

55. Interview with Dunu Roy, New Delhi, 12 August 2013.

56. Minutes of 29th National Technical Advisory Group Meeting, 25 February 2010. Originally available at http://jnnurm.nic.in/minutes-of-tag-meeting-2.html (accessed 6 August 2013; site discontinued).

57. Full text of the 'Address by the Hon'ble President of India, Pratibha Devisingh Patil, to Parliament', New Delhi, 4 June 2009. Available at http://pratibhapatil.nic.in/sp040609.html (accessed 3 August 2019). By one account, MoHUPA was not even consulted about the announcement in the President's speech, although the ministry thereafter moved quickly to draft a concept note and develop a model regulatory framework for a nationally uniform approach to according property rights to slum dwellers/urban poor ('Action Taken Report on 100 Days Agenda of Ministry of Housing Urban Poverty Alleviation, 1 September 2009. Originally available at http://mhupa.gov.in/w_new/100DaysAgenda.pdf (accessed 30 May 2013; link discontinued).

58. Interview with K. C. Sivaramakrishan, New Delhi, 8 August 2013.

59. 'Recommendations of the National Advisory Council – Reforms Proposed for the Rajiv Awas Yojana', 20 December 2011. Originally available at http://nac.nic.in/pdf/reforms_ray.pdf (accessed 17 September 13; link discontinued).

60. Originally available at http://nac.nic.in/press_releases/27_september_2013.pdf (accessed 1 October 13; link discontinued).

61. Available at http://pib.nic.in/newsite/erelease.aspx?relid=99202 (accessed 17 September 13).

62. 'Cities should get chance to plan their growth, says Modi', *The Hindu*, 25 June 2015. Available at http://www.thehindu.com/news/national/prime-minister-narendra-modi-launches-smart-cities-mission/article7353823.ece (accessed 1 September 17).

seven

Conclusion

In this book we have analysed the political and policy processes that led to the substantial expansion of India's welfare regime during the UPA-I and UPA-II governments. The expansion was not merely quantitative, introducing new programmes or expanding existing ones. Rather, India's welfare regime was radically transformed. For a long time, India's social security system was confined to 'labour aristocracies' in the formal sector of the economy, thus leaving more than 90 per cent of the workforce without any substantial form of social protection. Programmes for workers in the informal sector did exist—the PDS or the ICDS, for instance—but these were largely ineffective and fell far short in reaching the great majority of the population. After 2004, however, India's welfare regime changed in at least two important ways. First, the number of people that were entitled or able to access social protection programmes increased dramatically, mainly because of the gradual abandonment of having a BPL card as a criterion to access the State's support and because of the radical extension in coverage. Second, many of the policies introduced or reformed by the UPA government are now legal entitlements either because they are backed by legislation (like the MGNREGA or the NFSA) or because they are protected by Supreme Court orders (like the ICDS) (Drèze and Khera 2017a).

We showed how this transformation arose out of compulsions originating from India's democratic system. Competition between the Congress and the BJP created incentives for the former to give substance to the 'myth' that its electoral success in 2004 was due to a revolt of the poor against the 'arrogance' of the BJP's 'India Shining' campaign. This facilitated a post-poll alliance with the parties of the Left Front, which negotiated with the Congress Party a CMP that was, albeit partially, translated into reality in the following years.

The design of the UPA's anti-poverty initiatives benefited greatly from the openness and breadth of the policy community. The creation of the NAC—and its composition—marked a substantial break with the past in terms of how policies are designed and negotiated. Instead of formulating policies behind closed doors and within a restricted group of professional policy-makers, the UPA allowed progressive civil society individuals with a deep, on-the-ground experience on social policy implementation to play a major role, both in terms of policy-design and in terms of advocacy and lobbying. Crucially, these individuals and organisations—many of whom were associated with the Right to Food Campaign—could cooperate with other democratic institutions such as the Supreme Court and parliamentary committees to push for the adoption of progressive legislation and to ensure that fiscal conservatives and other opponents within government circles did not succeed in undermining the progressive character of the policies.

Finally, some influential political leaders were crucial in explaining why the anti-poverty initiatives of the UPA took the form they did. In particular, the UPA's chairperson, Sonia Gandhi, used her political capital to remove obstacles during the policy formulation process, defended the NAC by putting her weight behind it and letting her party members—particularly MPs—know that she was keen on translating into reality the promises of the CMP. Conversely, other important political leaders—like Prime Minister Manmohan Singh—had a more ambiguous role, at times supporting, at times opposing legislation and initiatives that would expand India's social policy commitments. But their contribution to explanations of the form taken by India's welfare regime remained important.

In this concluding chapter, we will look at the impact of the expansion of that welfare regime on India's human development. This chapter does not offer rigorous impact evaluations. Rather, we will show how—thanks to vigorous economic growth, coupled with the substantial expansion of welfare initiatives during the UPA years—the living conditions of a sizable portion of India's population changed for the better.

POVERTY AND INEQUALITY

A first, crude indication of the effectiveness of the UPA's policy initiatives is the quite sharp reduction of poverty between 2004 and 2014. Of course, economic growth, which averaged at 7.71 per cent[1] per year between 2004 and 2014, is a big part of the explanation for the sharp reduction in the number of people living below the poverty line (Table 7.1). This is not only because, despite the severe inequities in the distribution of the fruits of growth, most sections of society tend to benefit from it. It is also because higher growth results in higher revenues which can then be redistributed through higher expenditures in public services and social policies. Between 2002 and 2012, India's Central government's revenues increased from 17.73 to 19.72 per cent of the GDP, which amounts to an increase by about 300 per cent in absolute terms (Maiorano and Manor 2017).

As Table 7.1 shows, poverty levels and the intensity of poverty (as measured by the poverty gap) decreased sharply between 2004 and 2011 and at a much faster rate than in the previous 11 years (which were also years of sustained economic growth of 6 per cent per annum). The table uses the World Bank's poverty lines which, like any measure of poverty, are somewhat arbitrary. However, using different poverty lines would not change the picture significantly.

It should be noted, however, that as much as 60.4 per cent of the population still lives below the poverty line at 3.20 PPP US$/day. This means that there is a vast section of the population that lives on the edge of extreme poverty, and is just 'one illness away' from descending into it (Krishna 2011). This underscores the importance

TABLE 7.1: Poverty reduction between 1993 and 2011

	1993	*2004*	*2011*	*% Change 1993–2004*	*% Change 2004–2011*
Poverty headcount ratio at US$ 1.90 a day (2011 PPP) (% of population)	45.90	38.20	21.20	−16.7	−44.5
Poverty headcount ratio at US$ 3.20 a day (2011 PPP) (% of population)	81.10	75.20	60.40	−7.2	−19.7
Poverty gap at US$ 1.90 a day (2011 PPP) (% of population)	12.10	9.20	4.30	−23.9	−53.2
Poverty gap at US$ 3.20 a day (2011 PPP) (% of population)	34.40	29.80	19.70	−13.3	−33.8

Source: World Development Indicators.

PPP: purchasing power parity

of social safety nets like the MGNREGA, which prevented as many as 14 million families from falling back into poverty, according to a recent study (Desai, Vashishtha and Joshi 2015). The PDS, on the other hand, allows millions of families—67 per cent of the population, as per the NFSA—to purchase food at highly subsidised prices, thus sheltering them from fluctuations in market prices. Social policies are also important in reducing the incidence and depth of poverty. Klonner and Oldiges (2014), for instance, calculated that the MGNREGA reduced the poverty gap by about one-fifth. More generally, it is now widely accepted that economic growth does not automatically 'trickle down' to the poor, and that social policies play a substantial role in reducing and/or mitigating poverty (Barrientos 2013).

The expansion of India's welfare regime that we analysed in this book led to a substantial increase of the proportion of people who are able to access the State's support. According to calculations made by Drèze and Khera (2017), the three largest policies that we have analysed (MGNREGA, ICDS, PDS) led to an expansion of the population benefiting—from 92 per cent to 5,700 per cent between 2004/05 and 2011/12 (Table 7.2).

TABLE 7.2: Expansion of social protection programmes, 2004/05–2011/12

		2004/05	2011/12	Change 2004/05–2011/12
ICDS	Pregnant women accessing the services	20	53	+165%
	Children accessing the services	27	57	+111%
MGNREGA	Proportion of rural households that worked on MGNREGA or similar local public works in the past 12 months	0.5	29	+5,700%
PDS	Proportion of households that bought rice or wheat from the PDS in the last 30 days	27	52	+92%

Source: Drèze and Khera 2017: Table 1.

So the proportion of people entitled to benefit from government policies expanded substantially during the UPA years. For instance, the MGNREGA substituted for previous employment programmes that mostly targeted people possessing a BPL card, and made it a right of every Indian citizen residing in rural areas to get employment on demand. Similarly, the universalisation of the ICDS and the Midday Meal schemes effectively made access to these programmes a right of every eligible person. The RTF Act expanded the target population to two-thirds of Indian citizens. Table 7.2 shows that this expansion in coverage did not remain on paper—it was translated into a significant expansion of India's social security net.

Overall, the UPA's record at reducing poverty through a combination of solid economic growth and increased efforts to protect the poor was significant and probably better than that of any other previous Indian government, although countries like Brazil, China and South Africa reduced extreme poverty at an even faster pace (Maiorano and Manor 2017).

Much less impressive has been the UPA's record at reducing inequalities, an extremely difficult task, especially in periods of high growth. A panel survey of over 45,000 households across the country found that, between 2004–05 and 2011–12, the per capita income of India's poorer sections of society (SCs, STs and Muslims) increased significantly more than that of the most privileged social groups (upper-caste Hindus). The same study found that household incomes in rural areas had increased more between 2004 and 2012 than had urban household incomes (in percentage terms) (Desai, Vashishtha and Joshi 2015). Yet, while this means that the UPA's policies were reaching the poorest of the poor—a very difficult task in itself—income inequality actually increased (Table 7.3).

TABLE 7.3: Inequality measurers, 1993–2011

	1993	2004	2011
Gini coefficient (expenditure based)*	30.77	34.12	35.15
Gini coefficient (income based)**	NA	47.2	47.9
Income share top 10% ***	25.98	28.26	29.98
Income share bottom 10% ***	3.95	3.75	3.52

Source: *World Bank World Income Inequality Database.
**LIS Key figures (available at: http://www.lisdatacenter.org/data-access/key-figures/)
***World Bank Poverty and Equity Database

While both Gini coefficients indicate that income inequality increased during the UPA years, they present two rather different pictures of inequality in India. According to the first (expenditure-based) coefficient, India is a relatively low-inequality country. However, if we measure the Gini coefficient using income instead—the methodology used in most countries of the world—India's figure is close to Brazil's, one of the most unequal countries on the planet (which had a Gini of 49.48 in 2014). This would be consistent with data on wealth inequalities, in which the Gini coefficient increased from 77.8 to 83.1 between 2010 and 2015. Brazil's figure (83) was slightly lower than India's in 2015 (Credit Suisse 2015).

High and increasing inequalities, moreover, reinforce other types of inequalities, especially gender and caste. A recent study clearly shows how economic and social inequalities translate into startling differences in living conditions. Table 7.4 shows the average year of death of different sections of Indian society (Borooah 2018).

TABLE 7.4: Average year of death by social status, 2004–14

	2004	2014	% Change 2004–14
ST	45	43	−4.4%
SC	42	48	+14.3%
OBC Muslims	43	50	+16.3%
OBC non-Muslims	49	52	+6.1%
Upper caste Muslims	44	49	+11.4%
Upper caste non-Muslims	55	60	+9.1%

Source: Borooah 2018.

Scheduled Tribes live on average for as many as 17 years less than upper-caste non-Muslims. Clearly, the State must do much more to protect its more vulnerable citizens, starting with investments in health and education.

HEALTH AND EDUCATION

The poor record in health and education is perhaps the greatest failure of the Indian State. Youth literacy rates today are lower than in China in 1982, when the latter was not only immensely poorer than today's India, but also poorer than India at that time. Life expectancy in India today is only slightly higher than in China in 1985. This has much to do with very low levels of public expenditure on health and education since Independence.

The UPA governments did little to change the situation, despite the introduction of two important initiatives: the National Rural Health Mission and the Right to Education Act. As Table 7.5 shows, India's expenditure on health and education increased only marginally and remains lower than in most other countries in the world.

India has therefore, and in comparative terms, invested very little in crucial public services, focusing the bulk of its

TABLE 7.5: Health and education expenditure, 2004–13 (% of GDP)

		2000	2004	2013
Combined public expenditure on health and education	India	5.25	4.11	4.71
	Latin America	6.68	6.70	8.88
	Sub-Saharan Africa	5.03	5.71	6.32
	South Asia	3.47	3.31	3.83
	East Asia and Pacific	7.93*	8.20	8.72
	OECD	10.13	11.4	12.86
Public expenditure on health	India	0.86	0.71	0.86
	Latin America	2.82	2.95	3.53
	Sub-Saharan Africa	1.86	3.62	1.82
	South Asia	0.93	0.75	0.85
	East Asia and Pacific	4.38*	4.34	4.59
	OECD	5.27	6.36	7.61
Public expenditure on education	India	4.38	3.40	3.84
	Latin America	3.86	3.75	5.22
	Sub-Saharan Africa	3.17	2.09	4.50
	South Asia	2.55	2.56	2.98
	East Asia and Pacific	3.55*	3.85	4.12
	OECD	4.86	5.04	5.26

Source: World Development Indicators.

*Data are from 2001.

developmental expenditure on poverty-reduction programmes (Kapur and Nangia 2015), possibly because of their higher visibility and political returns, and the distribution of some resources along clientelistic chains from the top to the bottom of the system.

The UPA years were nevertheless a period of important progress when we consider a number of human development indicators. As Table 7.6 shows, there was a steep acceleration during these years, from an already positive trend, in the proportion of children attending school. This has much to do with the long overdue establishment of free and compulsory education through the Right to Education Act, 2009. But other policies helped to keep children in schools. Children from families participating in the MGNREGA, for instance, are more likely to attain higher education and have higher learning outcomes (Desai, Vashishtha and Joshi 2015).[2] Similarly, there is a wealth of evidence that nutritional programmes like the Midday Meal Scheme and the ICDS have had positive repercussions on children's education by promoting school attendance and by making children more focused in school as they get less distracted by hunger (Drèze and Khera 2017). Very importantly, moreover, India closed the gender gap in terms of the proportion of children out of school, and it has made substantial progress in terms of youth literacy levels. A major concern, however, remains the quality of education, which remains very low, particularly in rural areas (ASER 2019).

TABLE 7.6: Changes in key education indicators, 1990–2013

	1990			*2003*			*2013*			*Change 1990–2003*	*Change 2003–13*
	T	*F*	*M*	*T*	*F*	*M*	*T*	*F*	*M*	*T*	*T*
Children* out of school	22.5	34.6	11.2	11.3	12.7	10	2.3	1.6	2.9	−49.9%	−79.8%
	1991			*2001*			*2011*			*Change 1991–2001*	*Change 2001–2011*
	T	*F*	*M*	*T*	*F*	*M*	*T*	*F*	*M*	*T*	*T*
Literacy rates of youth**	62.9	49.3	73.5	76.4	67.6	84.2	86.1	81.9	90	+23%	+13%

Source: World Development Indicators.
*% of primary school age
**% of ages 15–24

There have been marked improvements in health outcomes as well (Table 7.7). Data on selective health indicators reveal a picture similar to those on education: a positive trend since the 1990s accelerated further during the UPA years. There has also been important progress in other dimensions of people's well-being like immunisation rates, children's nutritional status, and ante- and post-natal care.[3]

TABLE 7.7: Changes in key health indicators, 1990–2015

	1990			*2004*			*2015*			*Change 1990–2004*	*Change 2004–15*
	T	F	M	T	F	M	T	F	M	T	T
Life expectancy at birth	57.9	58.2	57.6	64.2	65	63.3	68.3	69.9	66.9	+10.8%	+6%
Mortality rate, infant (per 1,000 live births)	88.4	86.20	90.5	57.7	NA	NA	36.2	36.3	36	−34.7%	−37.2%
Mortality rate, under-5 (per 1,000 live births)	125.9	130.2	121.9	77.7	NA	NA	45.2	46.7	43.9	−38.2%	−41.8%
Maternal mortality ratio (national estimate, per 100,000 live births)	NA	NA	NA	NA	254	NA	NA	130	NA	NA	−48.8%

Source: World Development Indicators.

The UPA governments laid the foundations for a more inclusive welfare regime in India. This, coupled with robust economic growth, has translated into a significant betterment on a number of human development indicators. This does not mean that India's developmental problems have been solved. The newly released Multidimensional Poverty figures depict a still alarming picture: in 2012, as much as 41.3 per cent of the population was multidimensionally poor (OPHI 2017). The figure for rural India is 53.5 per cent. Furthermore, an additional 22 per cent is considered vulnerable to multidimensional poverty. The proportion of people in multidimensional poverty is only 4 per cent in China, 5.3 per cent in Brazil and 15.5 per cent in Indonesia. India's figures, rather than being comparable to those of other emerging economies, are similar to those of much poorer countries like Pakistan or Bangladesh and even Sub-Saharan African countries like Kenya or Namibia.[4] While there have been marked improvements in this measure of poverty as well—multidimensional poverty declined from 53.7 per cent in 2006 to 41.3 per cent in 2017—there clearly is an urgent need for the Indian State to increase its efforts to tackle poverty and other forms of deprivation, particularly in terms of the provision of essential public services. Failing to do so might extract a very high price, not only by depriving a very sizable part of its population from reaping the benefits of India's growth story, but also by preventing the fulfillment of its ambitions to become one of the pillars of the future world economic order. As Amartya Sen bitterly remarked, 'India is the only country trying to become a global economic power with an uneducated and unhealthy labour force'[5].

NOTES AND REFERENCES

1. In per capita terms, GDP grew at 6.20 per cent per year, on average.
2. Other studies confirmed these results, e.g. Mani et al. 2014. Another study, however, argued that participating in the MGNREGA reduces educational attainments of older children (aged 13–16), while effects on younger children remain significantly positive (Shah and Steinberg 2015).
3. See NFHS-4 (2017) for further details.
4. OPHI data tables. Available at: https://ophi.org.uk/multidimensional-poverty-index/global-mpi-2017/mpi-data/ (accessed 4 August 2019).
5. Sen 2015. Interview with Amartya Sen, conducted by Sonali Campion and Taryana Odayar, at the London School of Economics and Political Science, 6 November 2015. Available at: http://blogs.lse.ac.uk/southasia/2015/11/19/india-is-the-only-country-in-the-world-trying-to-become-a-global-economic-power-with-an-uneducated-and-unhealthy-labour-force-amartya-sen/ (accessed 5 August 2019).

Bibliography

Abreu, D. et al. 2012. Open Letter to the Prime Minister. 'Simplifying the National Food Security Bill'. *Outlook*. 12 March 2012. Available at http://www.scribd.com/doc/85054632/Simplifying-the-NFS-948744a (accessed 19 May 2012).

Accountability Initiative. 2013. *Budget Briefs. JNNURM, GOI, 2013–14*. New Delhi: Accountability Initiative, Centre for Policy Research. Available at http://accountabilityindia.in/sites/default/files/jnnurm_2013-14.pdf (accessed 8 March 13).

Afridi, F. and V. Iversen. 2014. 'Social Audits and MGNREGA Delivery: Lessons from Andhra Pradesh'. *India Policy Forum* 10(1): 297–341. April. National Council of Applied Economic Research.

Afridi, F., V. Iversen and M. R. Sharan. n.d. 'Women Political Leaders, Corruption and Learning: Evidence from a Large Public Program in India'. IZA Discussion Papers.

Aggarwal, A. and H. Mander. 2013. 'Abandoning the Right to Food'. *Economic and Political Weekly* 48(8): 23–25.

Ahmed, S. and A. Varshney. 2008. *Battles Half Won: The Political Economy of India's Growth and Economic Policy since Independence*. Washington: The World Bank.

Alderman, H., J. R. Behrman and C. Puett. 2017. 'Big Numbers about Small Children: Estimating the Economic Benefits of Addressing Undernutrition'. *The World Bank Research Observer* 32(1): 107–125.

Aiyar, Mani Shankar. 2009. 'The Politics of Poverty'. *India Today*. 13 August.

Aiyar, S. and A. Mody. 2011. 'The Demographic Dividend: Evidence from the Indian States'. IMF Working paper 11/38. Washington, DC: International Monetary Fund.

ASER. 2014. *Annual Status of Education Report*. New Delhi: ASER Centre.

———. 2019. *Annual Status of Education Report (Rural) 2018 – Provisional*. New Delhi: ASER Centre. 15 January. Available at img.asercentre.org/docs/ASER%202018/Release%20Material/aserreport2018.pdf (accessed 4 August 2019).

Balchand, K. 2012. 'Now, Planning Commission Lowers the Poverty Line'. *The Hindu*. 20 March. Available at http://www.thehindu.com/news/national/article3013870.ece (accessed 17 May 2012).

Balarajan, Y. and M. R. Reich. 2016. 'Political Economy of Child Nutrition Policy: A Qualitative Study of India's Integrated Child Development Services (ICDS) Scheme'. *Food Policy* 62: 88–98.

Bandi, M. 2013. 'Implementation of the Forest Rights Act: Undoing Historical Injustices'. *Economic and Political Weekly* 48(31): 22. 3 August; citing, 'India's Forest Rights Act of 2006 – Illusion or Solution?', a briefing paper by the Asian Indigenous and Tribal People's Network (AITPN), New Delhi, 15 December 2006.

Banerjee, A., E. Duflo, C. Imbert, S. Mathew and R. Pande. 2015. 'Can E-governance Reduce Capture of Public Programs? Experimental Evidence from India's Employment Guarantee'. *3ie Grantee Final Report*. New Delhi: International Initiative for Impact Evaluation (3ie).

Bardhan, Pranab. 2011. 'Challenges for a Minimum Social Democracy in India'. *Economic and Political Weekly* 46(10). 5 March.

Bardhan, P. and D. Mookherjee. 2006. *Decentralization and Local Governance in Developing Countries: A Comparative Perspective*. Cambridge, MA: MIT Press.

Barrientos, A. 2013. *Social Assistance in Developing Countries*. Cambridge: Cambridge University Press.

Baru, R. V., R. Dasgupta, M. Deshpande and A. Mohanty. 2008. 'Full Meal or Package Deal?'. *Economic and Political Weekly* 43(24): 20–22. 14 June.

Basole, A. and D. Basu. 2015. 'Fuelling Calorie Intake Decline: Household-Level Evidence from Rural India'. *World Development* 68: 82–95.

Berg, E., S. Bhattacharyya, D. Rajasekhar and R. Manjula. 2017. 'Can Public Works Increase Equilibrium Wages? Evidence from India's National Rural Employment Guarantee'. Working Paper. 21 September. Available at http://www.erlendberg.info/agwages.pdf (accessed 7 August 2019).

Besley, T., R. Pande and V. Rao. 2005. 'Political Selection and the Quality of Government: Evidence from South India'. Yale University Economic Growth Centre Discussion Paper 921.

Bhagwati, J. and A. Panagariya. 2014. *Why Growth Matters: How Economic Growth in India Reduced Poverty and the Lessons for Other Developing Countries*. Public Affairs: First Trade Paper Edition.

Biswas, J. and J. S. Verma. 2009. 'Tackling Child Undernutrition in India: Governance Challenges Need More Attention'. *IDS Bulletin* 40(4): 111–124.

Borooah, Vani Kant. 2018. 'Caste, Religion, and Health Outcomes in India, 2004–14'. *Economic and Political Weekly* 53(10). 10 March.

Bose, I. 2010. 'How Did the Indian Forest Rights Act Emerge?'. IPPG Discussion Paper 39. University of Manchester.

Brass, P. R. 1990. *The Politics of India since Independence*. Cambridge: Cambridge University Press.

Brecher, M. 1959. *Nehru: A Political Biography*. London: Oxford University Press.

Census of India 2011. Provisional Population Totals. Available at http://censusindia.gov.in/2011census/censusinfodashboard/index.html (accessed 21 May 2012).

Chambers, R. and G. Von Medeazza. 2013. 'Sanitation and Stunting in India'. *Economic and Political Weekly* 48(25): 15–18.

Chandrasekhar, C. P. 2012. 'Chronic Famishment'. *The Hindu*. 19 February.

Chatterjee, S. 1992. 'Motion of Thanks on the President's Address'. 3 April. Available at http://parliamentofindia.nic.in/lsdeb/ls10/ses3/1403049201.htm (accessed 21 May 2012).

Chaudhury, N., J. Hammer, M. Kremer, K. Muralidharan and F. H. Rogers. 2006. 'Missing in Action: Teacher and Health Worker Absence in Developing Countries'. *Journal of Economic Perspectives* 20(1): 91–116.

Checkel, J. T. 2006. 'Tracing Causal Mechanisms'. *International Studies Review* 8(2): 362–370.

Chopra, D. 2011a. 'Policy Making in India: A Dynamic Process of Statecraft'. *Pacific Affairs* 84(1): 89–107.

———. 2011b. 'Interactions of "Power" in the Making and Shaping of Social Policy'. *Contemporary South Asia* 19(2): 153–171.

———. 2014. 'The Indian Case: Towards a Rights-Based Welfare State?'. In *Development and Welfare Policy in South Asia*, eds. G. Koheler and D. Chopra. Oxford: Routledge.

Coffey, D. and P. Hathi. 2016. 'Underweight and Pregnant: Maternity Entitlements and Weight Gain during Pregnancy'. *Indian Journal of Human Development* 10(2): 179–190. 6 February.

Coffey, D. and D. Spears. 2017. *Where India Goes: Abandoned Toilets, Stunted Development and the Costs of Caste*. New Delhi: Harper Collins.

Coffey, D., A. Deaton, J. Drèze, D. Spears and A. Tarozzi. 2013. 'Stunting Among Children'. *Economic and Political Weekly* 48(34): 68–69.

Coffey, D., R. Khera and D. Spears. 2013. *Women's Status and Children's Height in India: Evidence from Joint Rural Households*. Princeton, NJ: Rice Institute.

Coffey, D., A. Gupta, P. Hathi, N. Khurana, D. Spears, N. Srivastav and S. Vyas. 2014. 'Revealed Preference for Open Defecation: Evidence from a New Survey in Rural North India. SQUAT Working Paper 1. Princeton, NJ.

Comptroller and Auditor General of India (CAG) 2013a. *Report No. 15 of 2012–13 – Performance Audit of Jawaharlal Nehru National Urban Renewal Mission*. Available at http://cag.gov.in/content/report-no-15-2012-13-%E2%80%93-performance-audit-jawaharlal-nehru-national-urban-renewal-mission (accessed 10 August 13).

———. 2013b. Report of the Comptroller and Auditor General of India on Performance Audit of the Integrated Child Development Services (ICDS) Scheme. New Delhi: CAG.

Constituent Assembly Debates, Vol. 2. Available at http://cadindia.clpr.org.in/constituent-assembly-debates/II/1947-01-22 (accessed 29 August 17).

Corbridge, Stuart and John Harriss. 2000. *Reinventing India: Liberalization, Hindu Nationalism and Popular Democracy*. Cambridge: Cambridge University Press.

Credit Suisse. 2015. *Global Wealth Report 2015*. Zurich: Credit Suisse Research.

Currie, J. 2008. 'Healthy, Wealthy, and Wise: Socioeconomic Status, Poor Health in Childhood, and Human Capital Development'. NBER Working Paper 13987. Washington, DC: National Bureau of Economic Research.

Das, S. K. 2013. *India's Rights Revolution: Has It Worked for the Poor?* New Delhi: Oxford University Press.

Das, U. 2015a. 'Can the Rural Employment Guarantee Scheme Reduce Rural Out-migration: Evidence from West Bengal, India'. *Journal of Development Studies* 51(6): 621–641.

Das, U. 2015b. 'Does Political Activism and Affiliation Affect Allocation of Benefits in the Rural Employment Guarantee Program: Evidence from West Bengal, India'. *World Development* 67: 202–217.

____. 2018. 'Rural Employment Guarantee Programme in India and its Impact on Household Educational Decisions: A Focus on Private Coaching'. 30 March. Available at SSRN: https://ssrn.com/abstract=3152927 (accessed 7 August 2019).

Dasgupta, A., K. Gawande and D. Kapur. 2017. '(When) Do Antipoverty Programs Reduce Violence? India's Rural Employment Guarantee and Maoist Conflict'. *International Organization* 71(3): 605–632.

Dasgupta, R., N. K. Arora, S. Ramji, S. Chaturvedi, S. Rewal, K. Suresh, V. Deshmuk and N. Thakur. 2012. 'Managing Childhood Under-Nutrition'. *Economic and Political Weekly* 47(16): 15–19.

Deaton, Angus and Jean Drèze. 2009. 'Food and Nutrition in India: Facts and Interpretations'. *Economic and Political Weekly* 44(7). 14 February. http://www.epw.in/special-articles/food-and-nutrition-india-facts-and-interpretations.html.

Deininger, K. and Y. Liu. 2013. 'Welfare and Poverty Impacts of India's National Rural Employment Guarantee Scheme: Evidence from Andhra Pradesh'. IFPRI Discussion Paper 1289. Washington.

Desai, S., P. Vashishtha and O. Joshi. 2015. *Mahatma Gandhi National Rural Employment Guarantee Act: A Catalyst for Rural Transformation*. New Delhi: National Council of Applied Economic Research.

Deshpande, R., K. K. Kailash and L. Tillin. 2017. 'States as Laboratories: The Politics of Social Welfare Policies in India'. *India Review* 16(1): 85–105.

Drèze, J. 2004. 'Democracy and Right to Food'. *Economic and Political Weekly* 39(17): 1723–1730. 24 April.

____. 2006. 'Universalisation with Quality: ICDS in a Rights Perspective'. *Economic and Political Weekly* 41(34): 3706–3715.

____. 2010a. 'The Middle Class Has Lost Track of How Poor This Country Is'. *Tehelka Magazine* 7(44). Available at http://www.tehelka.com/story_main47.asp?filename=Ne061110The_middle_class.asp (accessed 19 May 2012).

____. 2010b. 'The Task of Making the PDS Work'. *The Hindu*. 8 July. Available at http://www.thehindu.com/opinion/lead/the-task-of-making-the-pds-work/article504695.ece (accessed 7 August 2019).

Drèze, J. 2011. 'Employment Guarantee and the Right to Work'. In *The Battle for Employment Guarantee*, ed. Reetika Khera. 511. New Delhi: Oxford University Press.

Drèze, J. and R. Khera. 2015. 'Understanding Leakages in the Public Distribution System'. *Economic and Political Weekly* 50(7): 39–42. 14 February.

———. 2017a. 'Recent Social Security Initiatives in India'. *World Development* 98: 555–572.

———. 2017b. 'The PDS Turnaround in Chhattisgarh'. In *Sense and Solidarity: Jholawala Economics for Everyone*, Jean Drèze. New Delhi: Orient BlackSwan.

Drèze, J. and A. Sen. 1995. *India. Economic Development and Social Opportunity*. Oxford: Clarendon Press.

———. 2013. *An Uncertain Glory: India and Its Contradictions*. London: Allen Lane.

Duflo, E., R. Hanna and S. P. Ryan. 2012. 'Incentives Work: Getting Teachers to Come to School'. *American Economic Review* 102 (4): 1241–1278.

Dutt, R. C. 1901. 'The Economic Condition of India'. In *The Penguin Book of Modern Indian Speeches: 1877 to the Present*, ed. R. Batabyal. 43–55. New Delhi: Penguin Books, 2007.

EPW editorial. 2006. 'Right to Information: An Amendment Too Soon'. *Economic and Political Weekly* 41(31). 5 August.

———. 2010. 'Trivialising Food Security'. *Economic and Political Weekly* 45(16): 7–8. 17 April.

———. 2012. 'Running Down a Positive Law'. *Economic and Political Weekly*, 47(43). 27 October.

———. 2015. 'Death by Neglect'. *Economic and Political Weekly* 50(20). 16 May.

FOCUS. 2006. *Focus On Children Under Six Report*. New Delhi: Citizens' Initiative for the Rights of Children Under Six, Right to Food Campaign. December. Available at http://www.righttofoodindia.org/data/rtf06focusreportabridged.pdf (accessed 9 August 2019).

Frankel, F. R. 2005. *India's Political Economy 1947–2004*. New Delhi: Oxford University Press.

Friedman, S. and D. Maiorano. 2017. 'The Limits of Prescription: Courts and Social Policy in India and South Africa'. *Commonwealth and Comparative Politics* 55(3): 353–376.

Galasso, Emanuela and Robert Adam Stephen Wagstaff. 2018. 'The Aggregate Income Losses from Childhood Stunting and the Returns to a Nutrition Intervention Aimed at Reducing Stunting

(English)'. Policy Research Working Paper WPS 8536. Washington, DC: World Bank Group.

Gandhi, S. 2003. Keynote Address on 'The Indian Roadmap' to The Hindustan Times Conference on Peace Dividend in South Asia 12-12-2003. Available at https://www.inc.in/en/media/speech/keynote-address-on-the-indian-roadmap-to-the-hindustan-times-conference-on-peace-dividend-in-south-asia (accessed 8 August 2019).

———. 2005. HT Leadership Summit 2005 Building A Better Future. Speech of Congress President. Available at http://pressbrief.in/index.php/English-Speech-Text/Sonia-Gandhi.s-Speech-at-HT-Conclave-15-Nov-2005.html (accessed 21 May 2012; link discontinued).

———. 2010a. Chairperson's Address at the 10th Indira Gandhi Conference 2010 Friday, 19 November 2010: Teen Murti House. Available at http://aicc.org.in/new/cp_address_10th_indira_gandhi_conference_19th_nov_2010.php (accessed 20 May 2012; link discontinued).

———. 2010b. Speech at 83rd Plenary Session of INC concluding celebrations of its 125th anniversary, 19–20 Dec 2010, Rajiv Nagar, Burari, Delhi. Available at http://aicc.org.in/new/Full%20Text%20in%20English.pdf (accessed 20 May 2012).

George, Alexander L. and Andrew Bennett. 2005. *Case Studies and Theory Development in the Social Sciences*. Cambridge, Massachusetts: MIT Press.

Ghosh, Jayati. 2005. 'The Unsung Heroines of India'. *Frontline* 22(12). 4–17 June.

Gillespie, S., L. Haddad, V. Mannar, P. Menon and N. Nisbett. 2013. 'The Politics of Reducing Malnutrition: Building Commitment and Accelerating Progress'. *The Lancet* 382(9891): 552–569.

Gonsalves, C., V. Naidu, P. Ramesh Kumar and A. Bhat. 2004. *Right to Food*, Volume 1. New Delhi: Human Rights Law Network.

Gopalakrishnan, R. 2009. 'Slums and Economic Stimulus'. *The Economic Times*. 28 February. Available at https://economictimes.indiatimes.com/slums-and-economic-stimulus/articleshow/4203187.cms?from=mdr (accessed 8 August 2019).

———. 2011. 'Towards Social Development Zones'. *The Economic Times*. 10 June. Available at http://economictimes.indiatimes.com/towards-social-development-zones/articleshow/8795854.cms (accessed 31 October 13).

Gopalakrishnan, Shankar. 2017. 'The Forest Rights Act: Political Economy of "Environmental" Questions'. *Economic and Political Weekly* 52(31): 71–76. 5 August.

Government of India. 2004. Order No. 631/2/1/2004-Cab, May 31, 2004. Available at http://nac.nic.in/ (accessed 21 May 2012; site discontinued).

———. 2005a. Right to Information Act, 2005. Available at http://rti.gov.in/rti-act.pdf (accessed 19 May 2012).

———. 2005b. Mahatma Gandhi National Rural Employment Guarantee Act, 2005. Available at https://www.nrega.nic.in/netnrega/mgnrega_new/Nrega_home.aspx (accessed 8 August 2019).

———. 2011. *Economic Survey 2011–12*, p. 241. Available at https://www.indiabudget.gov.in/budget2012-2013/es2011-12/echap-10.pdf (accessed 8 August 2019).

Gragnolati, M., M. Shekar, M. Das Gupta, C. Bredenkamp and Yi-Kyoung Lee. 2005. *India's Undernourished Children: A Call for Reform and Action*. Health, Nutrition and Population (HNP) Discussion Paper. August. Washington, DC: World Bank Publications. Available at http://siteresources.worldbank.org/SOUTHASIAEXT/Resources/223546-1147272668285/IndiaUndernourishedChildrenFinal.pdf (accessed 8 August 2019).

Grant Thornton India. 2011. *Appraisal of Jawaharlal Nehru National Urban Renewal Mission (JnNURM) Final Report – Volume I*. March. Available at http://www.cmamp.com/CP/FDocument/JnNURMvolumeI.pdf (accessed 9 August 2019).

Gulati, Ashok, Jyoti Gujral, T. Nandakumar, Surbhi Jain, Sourabh Anand, Siddharth Rath and Piyush Joshi. 2012. 'National Food Security Bill: Challenges and Options'. *CACP Discussion Paper 2*, December. Commission for Agricultural Costs and Prices.

Gupta, R. 2011. 'Deconstructing the NAC'. 5 August. Available at http://kafila.org/2011/08/05/deconstructing-the-nac-ruchi-gupta/ (accessed 21 May 2012).

HANCHI. 2013. *The Hunger And Nutrition Commitment Index*. Brighton: Institute of Development Studies.

Harriss, J. 2011. *'Inclusive Growth': How is India Doing?* Singapore: Institute of South Asian Studies.

Hasan, Z. 2009. *Breaking New Ground: Congress and Welfarism in India*. Paris: Institut Français des Relations Internationales.

———. 2013. *Congress After Indira: Policy, Power, Political Change (1984–2009)*. New Delhi: Oxford University Press.

Hazards Centre. 2007. *Whither Indian Cities: Urban Reforms and Counter Strategies. A Documented Outcome of National Consultation on Jawaharlal Nehru National Urban Renewal Mission, 15th-16th April 2006, Mumbai*. New Delhi: Committee for the Right to Housing, Hazards Centre, Sanchal Foundation. Available at http://www.hazardscentre.com/hazards_publications/pdf/urban_governance_resistance/whither_indian_cities.html (accessed 30 May 13).

Headey, D., J. Hoddinott, D. Ali, R. Tesfaye and M. Dereje. 2015. 'The Other Asian Enigma: Explaining the Rapid Reduction of Undernutrition in Bangladesh'. *World Development* 66: 749–761.

HLRN. 2017. *India's Smart Cities Mission: Smart for Whom? Cities for Whom? A Human Rights and Social Justice Analysis of Smart City Proposals*. June. New Delhi: Housing and Land Rights Network. Available at http://hlrn.org.in/documents/Smart_Cities_Report_2017.pdf (accessed 30 September 2017).

Hungama. 2011. *The HUNGaMA Survey Report*. Hyderabad: Naandi Foundation.

IFPRI. 2014. *Global Nutrition Report 2014: Actions and Accountability to Accelerate the World's Progress on Nutrition*. Washington, DC: International Food Policy Research Institute.

———. 2016a. *2016 Global Hunger Index: Getting to Zero Hunger*. Bonn, Germany, Washington DC and Dublin, Ireland: Welthungerhilfe, IFPRI and Concern Worldwide.

———. 2016b. *Global Nutrition Report 2016: From Promise to Impact: Ending Malnutrition by 2030*. Washington, DC: IFPRI.

Imbert, C. and J. Papp. 2015. 'Labor Market Effects of Social Programs: Evidence from India's Employment Guarantee'. *American Economic Journal: Applied Economics* 7(2): 233–263.

Indian National Congress. 1999. *Manifesto 1999*. Available at http://aicc.org.in/new/manifesto-1999.php (accessed 17 May 2012; link discontinued).

———. 2004. *Manifesto 2004*. Available at http://aicc.org.in/new/manifesto-2004.php (accessed 17 May 2012; link discontinued).

Jain, M. 2015. 'India's Struggle Against Malnutrition—Is the ICDS Program the Answer?'. *World Development* 67: 72–89.

Jaffrelot, Christophe and Basim-U-Nissa. 2018. 'The Struggle of RTI Activists in Gujarat'. *Economic and Political Weekly* 53(33). 18 August.

Jayachandran, Seema and Rohini Pande. 2017. 'Why are Indian Children So Short? The Role of Birth Order and Son Preference'. *American Economic Review* 107(9): 2600–2629.

Jenkins, Rob. 1999. *Democratic Politics and Economic Reform in India*. Cambridge: Cambridge University Press.

Jenkins, R. and Anne Marie Goetz. 1999. 'Accounts and Accountability: Theoretical Implications of the Right-to-Information Movement in India'. *Third World Quarterly* 20(3): 603–622.

Jenkins, R. and J. Manor. 2017. *Politics and the Right to Work: India's Mahatma Gandhi National Rural Employment Guarantee Act*. New Delhi/London/New York: Orient BlackSwan/Hurst/Oxford University Press USA.

JNNURM Overview. 2005. Available at http://mohua.gov.in/upload/uploadfiles/files/1Mission%20Overview%20English(1).pdf (accessed 8 August 2019).

Kapur, A., E. Joshi and V. Srinivas. 2016. *ICDS 2016–17: Budget Briefs*, Vol. 8, No. 4. New Delhi: Accountability Initiative, Centre for Policy Research.

Kapur, D. and P. Nangia. 2015. 'Social Protection in India: A Welfare State sans Public Goods?'. *India Review* 14(1): 73–90.

Kapur, Devesh, Partha Mukhopadhyay and Arvind Subramanian. 2008. 'The Case for Direct Cash Transfers to the Poor'. *Economic and Political Weekly* 43(15): 37–43.

Kashwan, Prakash. 2017. *Democracy in the Woods: Environmental Conservation and Social Justice in India, Tanzania and Mexico*. New York: Oxford University Press.

Kelkar, V. L. 2004. 'India: On the Growth Turnpike'. In *The First Ten K. R. Narayan Orations*, ed. R. Jha. Canberra: Australian National University Press.

Kelland, K. 2013. 'About 48% of Children in India are Stunted: UNICEF'. *Livemint*. 7 June.

Khare, A., M. Sarin, N. C. Saxena, S. Palit, S. Bathla, F. Vania and M. Satyanarayana. 2000. *Joint Forest Management: Policy, Practice and Prospects*. London: International Institute for Environment and Development. Initially cited in Bose 2010.

Khera, R. 2011. 'Trends in Diversion of Grain from the Public Distribution System'. *Economic and Political Weekly* 46(21). 21 May.

———. 2013. *Democratic Politics and Legal Rights: Employment Guarantee and Food Security in India*. Working Paper 327. New Delhi: Institute of Economic Growth.

Khera, R. 2014. 'Cash vs. in-Kind Transfers: Indian Data Meets Theory'. *Food Policy* 46: 116–128. June. doi:10.1016/j.foodpol.2014.03.009.

———. 2017. 'Impact of Aadhaar in Welfare Programmes'. 29 September 2017. Available at SSRN: https://ssrn.com/abstract=3045235 (accessed 30 October 2017).

Klonner, S. and C. Oldiges. 2012. 'Employment Guarantee and its Welfare Effects in India'. University of Heidelberg Working Paper. 30 September.

Kohli, A. 1990. *Democracy and Discontent: India's Growing Crisis of Governability*. Cambridge: Cambridge University Press.

———. 2012. *Poverty Amid Plenty in the New India*. Cambridge: Cambridge University Press.

Kothari, A. 2011. 'Not Out of the Woods Yet'. *Frontline* 28(5). 26 February–11 March.

Krishna, Anirudh. 2011. *One Illness Away: Why People Become Poor and How They Escape Poverty*. Oxford: Oxford University Press.

Krishna, Sudhir. 2013. 'PPP is Essential for Urban Development'. *Inclusion* 4(1), January–March 2013. Available at http://inclusion.skoch.in/story/70/ppp-is-essential-for-urban-development-370.html (accessed 26 July 2019).

Kumar, A. 2008. 'Dissonance between Economic Reforms and Democracy'. *Economic and Political Weekly* 43(1): 54–60. 5 January.

Kumar, K., Neera M. Singh and Y. Giri Rao. 2017. 'Promise and Performance of the Forest Rights Act: A Ten-Year Review'. *Economic and Political Weekly* 52(25–26): 40–43. 24 June.

Kumar, P. J. Dilip. 2013. 'Village Communities and their Common Property Forests'. *Economic and Political Weekly* 48(35): 33–36. 31 August.

Kundu, A. 2011. 'Trends and Processes of Urbanisation in India'. September. London: IIED/UNFPA. Available at http://pubs.iied.org/pdfs/10597IIED.pdf (accessed 30 March 13).

Li, T. and S. Sekhri. 2013. 'The Unintended Consequences of Employment Based Safety Net Programs, 25–27.

Lowe, Matt. 2018. 'Types of Contact: A Field Experiment on Collaborative and Adversarial Caste Integration'. 10 January. Available at https://pdfs.semanticscholar.org/2f93/776c47632d3eee891d284cb160bd4a3c844c.pdf?_ga=2.109943937.545437632.1565332525-740644800.1565332525 (accessed 9 August 2019).

Lok Sabha. 2013. *Standing Committe of Food, Consumer Affairs and Public Distribution, Report on the National Food Security Bill*. New Delhi: Lok Sabha Secretariat.

Mahadevia, D. 2010. 'Urban Reforms in Three Cities: Ahmedabad, Bangalore and Patna'. In *Public Service Delivery in India: Understanding the Reform Process*, ed. Vikram Chand. New Delhi: Oxford University Press.

Maiorano, D. and J. Manor. 2017. 'Poverty Reduction, Inequalities and Human Development in the BRICS: Policies and Outcomes'. *Commonwealth and Comparative Politics* 55(3): 278–302.

Maiorano, D., U. Das and S. Masiero. 2018. 'Decentralisation, Clientelism and Social Protection Programmes: A Study of India's MGNREGA'. *Oxford Development Studies* 46(4): 536–549.

Maiorano, D. 2015. *Autumn of the Matriarch: Indira Gandhi's Final Term in Office*. London: Hurst and Co.

____. 2014. 'The Politics of the Mahatma Gandhi National Rural Employment Guarantee Act in Andhra Pradesh'. *World Development* 58: 95–105.

Maira, A. et al. 2012. *Report of the Committee on JNNURM-II: Clean Bastis, Safe Communities and People's Cities*. New Delhi: Planning Commission, Government of India.

Mani, Subha, Jere R. Behrman, Shaikh Galab and P. Prudhvikar Reddy. 2014. 'Impact of the NREGS on Schooling and Intellectual Human Capital'. *Grand Challenges Canada (GCC) Economic Returns to Mitigating Early Life Risks Project Working Paper Series*, 2014-10.

Mander, Harsh. 2012. *Ash in the Belly: India's Unfinished Battle Against Hunger*. New Delhi: Penguin.

Manor, J. 2005a. 'India's Reform Strengths'. In *Asia's Giants: Comparing China and India*, eds. E. Friedman and B. Gilley. New York: Palgrave Macmillan.

Manor, J. 2005b. 'User Committees: A Potentially Damaging Second Wave of Decentralisation?'. In *Democratic Decentralisation through a Natural Resource Lens*, eds. J. C. Ribot and A. M. Larson. 192–213. London and New York: Routledge.

____. 2007. 'Successful Governance Reforms in Two Indian States: Karnataka and Andhra Pradesh'. *Commonwealth and Comparative Politics* 45(4): 425–451.

____. 2011a. 'Did the Central Government's Poverty Initiatives Help to Re-Elect It?'. In *New Dimensions of Politics in India: The United Progressive Alliance in Power*, eds. L. Saez and G. Singh. London and New Delhi: Routledge.

____. 2011b. 'Perspectives on Decentralisation'. Working Paper 3. Visby, Sweden: International Centre for Local Democracy.

Manor, J. 2011c. 'The Congress Party and the "Great Transformation"'. In *Understanding India's New Political Economy: A Great Transformation?*, eds. S. Ruparelia, S. Reddy, J. Harriss and S. Corbridge. 204–220. London: Routledge.

———. 2013a. *When Local Government Strikes It Rich: Generous Funding is Necessary but Insufficient alongside an 'Accountability Deficit'*. Visby, Sweden: International Centre for Local Democracy.

———. 2013b. 'Post-Clientelist Initiatives'. In *Democratization in the Global South: The Importance of Transformative Politics*, eds. K. Stokke and O. Tornquist. Basingstoke: Palgrave Macmillan.

———. 2014. 'Comparing Efforts by Four Governments to Tackle Poverty and Inequality since 2002: Brazil, India, China and South Africa' (unpublished paper presented to the panel on 'The Politics of Tackling Poverty and Inequality in the BRICS: Lessons for Development Studies'). Development Studies Association Conference, London, 1 November.

———. 2015. 'Key Issues in the Study of State Politics in India'. In *Politics in South Asia: Culture, Rationality and Conceptual Flow*, eds. S. O. Wolf, J. Schottli, D. Fromherz, K. Furstenberg, M. Gallenkamp, L. Konig and M. Pauli. 73–86. Switzerland: Springer, Cham.

Manor, J. and J. Duckett. 2017. 'The Significance of Political Leaders for Social Policy Expansion in Brazil, China, India and South Africa'. *Commonwealth and Comparative Politics* 55(3): 303–327.

Markusson, T. 2011. 'Inequality and Political Clientelism: Evidence from South India'. *The Journal of Development Studies* 47(11): 1721–1738.

Mathur, N. 2016. *Paper Tiger: Law, Bureaucracy and the Developmental State in Himalayan India*. Cambridge: Cambridge University Press.

McKinsey Global Institute. 2010. *India's Urban Awakening: Building Inclusive Cities, Sustaining Economic Growth*. April. Available at https://www.mckinsey.com/global-themes/urbanization/urban-awakening-in-india (accessed 30 March 13).

Melo, M. A., N. Ng'ethe and J. Manor. 2010. *Against the Odds: Politicians, Institutions and the Struggle against Poverty*. London, New York: Hurst, Columbia University Press.

Ministry of Law and Justice. 2013. *The National Food Security Act, 2013, The Gazette of India*. 10 September. Available at http://www.egazette.nic.in/WriteReadData/2013/E_29_2013_429.pdf (accessed 10 July 2019).

Mittal, N. and J. V. Meenakshi. 2015. 'Utilization of ICDS Services and Their Impact on Child Health Outcomes—Evidence from

Three East Indian States'. Working Paper 247. Delhi School of Economics, Centre for Development Economics.

MOF. 2015. *Economic Survey 2015/16*. New Delhi: Ministry of Finance.

MORD. 2012. *MGNREGA Sameeksha*. New Delhi: Ministry of Rural Development.

MOSPI. 2015. *Millennium Development Goals – India Country Report*. New Delhi: MOSPI.

MWCD. 2012. *Report of the Working Group on Nutrition for the 12th Five Year Plan (2012–17)*. New Delhi: MWCD.

———. 2013. *ICDS Mission – Broad Framework for Implementation*. New Delhi: MWCD.

———. 2015. *Rapid Survey on Children*. New Delhi: MWCD.

Naoroji, D. 1893. 'Poverty of India'. In *The Penguin Book of Modern Indian Speeches 1877 to the Present*, ed. R. Batabyal. 38–43. New Delhi: Penguin Books, 2007.

———. 1901. *Poverty and Un-British Rule in India*. London: Swan Sonnenschein and Co.

Nair, K. R. G. 2007. 'Malnourishment among Children in India: A Regional Analysis'. *Economic and Political Weekly* 42(37): 3797–3803.

Nair, M., P. Ariana, E. O. Ohuma, R. Gray, B. De Stavola and P. Webster. 2013. 'Effect of the Mahatma Gandhi National Rural Employment Guarantee Act (MGNREGA) on Malnutrition of Infants in Rajasthan, India: A Mixed Methods Study'. *PloS One* 8(9): e75089.

National Advisory Council. 2004. Recommendations on ICDS. New Delhi: NAC.

———. 2005. Follow-up Recommendations on ICDS. New Delhi: NAC.

———. 2011. Recomendations for a Reformed and Strenghtened ICDS. New Delhi: NAC.

———. 2012a. 'Profiles'. Available at http://nac.nic.in/member.htm (accessed 19 May 2012; link discontinued).

———. 2012b. 'Vision'. 2012. Available at http://nac.nic.in/ (accessed 21 May 2012; link discontinued).

National Human Rights Commission. 2011. *Report on the ICDS, Gorakhpur, Uttar Pradesh*. New Delhi: NHRC.

National Social Watch Coalition (NSWC). 2009. *Citizens Report on Governance and Development 2008–09*. New Delhi: Daanish Books.

Nayak, B. P., P. Kohli and J. V. Sharma. n.d. *Livelihood of Local Communities and Forest Degradation in India: Issues for REDD*. 5.

New Delhi: Tata Energy Research Institute (TERI), MOEF, Norwegian Ministry of Foreign Affairs.

Nayak, N. and R. Khera. 2009. 'Women Workers and Perceptions of the National Rural Employment Guarantee Act'. *Economic and Political Weekly* 44(43): 49–57.

Nayak, N. and N. Saxena. 2006. 'Implementation of ICDS in Bihar and Jharkand'. *Economic and Political Weekly* 41(34): 3680–3684.

NNC. 2007. *National Nutrition Conclave: Book of Proceedings. A Nutrition-Secure India: How Do We Get There?* Chennai: M. S. Swaminathan Research Foundation.

Nehru, J. 1955. 'A Socialistic Pattern of Society'. In *The Penguin Book of Modern Indian Speeches 1877 to the Present*, ed. R. Batabyal. 499–504. New Delhi: Penguin Books, 2007.

———. 1961. *The Discovery of India*. Bombay: Asia Publishing House.

NFHS-3. 2007. *National Family Health Survey (NFHS-3), 2005–06, India: Volume 1*. September 2007. Mumbai: International Institute for Population Sciences (IIPS).

NFHS-4. 2017. *National Family Health Survey (NFHS-4), 20015–16: India*. Mumbai: IIPS and ICF. December 2017. Available at: http://rchiips.org/NFHS/nfhs4.shtml (accessed 4 August 2019).

Nilekani, N. 2008. *Imagining India: Ideas for the New Century*. New Delhi: Penguin Books.

Norman, D. 1985. *Indira Gandhi: Letters to a Friend 1950–1984*. London: Weidenfeld and Nicolson.

OECD. 2009. *What Students Know and Can Do*. Paris: OECD.

OPHI. 2017. 'India Country Briefing', *Multidimensional Poverty Index Data Bank*. Oxford Poverty and Human Development Initiative, University of Oxford. Available at: www.ophi.org.uk/multidimensional-poverty-index/mpi-country-briefings/.

———. 2018. 'Global MPI Data Tables for Winter 2017–2018'. Oxford Poverty and Human Development Initiative, University of Oxford. Available at: https://ophi.org.uk/multidimensional-poverty-index/global-mpi-2017/mpi-data/ (accessed 4 August 2019).

Palshikar, S. and Y. Yadav. 2009. 'Between Fortuna and Virtu: Explaining the Congress' Ambiguous Victory in 2009'. *Economic and Political Weekly* 44(39). 26 September.

Panagariya, A. 2013. 'Does India Really Suffer from Worse Child Malnutrition Than Sub-Saharan Africa?'. *Economic and Political Weekly* 48(18): 98–111.

Parekh, D. et al. 2008. *Report of the High Level Task Force on Affordable Housing for All*. December. Available at http://www.naredco.in/pdfs/report-high-level-task.pdf (accessed 9 August 2019).

Patel, Vikram. 2018. 'Starvation Deaths in 2018', *The Indian Express*, 26 July 2018.

Patnaik, Biraj. 2010. 'Chhattisgarh's Food for Thought'. *Livemint*. 21 April.

Peisakhin, L. and P. Pinto. 2010. 'Is Transparency an Effective Anti-corruption Strategy? Evidence from a Field Experiment in India'. *Regulation and Governance* 4(3): 261–280.

Pereira, C. and F. Bertholini. 2017. 'Beliefs or Ideology: The Imperative of Social Inclusion in Brazilian Politics'. *Commonwealth and Comparative Politics* 55(3): 377–401.

Planning Commission. 1970. 'Preface' to the *Fourth Five Year Plan*, 18 July 1970. Available at http://planningcommission.nic.in/plans/planrel/fiveyr/index9.html (accessed 21 May 2012).

———. 2008a. 'Foreword' to the *Eleventh Five Year Plan*, 25 June 2008. Available at http://planningcommission.nic.in/plans/planrel/fiveyr/index9.html (accessed 21 May 2012).

———. 2008b. *Eleventh Five Year Plan 2007–12, Vol. 2 Social Sector*. New Delhi: Planning Commission, Government of India.

———. 2010. *Addressing India's Nutrition Challenges. Report of the Multi-stakeholder Retreat*. New Delhi: Planning Commission, Government of India.

———. 2011a. *Evaluation Report on Integrated Child Development Services*. New Delhi: Planning Commission, Government of India.

———. 2011b. *Report of the Inter Ministerial Group on ICDS Restructuring*. New Delhi: Planning Commission, Government of India.

———. 2012. 'History'. Available at http://planningcommission.nic.in/aboutus/history/index.php?about=aboutbdy.htm (accessed 21 May 2012).

———. 2013. *Twelfth Five Year Plan 2012–2017, Vol. 2 Economic Sectors*. New Delhi: Planning Commission, Government of India.

POCUS. 2014. *Progress On Children Under Six Report*. New Delhi: Citizens' Initiative for the Rights of Children Under Six, Right to Food Campaign.

———. 2016: *Progress On Children Under Six Report*. New Delhi: Citizens' Initiative for the Rights of Children Under Six, Right to Food Campaign. Available at https://www.academia.edu/34406474/Progress_of_Children_Under_Six_POCUS_(accessed 9 August 2019).

Prasad, V. and D. Sinha. 2008. 'Childhood on Hold'. *The Hindu,* 21 September.

PRIA. 2009. *Study on Accessing Information under RTI: Citizen's Experience in Ten States*. New Delhi: Society for Participatory Research in Asia.

Pritchard, Bill, Anu Rammohan, Madhushree Sekher, S. Parasuraman and Chetan Choithani. 2014. *Feeding India: Livelihoods, Entitlements and Capabilities*. Abingdon, Oxon: Routledge.

Puri, Raghav. 2012. 'Reforming the Public Distribution System: Lessons from Chhattisgarh'. *Economic and Political Weekly* 47(5): 21–24. 4 February.

Rajivan, A. K. 2006. 'ICDS with a Difference'. *Economic and Political Weekly* 41(34): 3684–3688.

Ramalingaswami, V., U. Jonsson and J. Rohde. 2006. *The Asian Enigma: In the Progress of Nations*. New York: UNICEF.

Raman, Anuradha. 2013. 'Who Cares A Damn About Childcare!'. *Outlook*. 29 July.

Raman, V. V. 2006. 'Information Technology and Participatory Democracy: A Case Study of Bangalore City'. Ph.D. Thesis. Pennsylvania State University.

Rao, K. S. 2017. *Do We Care?: India's Health System*. New Delhi: Oxford University Press.

Rao, P. V. N. 1998. *The Insider*. New Delhi: Viking.

Ravindranath, N. V. and P. Sudha. 2004. *Joint Forest Management in India: Spread, Performance and Impact*. Hyderabad: Universities Press.

Ravallion, M. and Rinku Murgai. 2005. 'Employment Guarantee in Rural India: What Would It Cost and How Much Would It Reduce Rural Poverty?'. *Economic and Political Weekly* 40(31). 30 July.

Reich, Michael R. and Y. Balarajan. 2012. 'Political Economy Analysis for Food and Nutrition Security'. Health, Nutrition and Population (HNP) discussion paper. Washington, DC: World Bank.

Roberts, A. 2010. 'A Great and Revolutionary Law? The First Four Years of India's Right to Information Act'. *Public Administration Review* 70(6): 925–933.

Rogers, F. H. and E. Vegas. 2009. 'No More Cutting Class? Reducing Teacher Absence and Providing Incentives for Performance'. *World Bank Policy Research* Working Paper 4847.

Roy, A., J. Drèze and N. Dey. 2011. 'The Right to Transparent Governance'. In *Writings on Human Rights, Law and Society in India: A Combat Law Anthology*, ed. H. Dhobal. New Delhi: Human Rights Law Network.

Roy, D. ed. 2009. *Citizens' Review. Jawaharlal Nehru National Urban Renewal Mission. A Collective View from the Bottom. Half-Time Or Time-Out*. New Delhi: Hazards Centre. Available at http://www.hazardscentre.org/hazards_publications/pdf/sustainability_planning/half_time_out.html (accessed 30 September 13).

RTF. 2007. *Strategies For Children Under Six: A Framework for the 11th Plan*. New Delhi: Right to Food.

———. 2012. *Strategies For Children Under Six: Update and Recommendations for the 12th Plan*. New Delhi: Right to Food .

Rudolph, Lloyd and Susanne Hoeber Rudolph. 1987. *In Pursuit of Lakshmi: The Political Economy of the Indian State*. Chicago and London: University of Chicago Press.

Ruparelia, S. 2013. 'India's New Rights Agenda: Genesis, Promises, Risks'. *Pacific Affairs* 86(3): 569–590.

Sahu, Geetanjoy, Tushar Dash and Sanghamitra Dubey. 2017. 'Political Economy of Community Forest Rights'. *Economic and Political Weekly* 52(25–26): 45–47. 24 June.

Saxena, N. C. 1997. *The Saga of Participatory Forest Management in India*. Bogor, Indonesia: Centre for International Forest Research.

Saxena, N. C. 2012. 'Hunger and Malnutrition in India'. *IDS Bulletin* 43: 8–14. 8 July. Available at doi:10.1111/j.1759-5436.2012.00341.x (accessed 30 September 13).

———. 2013a. 'NGOs and the State in India: An Uncomfortable Relationship'. Available at http://www.academia.edu/11326202/NGOs_and_the_State_in_India_An_Uncomfortable_Relationship (accessed 30 September 17).

———. 2013b. 'The Urban Poor in India' (unpublished manuscript).

Scacco, A. and S. S. Warren. 2018. 'Can Social Contact Reduce Prejudice and Discrimination? Evidence from a Field Experiment in Nigeria'. *American Political Science Review* 112(3): 654–677. August.

Sen, A. 2000. *Development As Freedom*. New Delhi: Oxford University Press.

———. 2015. 'India is the Only Country Trying to Become a Global Economic Power with an Uneducated and Unhealthy Labour Force'. Interview with Amartya Sen, by Sonali Campion and Taryana Odayar, at London School of Economics and Political Science, 6 November 2015. Available at: http://blogs.lse.ac.uk/southasia/2015/11/19/india-is-the-only-country-in-the-world-trying-to-become-a-global-economic-power-with-an-uneducated-and-unhealthy-labour-force-amartya-sen/ (accessed 5 August 2019).

Sen, Abhijit and Himanshu. 2011. 'Why Not a Universal Food Security Legislation?'. *Economic and Political Weekly* 46(12). 19 March. Available at https://www.epw.in/journal/2011/12/special-articles/why-not-universal-food-security-legislation.html (accessed 12 August 2019).

Shah, M. and B. M. Steinberg. 2015. 'Workfare and Human Capital Investment: Evidence from India' (No. w21543). September. National Bureau of Economic Research.

Shankar, S and R. Gaiha. 2013. *Battling Corruption: Has NREGA Reached India's Rural Poor?* New Delhi: Oxford University Press.

Sharma, M., B. L. Sarangi, J. Kanungo, S. Sahoo, L. Tripathy, A. Patnaik, J. Tewari and A. D. Rath. 2009. 'Accelerating Malnutrition Reduction in Orissa'. *IDS Bulletin* 40(4): 78–85.

Singh, Manmohan. 1992a. 'Budget 1992–93: Speech of Shri Manmohan Singh, Minister of Finance, 29th February, 1992'. Available at https://www.indiabudget.gov.in/doc/bspeech/bs199293.pdf (accessed 12 August 2019).

———. 1992b. 'Budget 1991–92: Speech of Shri Manmohan Singh, Minister of Finance, 24th July, 1991'. In *Recent Developments in Indian Economy with Special Reference to Structural Reforms, Pt. 1*, ed. U. Kapila. 275–290. Delhi: Academic Foundation. Available at https://www.indiabudget.gov.in/doc/bspeech/bs199192.pdf (accessed 12 August 2019).

———. 2004. 'Prime Minister's Address to the Nation, June 24, 2004'. Master Plan Implementation Support Group (MPISG). New Delhi: Architexturez Imprints. Available at https://architexturez.net/doc/az-cf-21868 (accessed 12 August 2019).

———. 2005. 'PM's Independence Day Address, 2005'. 15 August. Available at https://archivepmo.nic.in/drmanmohansingh/speech-details.php?nodeid=160 (accessed 12 August 2019).

———. 2008. 'PM's Independence Day Speech, 2008'. 15 August. Available at https://archivepmo.nic.in/drmanmohansingh/speech-details.php?nodeid=677 (accessed 9 August 2019).

———. 2009. 'PM's Independence Day Speech, 2009'. 15 August. Available at https://archivepmo.nic.in/drmanmohansingh/speech-details.php?nodeid=780 (accessed 9 August 2019).

———. 2011. 'PM's Independence Day Address, 2011'. 15 August. Available at https://archivepmo.nic.in/drmanmohansingh/speech-details.php?nodeid=1045 (accessed 9 August 2019).

Singh, Rani. 2011. *Sonia Gandhi. An Extraordinary Life, An Indian Destiny*. New York: Palgrave Macmillan.

Sinha, A. 2012. 'Health Evidence from the States'. *Economic and Political Weekly* 47(6). 11 February.

Sinha, D. 2006. 'Rethinking ICDS: A Rights Based Perspective'. *Economic and Political Weekly* 41(34): 3689–3694.

Sinha, S. 2006. 'Infant Survival: A Political Challenge'. *Economic and Political Weekly* 41(34): 3657–3660.

Sivaramakrishnan, K. C. 2010. 'The JNNURM Story'. New Delhi: Centre for Policy Research (unpublished manuscript).

———. 2011. *Re-visioning Indian Cities: The Urban Renewal Mission*. New Delhi: Sage.

———. 2015. *Governance of Megacities: Fractured Thinking, Fragmented Setup*. New Delhi: Oxford University Press.

Skocpol, Theda. 1992. *Protecting Soldiers and Mothers: The Political Origins of Social Policy in the United States*. Cambridge, Massachusetts: Harvard University Press.

SPARC (Society for the Promotion of Area Resource Centres). 2010–11. *SPARC Annual Review 2010–11*. Mumbai.

SPARC. 2011–12. *SPARC Annual Review 2011–12*. Mumbai.

State of the Nation. 2015. *State of the Nation: RTE Section 12(1)C*. Indian Institute of Management – Ahmedabad, Central Square Foundation, Accountability Initiative (Centre for Policy Research) and Vidhi Centre for Legal Policy. Available at: www.dise.in/Downloads/State-of-the-Nation-Section-12-1-c-CSF-March-2015.pdf (accessed 12 August 2019).

South Asia Terrorism Portal. 2014. 'Fatalities in Left-wing Terrorism: 2005–2014'. Available at http://www.satp.org/satporgtp/countries/india/maoist/data_sheets/fatalitiesnaxal05-11.htm (accessed 15 September 2014).

Spears, D. 2012. 'Height and Cognitive Achievement among Indian Children'. *Economics and Human Biology* 10(2): 210–219.

———. 2013a. 'How Much International Variation in Child Height Can Sanitation Explain?'. *World Bank Policy Research Working Paper* 6351. Washington, DC.

———. 2013b. 'The Long and Short of Open Defecation'. *The Hindu*, 14 March.

Srivastava, Kavita. 2012. 'Letter: Expand the Food Security Bill'. *Economic and Political Weekly* 47(16): 4–5. 21 April.

Suryanarayana, M. H. and S. Geetha. 1993. 'Revamping PDS: Some Issues and Implications'. *Economic and Political Weekly* 28(41): 2207–2213. 9 October.

Svedberg, Peter. 2012. 'Reforming or Replacing the Public Distribution System with Cash Transfers?'. *Economic and Political Weekly* 47(7). 18 February.

Swaminathan, M. S. 2012. 'Food as People's Right', *The Hindu*. 3 January. Available at https://www.thehindu.com/opinion/lead/food-as-peoples-right/article2769348.ece (accessed 10 July 2019).

HPEC. 2011. *Report on Indian Urban Infrastructure and Services*. The High Powered Expert Committee (HPEC) for Estimating the Investment Requirements for Urban Infrastructure Services. Available at icrier.org/pdf/FinalReport-hpec.pdf (accessed 5 August 2013).

Tillin, Louise, Anupama Saxena and Yatindra Singh Sisodia. 2015. 'Comparing the Politics of Food Subsidies in Chhattisgarh and Madhya Pradesh'. In *Politics of Welfare: Comparisons across Indian States*, eds. Louise Tillin, Rajeshwari Deshpande and K. K. Kailash, 102–134. New Delhi: Oxford University Press.

Tillin, Louise, Rajeshwari Deshpande and K. K. Kailash, eds. 2015. *Politics of Welfare: Comparisons across Indian States*. New Delhi: Oxford University Press.

Tillin, L. and J. Duckett. 2017. 'The Politics of Social Policy: Welfare Expansion in Brazil, China, India and South Africa in Comparative Perspective'. *Commonwealth and Comparative Politics* 55(3): 253–277.

Tontisirin, K., Y. Kachondham and P. Winichagoon. 1992. 'Trends in the Development of Thailand's Nutrition and Health Plans and Programs'. *Asia Pacific Journal of Clinical Nutrition* 1: 231–238.

UNICEF. 2013. *Committing to Child Survival: A Promise Renewed.* New York: UNICEF.

Veeraraghavan, R. 2015. 'Open Governance and Surveillance: A Study of the National Rural Employment Program in Andhra Pradesh, India'. Ph.D. Thesis, University of California, Berkeley.

Vellakkal, S., A. Gupta, Z. Khan, D. Stuckler, A. Reeves, S. Ebrahim, A. Bowling and P. Doyle. 2017. 'Has India's National Rural Health Mission Reduced Inequities in Maternal Health Services? A Pre-post Repeated Cross-sectional Study'. *Health Policy and Planning* 32(1): 79–90. February. Available at https://doi.org/10.1093/heapol/czw100 (accessed 12 August 2019).

Venkataramakrishnan, R. 2015. 'Everyone in India Thinks They Are "Middle Class" and Almost No One Actually Is'. Available at https://scroll.in/article/740011/everyone-in-india-thinks-they-are-middle-class-and-almost-no-one-actually-is (accessed 1 September 2017).

Venugopal, K. R. 2012. *The Integrated Child Development Services: A Flagship Adrift*. New Delhi: Konark Publishers.

Victora, C. G., L. Adair, C. Fall, P. C. Hallal, R. Martorell, L. Richter and H. S. Sachdev. 2008. 'Maternal and Child Undernutrition: Consequences for Adult Health and Human Capital'. *The Lancet* 371(9609): 340–357.

Vir, S. C. 2016. 'Improving Women's Nutrition Imperative for Rapid Reduction of Childhood Stunting in South Asia: Coupling of Nutrition Specific Interventions with Nutrition Sensitive Measures Essential'. *Maternal and Child Nutrition* 12(S1): 72–90.

Vogl, T. S. 2014. 'Height, Skills, and Labor Market Outcomes in Mexico'. *Journal of Development Economics* 107: 84–96. March.

Wallace, P. 1978. 'Centralisation and Depoliticisation in South Asia'. *The Journal of Commonwealth and Comparative Politics* 16(1): 3–21.

WHO. 2006. *The World Health Report 2006 – Working Together for Health*. Geneva: World Health Organization.

World Bank. 2011. *Perspectives on Poverty in India*. Washington, DC: The World Bank.

———. 2013. *World Development Report 2014: Risk and Opportunity—Managing Risk for Development*. Washington, DC: The World Bank.

Index